Unworldliness in Twentieth Century German Thought

What happens when the world around us feels fragmented? How can a person continue to respond positively to their environment when it seems to have lost its internal coherence? These questions lie at the heart of this innovative interpretation of some of the most influential German philosophers of the twentieth century. The key figures in this study are the young Georg Lukács (1885–1971), Ernst Jünger (1895–1998), Ernst Bloch (1885–1977), Theodor Adorno (1903–1969), Max Kommerell (1902–1944), and Siegfried Kracauer (1889–1966).

By establishing an intellectual dialogue among these otherwise diverse thinkers, this study identifies a common interest: the question whether an unworldly, fragmented universe can nonetheless elicit a creative response from individuals. Together, these authors offer an alternative to what is considered the dominant trend in twentieth-century German philosophy: the phenomenological emphasis on humans' lived interactions with a shared and unified lifeworld. Special attention is given to six distinct interpretations of Miguel de Cervantes' novel *Don Quixote* and the unworldly actions of its main characters.

Unworldliness in Twentieth Century German Thought will appeal to researchers and advanced students interested in twentieth-century continental philosophy, German intellectual history, critical theory, and literature and philosophy.

Stéphane Symons is Full Professor of Philosophy of Culture and Aesthetics at the Institute of Philosophy at the KU Leuven, Belgium. His most recent publication is *Ludwig Binswanger and Fernand Deligny on the Human Condition: Wandering Lines* (2024).

Routledge Studies in Twentieth-Century Philosophy

Between Wittgenstein and Weil
Comparisons in Philosophy, Religion, and Ethics
Edited by Jack Manzi

The Turing Test Argument
Bernardo Gonçalves

Wittgenstein and Nietzsche
Edited by Shunichi Takagi and Pascal F. Zambito

The Event of Meaning in Gadamer's Hermeneutics
Carlo DaVia and Greg Lynch

Heidegger's Alternative History of Time
Emily Hughes and Marilyn Stendera

Power and Freedom in the Space of Reasons
Elaborating Foucault's Pragmatism
Tuomo Tiisala

Wittgenstein and Democratic Politics
Language, Dialogue and Political Forms of Life
*Edited by Lotar Rasiński, Anat Biletzki, Leszek Koczanowicz,
Alois Pichler, and Thomas Wallgren*

Unworldliness in Twentieth Century German Thought
Stéphane Symons

For more information about this series, please visit: www.routledge.com/Routledge-
Studies-in-Twentieth-Century-Philosophy/book-series/SE0438

Unworldliness in Twentieth Century German Thought

Stéphane Symons

NEW YORK AND LONDON

First published 2025
by Routledge
605 Third Avenue, New York, NY 10158

and by Routledge
4 Park Square, Milton Park, Abingdon, Oxon, OX14 4RN

Routledge is an imprint of the Taylor & Francis Group, an informa business

© 2025 Stéphane Symons

The right of Stéphane Symons to be identified as author of this
work has been asserted in accordance with sections 77 and 78 of
the Copyright, Designs and Patents Act 1988.

All rights reserved. No part of this book may be reprinted or
reproduced or utilised in any form or by any electronic, mechanical,
or other means, now known or hereafter invented, including
photocopying and recording, or in any information storage or
retrieval system, without permission in writing from the publishers.

Trademark notice: Product or corporate names may be trademarks
or registered trademarks, and are used only for identification and
explanation without intent to infringe.

Library of Congress Cataloging-in-Publication Data
Names: Symons, Stéphane (Philosopher), author.
Title: Unworldliness in twentieth century German thought /
    Stéphane Symons.
Description: 1. | New York, NY : Routledge, 2025. |
    Series: Routledge studies in twentieth-century philosophy |
    Includes bibliographical references and index.
Identifiers: LCCN 2024037130 (print) | LCCN 2024037131
    (ebook) | ISBN 9781032304595 (hardback) | ISBN 9781032427294
    (paperback) | ISBN 9781003364009 (ebook)
Subjects: LCSH: Philosophy, German—20th century.
Classification: LCC B3181 .S96 2025 (print) | LCC B3181 (ebook) |
    DDC 193—dc23/eng/20240924
LC record available at https://lccn.loc.gov/2024037130
LC ebook record available at https://lccn.loc.gov/2024037131

ISBN: 978-1-032-30459-5 (hbk)
ISBN: 978-1-032-42729-4 (pbk)
ISBN: 978-1-003-36400-9 (ebk)

DOI: 10.4324/9781003364009

Typeset in Sabon
by Apex CoVantage, LLC

Contents

Acknowledgments		*vi*
Introduction		1
1	Strange Bedfellows: The Young Georg Lukács and Ernst Jünger: Don Quixote, The Knight of Faith	32
2	Ernst Bloch Meets Theodor Adorno: *Don Quixote*, or Hope in Dark Times	61
3	The Missed Conversation Between Max Kommerell and Siegfried Kracauer: Sancho Panza, The Man Without Convictions	95
Index		*139*

Acknowledgments

I thank Dmitri Nikulin and his students at the New School for Social Research and Nathan Ross and his students at Adelphi University for the invitation to present some of my ideas, and for the valuable feedback I received on these occasions. I also thank Humboldt University's Institut für Philosophie and Institut für deutsche Literatur for hosting me during my research stays in Berlin.

This book originated in the project G030023N: The Frankfurt School meets Phenomenology (funded by the Research-Council Flanders) and the project C14/18/048: Space Thought and Taught (funded by BOF KUL).

I dedicate this book to Tammy Castelein and Arthur Francis Symons.

Introduction

I

In his early essay, 'Bedrooms', Marcel Proust describes what happens when we wake up: we are confused. 'Sometimes my sleep was so deep, or had taken me so suddenly, that I had lost track of where I was'.[1] This disorientation makes itself felt, first of all, through the suspension of the lived interaction with the actual space and the objects one is surrounded by. A bed, closet, door, or wall will now no longer be encountered as the intimately known thing that, in relation with other intimately known things, sets up the environment one calls home and which makes one feel at ease. In Proust's view, this suspension of the lived connection with our environment results from the disruption of our habits, 'that skillful but unhurrying manager . . . without [whose] help, [our mind] would be powerless, by its own efforts, to make any room seem habitable'.[2] The process of awakening adjourns the intuitive process of projecting meaning onto our daily surroundings and thereby confronts us with the mere being-there of physical things and phenomena. When our habits are suspended, these things and phenomena no longer appear clothed by our feelings, beliefs, and associations. Instead of being aligned with our own emotional universe, the physical environment in which we go about our ordinary existence now radiates an eerie distance, as if it was never fully known to begin with.

> Our soul is obliged to fill and repaint any new space offered to it, to spray its perfumes and tune its sounds, and until then I know what we can suffer on the first evenings, as long as our soul is isolated and has to accept the color of the armchair, the ticking of the clock, the smell of the bedspread.[3]

In Proust's view, famously, these disorienting experiences are the breeding ground of *creativity*. The moment of awakening, for instance, can open the vaults of memory, unleashing a series of recollections in which the

DOI: 10.4324/9781003364009-1

2 Unworldliness in Twentieth Century German Thought

bedrooms of one's childhood, long-lost and forgotten, resurface, along with the moments of awakening that were experienced within them. All of a sudden, not only the bedroom in the house of his grandparents, with its crucifix and alcove, floods Marcel's consciousness but also a pyramid-shaped room in Dieppe, where he was brought to convalesce, a rotan seat in an Auteuil garden, a salon in Evian, and the castle of Réveillon. In other words, the suspension of habit marks the possibility of a *metamorphosis*. When it jolts into motion one's memory, it does not so much bring back a *lived past* as that it presents the truly *new*: the interruption of our intuitive interaction with our surroundings brings out an unknown dimension and unsuspected richness within seemingly insignificant objects. In a sentence in 'Bedrooms' that he will reproduce almost word by word in the famous overture to the first volume of *In Search of Lost Time*, Proust puts it as follows: 'I sometimes wonder if the immobility of things around us is not imposed on them by our certainty that they are them and not others'.[4] In the liminal state where sleep and wakefulness blend together, what was believed to be well-known does indeed play tricks with our sense of certitude and becomes *young* again.[5] Upon awakening, the space of our bedroom, so intimately known that it had enabled us to fall asleep, resonates with an inexhausted potential to become other to what it was.

> So my body erects room after room around it, the winter ones where one likes to be separated from the outside, where one keeps a fire going all night, or keeps tied around one's shoulders a dark, smoky cloak of warm air, crossed by gleams, the summer ones where one likes to be united with the gentleness of nature, where one sleeps, a room where I slept in Brussels and whose shape was so elated, so vast and yet so closed-off that you felt hidden as in a nest and free as in a world.[6]

In in-between mental states like awakening, the things that normally yield an unproblematized feeling of recognition are released or, if one will, emancipated, from such overarching contexts of meaning. They are unexpectedly perceived to stand apart and acquire a monadic dimension: they present universes that far surpass the limits of the actual room in which one finds oneself.

According to Proust, this disruption of habit is marked by a second type of confusion. The process of awakening, to return to the same example, does not just suspend the lived interaction with one's external environment but also momentarily interrupts one's sense of self. In 'Bedrooms' Proust describes how one's self-perception can be shaken along with the intimate bond to well-known things. For the briefest of moments, we get the feeling that we are no more known to ourselves than the physical objects that

Introduction 3

surround us. It seems, in fact, that we are but a thing among other things. Waking up from deep sleep, we perceive ourselves as a sheer 'particle in a sleeping whole'.

> In these short awakenings, I was nothing more than an apple or a jar of jam, which, on the board where they were placed, would be called for a moment to a vague consciousness, and which, having found that it was dark in the sideboard . . . would have nothing more urgent than to return to the delicious insensibility of other apples and other jars of jam.[7]

For Proust, in other words, the lived interaction with the outside world is inseparable from a lived interaction with the intimate core of our sense of self and, consequently, the disruption of this interaction with our physical environment inevitably results in a disrupted self-perception. But, once more, Proust draws attention to the creative potential that comes together with such an unstable sense of self. In the opening section of *Swann's Way*, the above-quoted statement, from 'Bedrooms', that Marcel 'had lost track of where [he] was' will receive an important addition:

> when I awoke at midnight, not knowing *where* I was, I could not be sure at first *who* I was; I had only the most rudimentary sense of existence, such as may lurk and flicker in the depths of an animal's consciousness; I was more destitute of human qualities than the cave-dweller.[8]

This encounter with the self as a non-human is not a merely alienating feat according to Proust. While it can obviously confront us with the inevitable transience of existence, this feeling of self-alienation can equally well yield a sense of transformation, not unlike the possibility of metamorphosis that was described earlier. Through the feeling that it is, at times, our own intimate self that slips through our fingers, we can replenish the feeling that we, along with our intimate surroundings, can become *different*. It is, of course, no coincidence that Proust starts his cycle of novels with the description of precisely this creative potential of self-differentiation. One could even argue that the feeling that our existence is made up of multiple selves that are replaced one by one is *the* central topic of *In Search of Lost Time*. In *The Fugitive*, for instance, Proust puts it as follows:

> [M]y life appeared to me to be something . . . lacking the support of an individual, identical and permanent self, . . . something . . . easy for death to terminate here or there without any kind of conclusion.[9]

This statement does not testify to mere melancholy, and it surpasses the mournful awareness of inevitable finitude. In Proust's works, such

4 Unworldliness in Twentieth Century German Thought

descriptions of transient selves can just as well be connected to the irreducible potential of change. It is for this reason that he ends his cycle by highlighting the importance of *artistic* creation. In the final novel, *Time Regained*, Proust famously states that 'real life, life at last laid bare and illuminated – the only life in consequence which can be said to be really lived – is literature, and life thus defined is in a sense all the time immanent in ordinary men no less than in the artist'.[10] While, in real life, no one is granted a stable and permanent individual self, the act of artistic creation does enable the salvation of this series of transient selves. The novel itself, that is, remains autonomous from our lived experiences but, for that very reason, gathers our past selves in the not actually existing realm of *art*. By virtue of its *not* being an actual thing, the artwork thus grows capable of, so to speak, rejuvenating the feeling that a profound metamorphosis of the self remains possible after all.

The idea that our interaction with objects is inherently entwined with our self-perception, and that the suspension of the former will therefore inevitably result in an unstable sense of self, was not just dear to Proust. In the same period when Proust was working on his cycle of novels, early phenomenologists were grappling with philosophical intuitions that would, to a certain extent, go in the same direction. In fact, 1927 was the year when not only *Time Regained*, Proust's final novel, was (posthumously) published but also Martin Heidegger's *Being and Time*. In the third chapter of the first division of that study, Heidegger will coin his own term to denote the meaningful unity that takes shape when we establish a lived connection with our immediate environment: worldliness. The world, that is, is according to Heidegger not just a collection of various physical things. 'Thus, the first step is to enumerate the things which are "in" the world: houses, trees, people, mountains, stars. We can describe the "outward appearance" of these beings and tell of the events occurring with them. But that is obviously a pre-phenomenological "business" which cannot be phenomenologically relevant at all'.[11] With the concept of 'worldliness' Heidegger denotes the *structure of relationships* through which the various things that are 'in' the world refer to one another. Like the bedroom that Proust describes, such a structure sets up an intuitively known *network* of things. It is only on account of this internal unity that our world, and the objects within it, can be encountered in an intimate, as it was homely, manner. The role of the human being is, of course, crucial in this regard. It is only by virtue of our interaction with these objects, and our ability to engage with the relations that connect them to each other, that the outside world can acquire such a unified and intimately known presence. In a series of lectures given in the same year (1927), Heidegger states that the world is '*a moment in the structure of Dasein's mode of being*. The world is, so to speak, Dasein-ish'.[12] He even goes as far as to state that '[t]he world is something "subjective," presupposing that we correspondingly define subjectivity with regard to this phenomenon of world. . . . *So far as the Dasein exists a world is cast forth with the Dasein's being*'.[13] For Heidegger, this lived interaction with physical objects, and the human ability to meet them as parts of a larger whole, revolves around 'use'.

> Strictly speaking, there "is" no such thing as a useful thing. There always belongs to the being of a useful thing a totality of useful things in which this useful thing can be what it is. A useful thing is essentially "something in order to." The different kinds of "in order to" such as serviceability, helpfulness, usability, handiness, constitute a totality of useful things. The structure of "in order to" contains a reference of something to something.[14]

Practical use entails a pre-reflective understanding ('circumspection') of how one object refers to a whole series of other objects. When we use a hammer, this practical comportment carries within itself a pre-theoretical grasp of the overarching unity of the world that surrounds us, and the manner in which a series of things (hammer, nail, hand, a piece of wood, etc.) clings together. For Heidegger, as well, this lived interaction with a unified, external world goes hand in hand with a lived sense of self. For it is only by virtue of this feeling for the unity of the world, its worldliness, that the human being becomes worthy of the crucial task that rests on her shoulders. In Heidegger's view, 'worldliness is itself an existential'.[15] With this he means that grasping the unity of the surrounding world is a prerequisite for a reconnection with the even more foundational unity of *Being* and the establishment of an 'authentic' self. In other words, our lived interaction with a unified world is not just a practical matter but it is believed to potentially open both an ontological and an existential dimension. '"World" is ontologically not a determination of *those* beings which Da-sein essentially is *not*, but rather a characteristic of Da-sein itself'.[16] With the concept of 'being-in-the-world', developed in the fourth chapter of the first division of *Being and Time*, Heidegger further explores this connection between, on the one hand, the lived interaction with the surrounding world and, on the other, an 'authentic' sense of self. The human being is the sole creature that is capable of establishing a 'caring' attitude toward things, a genuine 'being-with' other human beings, and a conscious relation with its own 'throwness' and finitude. 'Being-in-the-world' therefore denotes a most fundamental feature of the human condition. 'The clarification of being-in-the-world showed that a mere subject without a world "is" not initially and is also never given'.[17] The human being finds herself always already surrounded by an environment that she inevitably needs to reckon with, and it is only from within this inextricable bond

6 *Unworldliness in Twentieth Century German Thought*

with an outside world that she both reconnects with the overarching horizon of Being and builds up a proper sense of self. In short, according to Heidegger, there can be no talk of a unified world without considering an authentic self, nor vice versa.

In spite of seeming affinities, there are at least two fundamental differences between Proust's and Heidegger's approach. First of all, in Heidegger's view, the interruption of our intuitive grasp of outside objects does not at all jeopardize the lived experience of a unified world. While Proust understands such a momentary suspension as a deeply confusing experience ('I had lost track of where I was'), for Heidegger, our failure to spontaneously interact with the external world sets the stage for the very experience of its 'worldliness'. For it is in his view precisely when a given object becomes use*less*, for instance, because it breaks down, that we gain the possibility of truly understanding how that object forms part of a larger structure of relationships with other objects. 'Tools turn out to be damaged, their material unsuitable. . . When we discover its unusability, the thing becomes conspicuous. . . [In the conspicuousness of what is unusable,] [h]andiness shows itself once again, and precisely in doing so the worldly character of what is at hand also shows itself, too'.[18] According to Heidegger, the deep coherence and unity of the world manifests itself most powerfully at the precise instant when one of its objects can no longer be used and thus seemingly detaches itself from that unity. 'As a deficient mode of taking care of things, the helpless way in which we stand before [an unusable thing] discovers the mere objective presence of what is at hand. . . . Unhandy things are disturbing and make evident the obstinacy of what is initially to be taken care of before anything else. With this obstinacy the objective presence of what is at hand makes itself known in a new way as the being of what is still present and calls for completion'.[19] The suspension of the interaction with the outside world ought therefore in Heidegger's view not to be considered a truly disorienting experience, as Proust would have it. To the contrary, such limit-experiences are, according to Heidegger, the seed of an insight with ontological and existential weight. In Heidegger's view, the sudden disruption of our habits results in a further confirmation that the world can and should be encountered as an integral whole, whereas, in Proust's view, this disruption renders the experience of such a unity impossible. Similarly, the destabilizing effect that such limit-experiences have on our self-perception is, in Heidegger's view, first and foremost the mark of an authentic self that does not shy away from looking at the dark truths of human existence in the eye. While, for Proust, such disorienting experiences shake the foundations of a stable self and result in an internal splitting ('I could not be sure at first *who* I was; I had only the most rudimentary sense of existence'), for Heidegger, these limit-experiences are, paradoxically, the indispensable building blocks of

Introduction 7

a more rooted sense of existence. They come together with a pronounced 'anxiety' but, rather than jeopardizing our self-perception, this anxiety is, notoriously, a 'foundational feeling' that enables a fuller grasp of the unique human being we are. In Heidegger's view, that is, there can be no such thing as a Proustian multiplicity of selves since each human being is characterized with an irreplaceable and un-shareable (individual) essence that she needs to fully embrace.

> Da-sein is a being which I myself am, its being is in each case mine. . . . Even if one rejects a substantial soul, the thingliness of consciousness and the objectivity of the person, ontologically one still posits something whose being retains the meaning of objective presence, whether explicitly or not.[20]

A second and equally fundamental point of difference between Proust and Heidegger revolves around the possibility that this loss of the lived unity of the world, and the accompanying destabilization of the sense of self could be a positive event. According to Proust, the suspension of our habitual engagement with our surroundings and the concomitant destabilization of self-perception replenish our belief in transformation and form the core of artistic creation. For Heidegger, however, such types of *un*-worldliness and *de*-selfing clearly run counter to the ontological and existential significance he is after. Introducing the concept of 'de-worlding' (*Entweltlichung*), he refers to a decontextualized perspective on a 'homogeneous' space, that is, a merely objective environment that has become isolated from human intentionality altogether. Such a space lacks the 'worldliness' that was described earlier: it has shed the internal unity that connects various phenomena and impedes the lived interaction through which the human being encounters her surroundings as genuinely meaningful. A 'deworlded' space presents a mere series of indiscriminate possibilities and no longer invites a deeply felt response on the part of the individual. For instance, '[w]here space is discovered non-circumspectly by just looking at it, the regions of the surrounding world get neutralized to pure dimensions'.[21] According to Heidegger, unworldliness suspends our spontaneous connection with objects, but, in opposition to the truth-bearing perception of 'unusable things' that was outlined earlier, it does not lead to any ontological or existential insight at all: a 'deworlded' space yields but a feeling of disconnectedness, fragmentation, and arbitrariness. 'The places and the totality of places of useful things at hand which are circumspectly oriented are reduced to a multiplicity of positions for random things. The spatiality of innerworldly things at hand thus loses its character of relevance'.[22] Admittedly, Heidegger's notion of 'de-worlding' refers to phenomena that are unrelated to what is described in Proust's

8 Unworldliness in Twentieth Century German Thought

essay 'Bedrooms' and the overture to his cycle of novels. When Heidegger draws attention to the danger that the 'worldly character of what is at hand gets specifically deprived of its worldliness', he targets, above all, the Cartesian outlook on the world. Founding his philosophical project in the problematization of the lived ties with the outside world, Descartes is taken to task for reducing this outside world to a collection of *res extensae* that no longer resonate with human significance. While such a worldview prepared the ground for the natural sciences and modern physics and enabled a study of phenomena as they factually *are*, it simultaneously blocked the path to a true, that is, *human* understanding of nature. In a series of lectures from 1925, Heidegger therefore claims that

> [e]very explanation, when we speak of an explanation of nature, is distinguished by its involvement in the *incomprehensible*. . . . Nature is what is in principle explainable and to be explained because it is in principle incomprehensible. . . . And it is incomprehensible because it is the *"deworlded" world*, insofar as we take nature . . . as it is discovered in physics.[23]

In spite of the specific context to which it belongs, Heidegger's concept of 'deworlding' does allow us to put our finger on an irreducible difference with Proust's project. For Proust, the process of de-worlding opens a productive dynamic in which specific objects and phenomena are released from the overarching context to which they ordinarily belong. This disruption of our habits yields a deeply rejuvenating effect: when objects and phenomena can somehow take leave of their most natural network of relationships, they replenish our belief in change. For Heidegger, however, such a collapse of the world's inner unity is a troubling and alienating feat: it yields but an impression of mere randomness and throws the human being back upon herself.

II

Heidegger's rejection of the creative potential of unworldliness builds on an important intellectual trend in German thought and will in its turn receive an influential intellectual heritage. The seeds of Heidegger's negative view of 'de-worlded' space can be found in Edmund Husserl's early texts, written during the first decades of the twentieth century. As is well known, in the 1920s, Heidegger supplants Husserl's phenomenological focus on human consciousness with an analysis of human *existence* and an *ontological* inquiry. But it is Husserl who has shown him the importance of our lived interactions with a unified world and clarified why they are unthinkable without the constitutive role of a stable subject. In his early texts, Husserl already introduces the foundational opposition between the 'natural attitude', which takes the existence of an external world for granted, and the phenomenological method which, 'bracketing' this existence of the external world, analyzes the meaning-giving capacities of human thought. In this manner, Husserl, like Heidegger, rejects positivism and instead emphasizes the human being's crucial role in shaping an internally coherent horizon of meaning. In *Ideas II*, for instance, Husserl writes that

> the actual surrounding world of any person whatsoever is not physical reality pure and simple and without qualification, but instead it is the surrounding world only to the extent he "knows" of it, insofar as he grasps it by apperception and positing or is conscious of it in the horizon of his existence as co-given and offered to his grasp – clearly or unclearly, determinately or indeterminately – precisely in accordance with the way it happens to be posited by consciousness.[24]

And, one page later, he adds that

> [s]peaking quite universally, the surrounding world is not a world "in itself" but is rather a world "for me," precisely the surrounding world of its Ego-subject, a world experienced by the subject or grasped consciously in some other way and posited by the subject in his intentional lived experiences with the sense-content of the moment.[25]

In these early stages of Husserl's thought, the discussion about the surrounding world and the ego, and the connection between both, primarily revolves around a quest for *mental* essences, which renders the inquiry into the lived interactions with an empirically real environment less philosophically urgent. But in a later work such as *The Crisis of European Sciences and Transcendental Phenomenology: An Introduction to Phenomenological Philosophy* (1936), Husserl moves closer to Heidegger and analyzes the ways in which a human being shapes empirically real surroundings into a meaningful human environment. This means that his rejection of positivism is deepened, along with his negative stance toward worldviews that do not reckon with the subject's constitutive and meaning-giving role. The notion of 'lifeworld' is of crucial importance here. 'The contrast between the subjectivity of the life-world and the "objective", the "true" world', writes Husserl in *Crisis*, 'lies in the fact that the latter is a theoretical-logical substruction, the substruction of something that is in principle not perceivable, in principle not experienceable in its own proper being, whereas the subjective, in the life-world, is distinguished in all respects precisely by its being actually experienceable'.[26] Endorsing a self-confessed 'return to the

10 *Unworldliness in Twentieth Century German Thought*

naïveté of life', Husserl criticizes the 'objective sciences' for their failure to reconnect with a human being's lived response to her surroundings.

Husserl and Heidegger's emphasis on the interactions with a lifeworld will become a dominant trend in twentieth-century German thought, as will be their dismissal of the creative potential of experiences of *un*-worldliness and *de*-selfing. This can be illustrated through three very different thinkers, active within the domains of, respectively, existential psychiatry, political philosophy, and philosophy of culture. A first figure who illustrates the *Nachleben* of Husserl and Heidegger's focus on worldliness, and their concomitant rejection of 'deworlded' space, is Ludwig Binswanger. In both his writings and his therapeutic practice, Binswanger founds his psychiatric insights in a *Daseinsanalyse*, the main assumption being that each patient is a unique individual, marked by a unique being-in-the-world and 'motivational structure'. This entails that symptoms should not be considered as mere deficiencies since they point, above all, to a specific manner of interacting with one's surroundings. It is not until this lived connection with the patient's lifeworld is scrutinized that a clear diagnosis can be made, and that the therapeutic process can take a start. According to Binswanger, 'The sick person is in a sense closer to the Dasein than we are – even if they are caught in a veritable dizziness of this Dasein'.[27] The therapist must prevent the patient from isolating herself from her environment and should assist the patient in realizing that her mental state, even during illness, provides a unique perspective on a lifeworld. In the case of eccentricity, for example,

> what we call psychotherapy is essentially no more than an attempt to bring the patient to a point where they can "see" how the totality of human existence or "being-in-the-world" is structured and to see at which of their nodes they have gone beyond himself. That is, the goal of psychotherapy is to bring the patient out of their eccentricity and safely "back to earth". Only from this point is a new *departure* and a new *ascent* possible.[28]

In this manner the *idios kosmos* of a closed-off individual can be opened toward the external *kosmos koinonia* that is shared with other human beings. Binswanger opposes the patient's risky tendency to 'lose themselves in pure subjectivity' with their capacity to open up to a communal universe. The patient's quest for an 'other' universe can only make the therapist 'wince' because 'the meaning of life is always something transsubjective, something universal, "objective" and impersonal'.[29] Binswanger is convinced that the construction of a stable self is indispensable in setting up these lived interactions with a shared world. A therapist can, and should, discover the fragments of a self that is buried underneath a seemingly aberrant behavior, which she can, together with the patient, reconstruct into a

Introduction   11

coherent identity. In his view, every human being is characterized by her own 'inner life history'. This inner life takes shape over time and creates a unified narrative out of a long series of lived experiences: '(O)ur interest is . . . in . . . the unique, temporal sequence of the contents of lived experience'. That life path points to 'the individual spiritual person' and is 'the origin or core of all experience, in short, *the inner history of the person's life*'.[30] One of the key differences with Freudian psychoanalysis, which Binswanger, after the example of Heidegger, calls 'naturalistic', is therefore that he refuses to consider the body as a (Cartesian) mechanism of blind impulses. Dreams, for instance, are not driven by anonymous drives that operate in a deworlded space. They are the products of a unique individual's engagement with an internally consistent world and thus carry *existential* weight.

In a wholly different subdiscipline of philosophy, political philosophy, Hannah Arendt's diagnosis of 'world-alienation' bears similar traces of Husserl and Heidegger's emphasis on worldliness, and their rejection of deworlded space. As is well known, Arendt came under the influence of Heidegger while studying in Marburg in 1925. While her concept of world-alienation was developed much later, it cannot be fully understood without laying bare the connection with Husserlian phenomenology. The first line of the prologue of the *Human Conditions* runs as follows:

> In 1957, an earth born object made by man was launched into the universe, where for some weeks, it circled the earth according to the same laws of gravitation that swing and keep in motion the celestial bodies – the sun, the moon, and the stars.[31]

When human beings lose their capacity to collectively *be-in-the-world*, they are reduced to mere physical entities. We have become, Arendt writes, 'universe dwellers instead of earth-dwellers':

> It is in the nature of the human surveying capacity that it can function only if man disentangles himself from all involvement in and concern with the close at hand and withdraws himself to a distance from everything near him. The greater the distance between himself and his surroundings, world or earth, the more he will be able to survey and to measure and the less will worldly, earth-bound space be left to him. The fact that the decisive shrinkage of the earth was the consequence of the invention of the airplane, that is, of leaving the surface of the earth altogether, is like a symbol for the general phenomenon that any decrease of terrestrial distance can be won only at the price of putting a decisive distance between man and earth, of alienating man from his immediate earthly surroundings.[32]

12   *Unworldliness in Twentieth Century German Thought*

World-alienation is to Arendt a specifically *modern* threat that can be described in various ways. First of all, it refers to the decline of the public sphere for political action. In Arendt's view the shared space in which human beings can actively deliberate and collectively decide about their destiny is put under severe pressure. Second, excessive privatization and isolation result in an excessive focus on merely personal concerns. Third, the natural sciences have become the main driving force behind processes of modernization, which results in the prominence of instrumental rationality and values like efficiency and utility. Fourth, world-alienation is characterized by a loss of authenticity, that is, an alienation from our true selves through the uncritical embrace of societal norms and standards. The last two of these four elements resonate strongly with the concerns of Husserl and Heidegger (and Binswanger). Like them, Arendt puts forward the double, and inseparable, ideal of being-in-the-world and true selfhood. Arendt does put the emphasis on a *collective* being-in-the-world and sees this not as an *existential given* but as the correlate of *political action*. Still, like Husserl and Heidegger, she highlights, on the one hand, the entwinement between lived interactions with a shared and unified world and, on the other, a stable sense of self. 'What makes mass society so difficult to bear is not the number of people involved, or at least not primarily, but the fact that the world between them has lost its power to gather them together, to relate and to separate them'.[33]

Hans Blumenberg is a third and, again, altogether different thinker whose work can nonetheless be situated within this same context. He, as well, gives critical weight to the concept of lifeworld. In Blumenberg's view, it is first and foremost a limit-concept that describes the flawless reconciliation between a human being and her surroundings. It refers to the perfect alignment between human consciousness and external reality since our interactions with the lifeworld remain unproblematized: when experienced as a lifeworld, the external world is deemed fully identical with our conception of it. For this reason, Blumenberg actually goes as far as to suggest that we cannot truly 'live' a lifeworld.[34] Rather, the lifeworld is marked by the fact that it does *not* meet the threshold of lived interaction and remains, strictly speaking, unnoticed. On account of this frictionless alignment with our expectations, it cannot even be 'described from within' and will only be brought to full awareness when we can somehow take a position *outside* of it. This is why Blumenberg painstakingly analyzes what happens when the self-evidentiality of a specific lifeworld is challenged on account of the entry of a *temporal* dimension, for instance, through historical events and societal evolutions. Describing the subtle transformations that recast entire historical and cultural periods, Blumenberg reconstructs how these have given way to novel ones. In spite of these specificities, his concept of lifeworld is in an essential

Introduction 13

manner derived from Husserlian phenomenology. Blumenberg is most fascinated with what he calls 'reality-concepts', that is, the myths and metaphors that shape our interactions with the lifeworld and result in an internally coherent worldview. Such 'reality-concepts' cannot be believed to accurately reproduce a non-human, purely external reality.[35] Like Husserl and Heidegger, Blumenberg carves out the difference between such vehicles of human thought and a mere, supposedly 'objective' reproduction of facts. As a consequence, myths and metaphors will never be supplanted by, for instance, a purely scientific instrumentarium. Blumenberg even goes further than Husserl in this regard. *Pace* Husserl, Blumenberg claims that the concept of lifeworld should only be used in plural to underscore their historical and cultural dimension. Husserl's promise of a 'rigorous science' that uncovers unshakeable (mental) truths is therefore replaced with an emphasis on the contingency of cultural and historical phenomena, the finitude of human endeavors and, crucially, the ability of the human being to acquire an understanding of both. In Blumenberg's view, there is no 'neutral' perspective that would enable us to analyze the universal essences of human thought. In an attempt to rid Husserlian phenomenology of all 'metaphysical remnants' (Blumenberg even writes about the 'cryptotheological' currents in early phenomenology)[36] he seeks above all to make phenomenology fruitful for anthropological, historical, and cultural research. Still, Blumenberg does concur with Husserlian phenomenology in considering deworlded space a major threat to the meaning-giving capacities of the human being. With his concept of the 'absolutism of reality', Blumenberg singles out the moment when the human being started walking upright. This radically transformed her outlook on the outside world since it expanded her field of vision and action. Becoming a biped confronted the human organism with an environment that was indifferent to her projects and created the awareness that one was visible to all kinds of opponents. Described as 'intentionality of consciousness without an object', the confrontation with such an indifferent and inhuman reality is, according to Blumenberg, the trigger of a deep-seated anxiety and even blind panic.[37] But, '[w]hat has become identifiable by means of a name is raised out of its unfamiliarity by means of metaphor and is made accessible, in terms of its significance, by telling stories. Panic and paralysis, as the two extremes of anxiety behavior, are dissolved by the appearance of calculable magnitudes to deal with and regulated ways of dealing with them'.[38] In his view, therefore, the construction of 'reality-concepts', a lifeworld and, by extension, culture at large is a neutralization of the anxiety provoked by the threat of unworldliness and de-selfing. This situation in which 'the whole horizon becomes equivalent as the totality of the directions from which 'it [i.e. danger] can come at one'[39] can and needs to be overcome through the

14　*Unworldliness in Twentieth Century German Thought*

setting-up of what Blumenberg calls a 'cosmos'. It is at this moment that the properly human ability to give shape to internally coherent worlds comes into existence.

III

In spite of all this interesting work that revolves around our lived interaction with a shared world, it is its conceptual antithesis, *un*worldliness, that is central to this book. Its main starting point is the idea that a deworlded space can result in a creative dynamic and need not be cast aside as a merely negative feature. The positive potential of the concept of unworldliness rests in the suggestion that a felt absence of unity or overarching meaningfulness can nonetheless trigger an experience that is no less profound and important than the lived experience of worldliness that is singled out in Husserlian phenomenology. The perceived absence of a unifying ground within the world, that is, can lay bare an unexpected potential *to change and be changed*. Though experienced as fragmented, such an 'unworldly world' can thus yield much more than a merely mournful or nostalgic quest for lost totalities: a world without a foundational meaning can instill the feeling that metamorphosis is possible. The subjective correlate of such a fragmented-but-changeable world is a process of de-selfing, not the world-constituting activity of a self-identical ego. For the awareness that human beings, as well, lack a unifying ground need not be a negative feature either. The experience of split selves or multiple identities might shake the stability of our self-perception, but this instability itself can have a deeply rejuvenating effect.

In the twentieth century this creative potential of unworldliness and de-selfing has primarily been tapped by post-war *French* philosophers. Though their projects are in no way identical, post-phenomenological and post-structuralist thinkers like Jacques Derrida, Michel Foucault, and Jean-François Lyotard have joined forces in rejecting the importance of a unified worldview that co-originates with a stable self.[40] Since human consciousness is always mediated by language and cannot ever be made fully transparent, since subjectivation is always a product of structures of knowledge and power, and since our (historical, political, social) lifeworld has disconnected itself from overarching, internally coherent 'master-narratives', the jargon of phenomenology has not survived the twentieth century unscathed. For Derrida, 'lived experience' is an 'unwieldy' concept that 'belongs to the history of metaphysics, and we can only use it under erasure', for Foucault, a 'de-subjectifying undertaking, the idea of a "limit-experience" that tears the subject from itself . . . is [a] fundamental lesson', and for Lyotard, 'the idea of the I and that of experience which is associated with it are not necessary for the description of reality'.[41] Indeed, it would make much sense to read the history of post-war French thought as one long critical comment vis-à-vis pre-war German phenomenology and its heirs. Levinas' positive remarks about the success of the first journey into outer space, for instance, can then be interpreted as a corrective to Arendt's Heidegger-influenced criticism of the same events. In 'Heidegger, Gagarin and Us', Levinas rejects the phenomenological ideal of being-in-the-world and the primordiality of rootedness and earthliness:

> I'm thinking of a prestigious current of modern thought, originating in Germany and flooding the pagan corners of our Western soul. I'm thinking of Heidegger and the Heideggerians. They want man to rediscover the world. Men would have lost the world. All they would know is the matter set before them, objecting in some way to their freedom; they would know only objects.[42]

Levinas counters this Heideggerian and Arendtian criticism through a remarkable defense of modern science and, indeed, a celebration of man's ability to literally *not*-be-in-the-world. 'Perhaps what matters most of all is to have left the Place. For an hour, a man existed outside any horizon – all was sky around him, or, more precisely, all was geometric space. A man existed in the absolute of homogeneous space'.[43] In Levinas' view, it is this *non*-lived and *external* perspective on the earth which reinstalls the Jewish desire to be 'free in relation to places' and to demystify nature. Levinas highlights the importance of dispelling the romantic idealization of the earth and worldliness and of rupturing the texture of an internally unified world, thereby liberating the ethical and transcendent 'nakedness of the face'. Coming from entirely different philosophical corners than Levinas, and wedded to a philosophy of radical immanence, Gilles Deleuze's concept of 'milieu' can just as much be pitted against the conceptual jargon of Husserlian phenomenology. In opposition to the notion of lifeworld, which conceptualizes the alignment of our surroundings to our supposedly constitutive capacities, Deleuze opens up the distance between both *and* makes this distance productive. In opposition to an *Umwelt*, a milieu is perceived as a multiplicity of different and a-subjective parts-without-a-whole. Rather than a unified horizon of meaning, a milieu is fragmented into 'qualities, substances, powers, and events: the street, for example, with its materials (paving stones), its noises (the cries of merchants), its animals (harnessed horses) or its dramas (a horse slips, a horse falls down, a horse is beaten . . .)'.[44] In Deleuze's view, human desire thrives on precisely such a-subjective parts-without-a-whole since our libidinal investment in the world and its objects is nourished by this irreducible multiplicity and unceasing variation. The numerous 'connections' that link a person to the characteristics and experiences of their environment are inherently flexible

16   *Unworldliness in Twentieth Century German Thought*

and open to transformation. These connections possess a dynamic energy that surpasses an individual's limitations or societal taboos. It is through these unanticipated interactions with their surroundings that human desire is sparked and can evolve into a powerful force for change. Here again, the ideal of a stable self that 'lives' the surrounding world as a meaningful unity is supplanted by a dynamic of de-selfing: above all, we are 'desiring-machines' marked by a potential to always become other.

The present book explores how this positive potential of unworldliness is dealt with in key instances of twentieth-century *German* thought. Though the rejection of this potential is the dominant trend in twentieth-century German thought, there is an important undercurrent of thinkers who do regard it as a positive feature. This is not to say that the book uncovers a hidden paradigm or one single intellectual agenda that is set forth by all of its protagonists. The philosophical projects that this book focuses on are as wide-ranging as the illustrations of French post-phenomenological thought given earlier. Their proponents often have very different intellectual, ideological, and biographical backgrounds and nourish very different philosophical ambitions. Reconstructed in detail, these differences will play a key role in the central argument, while carefully avoiding the reduction of text to context. The biographical, historical, and societal origins of philosophical arguments are crucial for a better understanding of their relevance, but these arguments always retain an important sense of autonomy. As intellectual historian Stefanos Geroulanos writes,

> Regardless of how they are puppeteered, concepts strung together in a given space have a temporality and a life of their own, one not quite attached to specific intellectuals, or to social-political circumstances and events. More often than not they structure, clothe, stage these circumstances and events in manners that historians are often eager to ignore. Concepts do not rest among clouds, to be stared at, "contextualized," or "historicized" from the "real" vantage point of society; rather they thread together the experience of knowledge, reading, speech, and belief. They cannot be experienced in the absence of this articulation, "without strings", apart from one another.[45]

Exposing some of the differences between the discussed philosophical projects therefore does not at all mitigate the central argument that a series of influential German thinkers has shared an affinity for the creative potential of unworldliness. To the contrary, by pointing to unexpected similarities in the writings of markedly left-wing (Lukács, Kracauer) and right-wing thinkers (Jünger, Kommerell) or, vice versa, by bringing to the surface often overlooked oppositions between otherwise like-minded thinkers (Adorno, Bloch), this study unpacks some of the various ways in

Introduction 17

which the concept of unworldliness has been given philosophical content. Only in this manner can the conceptual richness of the notion of unworldliness, and the various 'strings' that connect it to other notions, rise to the surface: taking recourse to similar concepts, very different authors nonetheless set out to do very different things. On account of this conceptual richness, no attempt was made to render an *exhaustive* overview of the importance of unworldliness in twentieth-century German thought. The three chapters each revolve around a conversation that is worth drawing attention to, but undoubtedly many more of such conversations would deserve to be reconstructed in the future. This future research will not in my view weaken the central hypothesis of the book but only give it more substance since it will most likely come together with extra arguments in favor of the positive meaning of the concept of unworldliness.

Having let go of the quest for an exhaustive *Auseinandersetzung* with the positive meaning of the concept of unworldliness, I have instead selected Miguel de Cervantes' *Don Quixote* and the themes that are raised in it as a running thread that brings coherence to the book. *Don Quixote* is often named the first novel and plays a remarkable role in continental philosophy, having received notable interpretations by very diverse philosophers such as Georg Wilhelm Friedrich Hegel, Friedrich Schlegel, Friedrich Nietzsche, Hermann Cohen, Miguel de Unamuno, José Ortega y Gasset, and Mikhail Bakhtin, and authors such as Fyodor Dostoyevski, Ernst Toller, Vladimir Nabokov, Jorge Luis Borges, and Salman Rushdie. The six protagonists of this book, Georg Lukács, Ernst Jünger, Ernst Bloch, Theodor Adorno, Max Kommerell, and Siegfried Kracauer, have all at some point turned to this text as well. Revealing how these six authors have come up with very different interpretations of one and the same book helps to bring out their different views of unworldliness. Don Quixote, surely the most well-known of all unworldly characters, and his companion Sancho Panza, usually associated with a down-to-earth attitude and common sense, can therefore be regarded as what Deleuze and Guattari have called 'conceptual personae'.[46] They are no mere fictional characters in a novel but 'perform' philosophical thought. Conceptual personae embody the tensions and challenges that render a specific problem *vital*, plugging it back into the societal, historical, political, and intellectual fabric in which it originates but without losing sight of its properly *philosophical* dimension. As such, the conceptual personae of Don Quixote and Sancho Panza point out both the possibilities *and* limitations of the philosophical positions laid out in this study.

Theodor Adorno's criticism of Husserlian phenomenology plays a pivotal role in navigating the positive appraisal of unworldliness in twentieth-century German thought. It is often forgotten that Adorno was a reader of Husserl from an early stage onward (1924) and devoted some

18 *Unworldliness in Twentieth Century German Thought*

of his most important early essays and lectures to his thought. During the first years of his exile in Oxford (1934–1937), he planned to write a second doctorate about Husserlian phenomenology and later counted this preparatory research, which would result in the 1956 study *Against Epistemology*, among his most important accomplishments. Moreover, there is a direct conceptual line that goes from this early research on Husserl to his post-war critical study of Heidegger, *The Jargon of Authenticity*, and his groundbreaking work *Negative Dialectics*. Though Adorno does not take explicit recourse to the term *worldliness*, one could argue that his rejection of Husserlian phenomenology, to which Heidegger's work belongs as well, revolves around an analysis of the following paradox: for the very reason that it focuses on the issue of worldliness, a genuine interaction with the outside world has become all but unthinkable in Husserlian phenomenology. For, in spite of the rhetoric about the inherent 'openness' of human consciousness and existence, according to Adorno, Husserlian phenomenology retreats into a sterile and ultimately untenable form of immanence. In his view, Husserlian phenomenology is above all a far heir to German idealism, which absolutizes the distance between the subject's meaning-giving capacities on the one hand and a purely external world on the other.[47] Because it is (transcendental) subjectivity that is deemed constitutive for our interactions with the world, Husserlian phenomenology fails to reckon with the many ways in which the outside world shapes our thoughts and actions. 'The positing of a transcendent [i.e. external] world . . . contradicts the presupposition of consciousness as the "sphere of being of absolute origins". It contradicts the basic principle of transcendental idealism'.[48] Seeking a direct understanding of *mental* essences and *existential* universals, Husserl and Heidegger are deemed guilty of a pernicious *inward turn* that cannot shed any light on our genuine, empirical interactions with the world. 'The outset of contemporary ontology', writes Adorno, 'coincides with the cult of inwardness. The retreat of ontology from the course of the world is also a retreat from the empirical content of subjectivity'.[49] Adorno therefore claims that the only 'truth' that can be derived from Husserl and Heidegger's 'untruths' is a societal one: the subject-position that both thinkers presuppose reveals in very clear terms how bourgeois individuals seek to constantly isolate themselves from their surroundings and other people. The final lines of his Husserl-book therefore read as follows:

> The intertwining of illusion and necessity in idealism has seldom become clearer in its history than with Husserl. . . . The ground of the paradox, the monadological constitution of man, could only be sublated if consciousness were at some time finally to rule over being, which it constantly only with untruth asserts is grounded in consciousness.[50]

Introduction 19

For Adorno, reality is above all historically and socially produced and, as such, contingent. For this reason, it is crucial to come to terms with the fact that even our most intimate feelings are 'mediated' by historical and societal developments that can, and most often should, be changed. Husserlian phenomenology, however, gets stuck in its quest for 'immediacy'. Underlying the project of Husserlian phenomenology is a master-ego that forms the outside world after its own likeness and cannot come to terms with anything that does not fit that image. This explains why Husserlian phenomenology revolves around the idea that only essences and totalities or, indeed, internally coherent lifeworlds, are meaningful, and this is because they resonate with a strong sense of necessity and completeness. Who scratches the surface of this supposedly universal, meaning-giving, and world-constituting subject will, according to Adorno, easily uncover a deep-seated anxiety that shakes the self to the core.

> Dread stamps the ideal of Husserlian philosophy as one of absolute security, on the model of private property. Its reductions aim at the secure: viz. the immanence to consciousness of lived experiences whose title deeds the philosophical self-consciousness to which they "belong" should possess securely from the grasp of any force; and essences which, free from all factical existence, defy vexation from factical existence. . . . Security is left as an ultimate and lonely fetish like the number, one million, on a long deflated bank note. More overtly than anywhere else the late bourgeois resigned quality of phenomenology becomes evident.[51]

The stable subject that figures prominently in Husserlian phenomenology as the seat of lived experiences is in no way prepared, nor capable, of accepting that the surrounding world refuses to be tuned to its terms. In truth, therefore, the stable ego that is presupposed in Husserlian phenomenology is not so stable after all: it falls prey to ceaseless attempts to discover unshakeable essences, to shape ever new totalities and to meet its surroundings as 'worldly' for the main reason that a confrontation with genuine alterity would be too much to bear. What goes lost in such a view of man and world is the genuinely *critical* potential of human thinking and acting. For Adorno, human beings may not be able to shape reality after their own likeness, but they *are* capable of exposing its aberrations and injustices. To him, the contestation of the present reality in its fragmented state matters infinitely more than the supposed constitution of a unified lifeworld that would be shared by all. It is at this point that Adorno's (implicit) embrace of the positive value of unworldliness comes into view. Adorno does not replace the strong subject-object dualism of Husserlian phenomenology by a monist view where man and world can be wholly reconciled. In his early thoughts on Husserl, already, his dialectics are

20 *Unworldliness in Twentieth Century German Thought*

above all *negative*, driven by the awareness of contradiction rather than the search for synthesis. This entails that Adorno, in contrast to Husserl, seeks to make the very distance between man and world productive. In his view, the human being is characterized by the ability to react to a world that is perceived as inhuman. It is in this ability that Adorno situates both the starting-point of the fight for justice and equality *and* the irreducible kernel of hope that resides within an otherwise hopeless world. For, anticipating his later philosophy of the non-identical, the early Adorno already identifies an intention*less* reality as the true correlate of human thought. The encounter with an undeniable reality that cannot be translated back into an overarching totality of meaning enables the human being to say 'no' *and* replenishes the hope that even such a situation can at some point change and be changed. Following his friend Walter Benjamin's claim that 'truth is the death of intention', Adorno highlights that it is precisely when reality does *not* resonate with human meaning that our thinking and acting matter most. The realization that a given state of affairs does not bear the traces of human significance is a prerequisite both for our sharp rejection of it and for the awareness that is 'not yet complete' and can therefore be made different.

Adorno's criticism of Husserlian phenomenology brings us to at least one provisionary conclusion: an appraisal of the potential of unworldliness cannot be identified with a longing for supra-worldly transcendence, let alone with the quest for a 'view from nowhere'. The notions of unworldliness that are central to this study have nothing to do with the premodern ideals of divine wisdom or supra-human insight, nor do they square with the secularized version of such ideals through, for instance, the defense of a non-embodied, Archimedean viewpoint or the invention of linear perspective. To the contrary, the various concepts of unworldliness that this book will draw attention to build on the potential of a certain type of being-in-the-world, albeit one that is very different from the one propounded by Husserlian phenomenology. While Husserlian phenomenology derives its analysis of being-in-the-world from the human being's supposed intentionality vis-à-vis a unified and shared horizon of meaning, this study seeks above all to describe how human beings continue to relate to *non*-unified and, to a certain extent, meaning*less* realities: a different notion of being-in-the-world is needed for a being-in-a-world-that-will-always-remain-different. Authors who embrace the positive meaning of the notion of unworldliness coin the human being as a creature that seeks out elements and motifs that do not seemingly *belong*. According to these authors, we do not shy away from what is perceived as genuinely *other* but are drawn to it, even if and when such experiences shake up the stability of our self-perception. If the dominant, 'worldly' trend in German philosophy has led us from Husserl and Heidegger to Binswanger, Arendt,

Introduction 21

and Blumenberg, its 'unworldly' countercurrent can lead us from Adorno to Aby Warburg and Alexander Kluge and Oskar Negt.

Warburg (1866–1929) is mostly known as a specialist of early modern European art and culture. His interest goes out to artistic motifs, fragments, and details that do *not* match with the overall totality of the paintings and artworks from which they are a part. In his analyses of early Renaissance painting and, later, in his famous *Atlas Mnemosyne*, Warburg focuses, for instance, on the folds in clothing, the effects of a sudden gush of wind, the movements of hair and the 'gestures' that destabilize the internal calmness and unity of well-known and lesser-known artworks and images.[52] Warburg does not consider them as revelations of a discursive meaning (logos) that would lie dormant within the image (icon): as the founding father of icono*graphy*, his method differs in a crucial way from the icono*logical* project that was launched by some of his disciples, most importantly Erwin Panofsky. Instead, Warburg treats these motifs, fragments, and details as the expression of deep-seated and irresolvable tensions that can be monitored in a 'science without name' and 'art-history without text'. Warburg calls them *Pathosformeln* and dynamograms to highlight that they are first and foremost the visualization of an irrational impulse and an unceasing movement. Though he was most likely not familiar with Adorno's criticism of Husserlian phenomenology and, on August 15, 1923, even received a visit of Edmund Husserl himself while he was hospitalized in Ludwig Binswanger's mental asylum in Kreuzlingen,[53] his conceptual framework runs counter to that of Husserlian phenomenology.[54] *Pathosformeln* and dynamograms interrupt the homogeneity of an overarching horizon of meaning. They dispel any sense of internal unification and, for this very reason, draw our attention to them. These 'formulas' are not even forms (morphès) but, first and foremost, embodied *meta*-morphoses: they illustrate that these images of the past have retained a dynamism that has not yet fully exhausted itself. *Pathosformeln* and dynamograms thus illustrate what we have so far called an 'unworldly' presence. The fascination for such instances of interruption and destabilization leads Warburg to the hypothesis of a 'survival of antiquity'. While the modern era, from the Renaissance to the present, is usually understood as the progressive victory of reason over unreason and science over superstition, Warburg discloses that, even within the heart of a humanistic and 'enlightened' society, our interactions with the world remain shot through with undetected affects and emotional responses. That Warburg's research cannot be squared with Husserlian phenomenology is most of all attested to by the anthropological writings that give conceptual foundation to his art-historical project. In contrast to Husserl and Heidegger, Warburg considers the human being a deeply unstable creature that lives in constant fear of losing her mental equilibrium. The encounter with *Pathosformeln* and dynamograms cannot

22   *Unworldliness in Twentieth Century German Thought*

therefore be properly called a 'lived experience': its prime marker is that it *jeopardizes* the world-constituting abilities of the ego and *impedes* our ability to say I. This analysis of deep-seated anxieties is surely connected to Warburg's own mental problems. Still, they are to him an anthropological given, resulting from the fact that we are all 'handling' organisms. When using tools for practical purposes, we are inevitably exposed to an external world that is felt to be profoundly inhuman.

> The starting point is the following; I consider man as an animal who handles things, whose activity consists in establishing connections and separations. This makes him lose his organic feeling of the self because indeed the hand allows him to seize concrete objects, which do not have a nervous apparatus because they are inorganic, but which nevertheless extend his self in an inorganic way. Here is the tragedy of the man who, by handling things, extends beyond his organic limit.[55]

The unavoidable connection with an inorganic universe pushes the self beyond its limits and unmasks the notion of a stable subject as, at most, a philosophical naivete. For Warburg, art creation and perception are essential in warding off this threat of mental collapse and ego-loss. He deems it possible that a human being interacts with an inorganic world in a creative manner, drawing psychic energy from what would otherwise be but anxiety-provoking. For this reason, it should come as no surprise that *Pathosformeln* and dynamograms can at times have an enlivening effect. In art creation and perception, the troublesome exposure of man to an inhuman world is not fully neutralized, but it is mediated through what Warburg calls 'distance-putting': art creation and perception are an 'intuitive touching/feeling/scanning without the will to appropriate' [*reflexmäßiges Abtasten ohne den Willen zur Annäherung*], an 'oscillating attentiveness', and a careful interaction between 'warding off and drawing near' [*abstossen and auslösen*]. Art therefore gives shape to a 'distance within the near-at-hand' [*Entfernung in der Greifnähe*] and a 'dynamic tension' [*dynamischer Spannungszustand*].[56] In art, in other words, the indifferent and fragmented state of the world is *dealt with*: it is neither repressed nor met as an overpowering presence. A world that is *not* attuned to the human being nonetheless, so to speak, allows itself to be played with.

It is no stretch to call the philosopher, filmmaker, storywriter, and public intellectual Alexander Kluge, who is one of Adorno's most prominent disciples, also an heir to Aby Warburg. Together with his intellectual companion and co-author Oskar Negt he, as well, has built a conceptual framework around the 'ability of feelings'. Like Warburg, Kluge and Negt single out the creative force of feelings and experiences that put pressure on our quest for a unifying grasp on our surroundings. According to Kluge

Introduction 23

and Negt, feelings can 'self-organize' and thereby acquire a presence and intensity that undercut our rational dealings with an 'actually existing' world. But this self-organization is endowed with a downright redemptive power: according to Kluge and Negt, feelings can disrupt the mechanisms of contemporary 'consciousness-industries' that seek to uniformize our thoughts and behavior.[57] In other words, our most spontaneous responses are believed to show up the emptiness behind the stereotypes and standardized behavior that are propagated in late capitalism. They can thus expose that it is the actual world itself that ought, in truth, to be considered *un*real. In the work of Kluge and Negt, therefore, only the disruptive and liberating power of feelings is described as genuinely 'real' and, moreover, as inherently collective. The 'ability of feelings' sets up a public sphere that revolves around the organization of shared experiences and not, as Jürgen Habermas would have it, the communication of rational individuals. This capacity to neutralize societal strategies of control and organize a 'proletarian' counter-public is due to a specific blindness and lack of adaptability on the part of human emotion. The phenomenological focus on the 'lived' nature of human experiences is rejected: their power to resist is believed to lie precisely in a suspension of the ties with the lifeworld. Kluge and Negt, rather, derive the 'ability of feelings' from their *in*ability to adapt to the world in its present, flawed condition. For lived interactions with our lifeworld run the risk of rendering it a sense of meaning that it, in the current society, does not at all deserve. Kluge and Negt even endow the unexpected intrusion of feeling with a 'historical' dimension, arguing that the uncontrollability of a single human body can have an enormous impact on the lives of many. In their book *History and Obstinacy*, for instance, they narrate the story of a pilot-fighter who was sent to Far East Asia in a mission to bomb what was believed to be a terrorist camp but afterward turned out to be an ordinary farm where a wedding ceremony was taking place. At the precise moment when he was ready to drop his bombs,

> the pilot experienced a convulsive evacuation of his bowels. . . . This irritated the young man ("he was filled with shame") and led him to yank at the controls of his fighter. The missiles landed in muddy fields where no one was injured.[58]

For Kluge and Negt, the lack of adaptability on the part of human feelings and experiences is standing proof for the contingency of all historical events. They turn to *non*-lived experiences to open an unexpected, utopian position: for them, it is crucial that even the greatest horrors are made visible as somehow *avoidable*. In the influential early text *Air Raid*, Kluge already describes how the ordinary behavior of visitors in a movie theater continues without seeming interruption, even when the building is being

24   *Unworldliness in Twentieth Century German Thought*

bombed by a pilot-fighter.[59] This mental and bodily inflexibility shows, according to Kluge, that it is always possible to take in a *different* perspective than the one that is seemingly dominant. In the view of Kluge and Negt, our embodied responses to the world are indeed marked by an 'obstinacy' and even 'antirealism' that surpass our conscious intentions but can nonetheless ward off greater harm. 'Antirealism of Feeling: Something within the subjective side of humans responds in the form of denial to a reality that injures them'.[60] Fantasy, as well, plays an important role in this analysis of the redemptive potential of human feeling. Through fantasy and wish-images, we are capable of dislocating the 'reality-principle' that presents a given state of events as valid and truthful, *for the simple reason that it exists*. Fantasy becomes productive when it pushes this actually existing world at a mental and bodily distance and renders it inoperative.

> In its unsublated form, as a mere libidinal counterweight to unbearable, alienated relations, fantasy is itself merely an expression of this alienation. Its contents are therefore inverted consciousness. Yet by virtue of its mode of production, fantasy constitutes an unconscious practical critique of alienation.[61]

According to Kluge and Negt, the human being is therefore no stable self that constitutes a coherent lifeworld but a 'power plant of feelings' that lacks any one governing principle. Kluge and Negt break down emotions into elemental 'microfeelings' that cannot be integrated into a whole. They thus emphasize that all human beings are internally split, but add that it is this inherent multiplicity of feelings that enables us to tap the potential of a world that is no less diverse and fragmented. What matters above all is 'the art of making difference'.[62] Like Warburg, Kluge and Negt describe such creative responses to a world-without-unity as a delicate balance between physical nearness and longed-for distance. Their most telling example of such a different being-in-the-world has much in common with Warburg's description of the 'oscillating attentiveness' that carefully mediates between 'warding off and drawing near' and creates a 'distance within the near-at-hand'. For Kluge and Negt, such a creative response becomes most visible in the act of fastening a screw, which should be neither too loose nor too tight. Simple as such an action might seem, it draws attention to the bodily intelligence and delicate interaction with the non-human that, for Kluge and Negt, lies at the heart of the proletarian counter-public they put forward. 'A German worker would have linguistic and political difficulties informing a Chinese worker about the experience of his social class; they could instantaneously and nonverbally compare notes on the skills required to repair a machine familiar to them both or to fasten a screw'.[63]

IV

Through their implicit and varied endorsement of the potential of unworldliness, Adorno, Warburg, Kluge, and Negt have set the stage for the six diverse authors who are the focus of this book.

In the first chapter, the young Lukács and Jünger are examined together despite their ideological differences. Both thinkers emphasize the significance of timeless (aesthetic, ethical, mythological) forms that endure despite the changing empirical world, reclaiming an internal necessity or even a sense of fate.

The first part of this chapter explores the intellectual development of the pre-war Lukács, who searches for ideals that remain untouched and uncontested by the external world. This quest leads him to embrace a radical sense of morality, champion the autonomy of art, and interpret Don Quixote as a hero who shields himself from the perceived meaninglessness of his surroundings. After his 'conversion' to Marxism, Lukács will take in a very different philosophical position.

The second part of the chapter highlights surprising parallels between the young Lukács' ideas and those of Ernst Jünger. Jünger, too, advocates for supposedly 'pure' forms and values that foster a heroic ethos and counteract the spiritual emptiness of the modern world. Jünger similarly views Don Quixote as a knight of faith who confronts his environment by affirming an untainted spiritual compass.

In the second chapter, the intellectual connections and distinctions between Ernst Bloch and Theodor Adorno are thoroughly explored. Unlike the heroic defiance of the world seen in Lukács and Jünger, Bloch and Adorno focus on a sustained critique of the world as it is, stemming from the necessity to engage with it. They thereby replace opposition with negation and the steadfast faith that underpinned Lukács and Jünger's beliefs with more fragile forms of hope.

Bloch's relationship with *Don Quixote* is ambivalent. He criticizes the character for his naivety and failure to confront reality, while simultaneously recognizing his capacity to revive a crucial kernel of hope.

Adorno, on the other hand, critiques Bloch for turning hope into a 'principle' and emphasizes the significance of *Don Quixote* as a *novel* and as a representation of 'semblance'.

The final chapter sets up an intellectual dialogue between two thinkers with very different ideological backgrounds, who likely never met: Max Kommerell and Siegfried Kracauer. Max Kommerell dismisses the positive potential of unworldliness. In his early work, he emphasizes the need for a shared, unified culture that, while not rationally comprehensible, must be emotionally experienced.

26 Unworldliness in Twentieth Century German Thought

Through an analysis of Kommerell and Kracauer's thoughts on friendship, the chapter examines how the early Kracauer, in contrast, moves away from *Lebensphilosophie* to become a sharp critic of Weimar culture. In the 1920s, Kracauer develops a theory that addresses the necessity of coming to terms with the fragmentation of contemporary society.

Following his split from Stefan Georg, Kommerell later adopts a more humanistic version of *Lebensphilosophie*. His analysis of Jean Paul and the 'free rhythms' of poets focuses on the significance of 'gestures' that express the belief in life's infinite richness and mystery. Kommerell finds an important example of this direct embrace of life's potential in the character of Sancho Panza.

After World War II, Kracauer's view on the positive potential of unworldliness has undergone an important change. His theories of film and history incorporate concepts from phenomenology (*Umwelt*) and Simmelian *Lebensphilosophie*. Although his position still differs somewhat from Kommerell's, Kracauer also emphasizes a return to the concreteness of our surroundings. He, too, looks to Sancho Panza as an example of a world-embracing attitude.

Notes

1 Marcel Proust, 'Chambres', in *Contre Sainte-Beuve* (Paris: Gallimard, Folio Essais, 1954), 58.
2 Marcel Proust, *In Search of Lost Time, Volume 1: Swann's Way*, transl. William C. Carter (New Haven and London: Yale University Press, 2013), 9.
3 Proust, 'Chambres', 60.
4 Proust, 'Chambres', 58–59.
5 For the topic of 'rejuvenation' in Proust, see Walter Benjamin, 'On the Image of Proust', in *Selected Writings. Volume 2: Part 1. 1927–1930*, ed. Michael Jennings, Howard Eiland and Gary Smith, transl. Rodney Livingstone et al. (Cambridge, MA and London: The Belknap Press of Harvard University Press, 2005), 237–247.
6 Proust, 'Chambres', 62.
7 Proust, 'Chambres', 58.
8 Proust, *Swann's Way*, 6 (emphasis added).
9 Marcel Proust, *In Search of Lost Time. Volume 5: The Fugitive*, transl. and intr. Peter Collier (London: Penguin, 2003), 558. See also my analysis of this idea in Stéphane Symons, *The Work of Forgetting: Or, How Can We Make the Future Possible?* (London and New York: Rowman and Littlefield, 2019), 98–102.
10 Marcel Proust, *In Search of Lost Time. Volume 6: Time Regained*, transl. Andreas Mayor and Terence Kilmartin, rev. D. J. Enright (New York: The Modern Library, 2003), 298.
11 Martin Heidegger, *Being and Time*, transl. Joan Stambaugh (Albany: SUNY Press, 1996), 59.
12 Martin Heidegger, *The Basic Problems of Phenomenology*, transl. Albert Hofstadter (Bloomington and Indianapolis: Indiana University Press, 1988), 166. See also Peter Eli Gordon, 'Realism, Science, and the Deworlding of the World', in

A Companion to Phenomenology and Existentialism, ed. Hubert L. Dreyfus and Mark A. Wrathall (Oxford and Cambridge: Blackwell, 2006), 425–444; Hubert L. Dreyfus, *Being-in-the-World: A Commentary of Heidegger's Being and Time, Division 1* (Cambridge, MA, and London: The MIT Press, 1995), 88–107.

13 Heidegger, *The Basic Problems of Phenomenology*, 168.
14 Heidegger, *Being and Time*, 64.
15 Heidegger, *Being and Time*, 60.
16 Heidegger, *Being and Time*, 60.
17 Heidegger, *Being and Time*, 109.
18 Heidegger, *Being and Time*, 68–69.
19 Heidegger, *Being and Time*, 69.
20 Heidegger, *Being and Time*, 108.
21 Heidegger, *Being and Time*, 104. See also Peter Eli Gordon's analysis of 'deworldedness' in Heidegger, 'Realism, Science, and the Deworlding of the World'.
22 Heidegger, *Being and Time*, 104.
23 Heidegger, quoted in Dreyfus, *Being-in-the-World*, 205. This same quote is discussed in Gordon, 'Realism, Science, and the Deworlding of the World', 438. The original passage can be found in Martin Heidegger, *History of the Concept of Time*, transl. Theodore Kisiel (Bloomington: Indiana University Press, 1985), 217–218 (note that the German term *Entweltlichung* has here been translated as unworldliness. I will be using both deworldedness and unworldliness and consider them to be synonyms).
24 Edmund Husserl, *Ideas Pertaining to a Pure Phenomenology and to a Phenomenological Philosophy. Second Book: Studies in the Phenomenology of Constitution*, transl. Richard Rojcewicz and André Schuwer (Dordrecht, Boston and London: Kluwer Academic Publishers, 1989), 195.
25 Husserl, *Ideas Pertaining to a Pure Phenomenology and to a Phenomenological Philosophy*, 196.
26 Edmund Husserl, *The Crisis of European Sciences and Transcendental Phenomenology*, transl. David Carr (Evanston, IL: Northwestern University Press, 1970), 127.
27 Ludwig Binswanger, quoted in Georges Didi-Huberman, *L'image survivante: Histoire de l'art et temps des fantômes selon Aby Warburg* (Paris: Les Éditions de Minuit, 2002), 386. For my discussion of Binswanger, and the connection with Heidegger and Husserl, see Stéphane Symons, *Ludwig Binswanger and Fernand Deligny on the Human Condition: Wandering Lines* (Cham, Germany: Palgrave Macmillan, 2024).
28 Ludwig Binswanger, 'Drei Formen missglückten Daseins', in *Ausgewählte Werke. Band 1: Formen mißglückten Daseins*, ed. Max Herzog (Heidelberg, Germany: Roland Asanger Verlag, 1992), 247. See also Ludwig Binswanger, 'Über Ideenflucht', in *Ausgewählte Werke. Band 1: Formen mißglückten Daseins*, ed. Max Herzog (Heidelberg, Germany: Roland Asanger Verlag, 1992), 151.
29 Binswanger, 'Traum und Existenz', in *Ausgewählte Werke. Band 3: Vorträge und Aufsätze*, ed. Max Herzog (Heidelberg, Germany: Roland Asanger Verlag, 1992), 106.
30 Ludwig Binswanger, 'Lebensfunktion und innere Lebensgeschichte', in *Ausgewählte Werke. Band 3: Vorträge und Aufsätze*, ed. Max Herzog (Heidelberg, Germany: Roland Asanger Verlag, 1992), 81.
31 Hannah Arendt, *The Human Condition* (Chicago and London: The University of Chicago Press, 1998), 1.

28 Unworldliness in Twentieth Century German Thought

32 Arendt, *The Human Condition*, 251.
33 Arendt, *The Human Condition*, 52–53.
34 Hans Blumenberg, *Lebenszeit und Weltzeit* (Frankfurt am Main, Germany: Suhrkamp, 1986), 23. My interpretation of Blumenberg's notion of lifeworld is based on Nicola Zambon's analysis in his 'Die Phänomenologie Hans Blumenbergs', in *Rivista di Filosofia Neo-Scolastica* CXV (1) (2023): 137–153.
35 Hans Blumenberg, *Phänomenologische Schriften. 1981–1988*, ed. Nicola Zambon (Frankfurt am Main: Suhrkamp, 2018), 11–14. See also Zambon's footnote 63 in his 'Die Phänomenologie Hans Blumenbergs'.
36 See Zambon, 'Die Phänomenologie Hans Blumenbergs', 139–142.
37 Hans Blumenberg, *Work on Myth*, transl. Robert M. Wallace (Cambridge, MA, and London: The MIT Press, 1985), 4.
38 Blumenberg, *Work on Myth*, 6.
39 Hans Blumenberg, *Work on Myth*, transl. Robert M. Wallace (Cambridge, MA, and London: The MIT Press, 1985), 4–5.
40 See Martin Jay, 'The Lifeworld and Lived Experience', in *A Companion to Phenomenology and Existentialism*, ed. Hubert L. Dreyfus and Mark A. Wrathall (Oxford and Cambridge: Blackwell, 2006), 91–92.
41 Derrida, Foucault and Lyotard, quoted in Jay, 'The Lifeworld and Lived Experience', 91–92.
42 Emmanuel Levinas, 'Heidegger, Gagarine et nous', in *Kainós* 3 (2003), www.kainos.it/numero3/disvelamenti/levinas-fr.html.
43 Levinas, 'Heidegger, Gagarine et nous'.
44 Gilles Deleuze, 'What Children Say', in *Essays Critical and Clinical*, transl. Daniel W. Smith and Michael A. Greco (Minneapolis: University of Minnesota Press, 1997), 61.
45 Stefanos Geroulanos, *Transparency in Post-War France: A Critical History of the Present* (Stanford, CA: Stanford University Press, 2017), 25.
46 Gilles Deleuze and Félix Guattari, *What Is Philosophy?* transl. Hugh Tomlinson and Graham Burchell (New York: Columbia University Press, 1994), 61–84.
47 Theodor W. Adorno, 'The Actuality of Philosophy', in *Telos* 31 (1977): 120–133. For an analysis of Adorno's interpretation of Husserlian phenomenology, see Peter E. Gordon, *Adorno and Existence* (Cambridge, MA, and London: Harvard University Press, 2016), Chapters 2–3; Jared A. Miller, 'Phenomenology's Negative Dialectic: Adorno's Critique of Husserl's Epistemological Foundationalism', in *Philosophical Forum* 40 (1) (2009): 99–125.
48 Theodor W. Adorno, 'Die Transzendenz des Dinglichen und Noematischen in Husserls Phänomenologie', in *Philosophische Frühschriften: Band 1*, red. Rolf Tiedemann (Frankfurt am Main, Germany: Suhrkamp, 1990), 17.
49 Theodor W. Adorno, *The Jargon of Authenticity*, transl. Knut Tarnowski and Frederic Will (Evanston, IL: Northwestern University Press, 1973), 54.
50 Theodor W. Adorno, *Against Epistemology: A Metacritique: Studies in Husserl and the Phenomenological Antinomies*, transl. Willis Domingo (Cambridge, UK: Polity Press, 2013), 234. Cf. also Gordon, *Adorno and Existence*, 63–70.
51 Adorno, *Against Epistemology*, 219.
52 See, e.g., Aby Warburg, 'Sandro Botticelli's *Birth of Venus* and *Spring:* An Examination of Concepts of Antiquity in the Italian Renaissance' (1893), in *The Renewal of Pagan Antiquity*, intr. Kurt W. Forster, transl. David Britt (Los Angeles: The Getty Research Institute for the History of Arts and the Humanities, 1999), 89; Aby Warburg, 'Dürer and Italian Antiquity', in *The Renewal*

of Pagan Antiquity, intr. Kurt W. Forster, transl. David Britt (Los Angeles: The Getty Research Institute for the History of Arts and the Humanities, 1999), 555.

53 See Thomas Vongehr, 'Aus dem Schatzkästlein des Husserl-Archivs: Am Bodensee 1923. Husserl und die Psychiatrie. Husserl trifft Ludwig Binswanger und Aby Warburg', in *Husserl Archiv Mitteilungsblatt* 33 (2010): 11–16.

54 See also the coda to my *Ludwig Binswanger and Fernand Deligny on the Human Condition*.

55 Aby Warburg, 'Reise-Erinnerungen aus dem Gebiet der Pueblo Indianer', in *Werke*, ed. Martin Treml, Sigrid Weigel and Perdita Ladwig, with Susanne Hetzer, Herbert Kopp-Oberstebrink and Christina Oberstebrink (Frankfurt am Main, Germany: Suhrkamp, 2018), 580.

56 Aby Warburg, 'Symbolismus als Umfangsbestimmung', in *Werke*, ed. Martin Treml, Sigrid Weigel and Perdita Ladwig with Susanne Hetzer, Herbert Kopp-Oberstebrink and Christina Oberstebrink (Frankfurt am Main, Germany: Suhrkamp, 2018), 624–626.

57 Oskar Negt and Alexander Kluge, *Public Sphere and Experience: Towards an Analysis of the Bourgeois and Proletarian Public Sphere*, transl. Peter Labanyi, Jamie Owen Daniel and Assenka Oksiloff (Minneapolis and London: University of Minnesota Press, 1993), Chapter 4.

58 Alexander Kluge and Oskar Negt, *History and Obstinacy*, transl. Richard Langston et al., ed. and intr. Devin Fore (New York: Zone Books, 2014), 204.

59 I thank Roland Breeur for drawing attention to this idea.

60 Kluge and Negt, *History and Obstinacy*, 414.

61 Negt and Kluge, *Public Sphere and Experience*, 33.

62 Alexander Kluge, *Die Kunst, Unterschiede zu machen* (Frankfurt am Main, Germany: Suhrkamp, 2016).

63 Kluge and Negt, *History and Obstinacy*, 488.

Bibliography

Adorno, Theodor W. 'The Actuality of Philosophy', in *Telos* 31: 120–133 (1977)

Adorno, Theodor W. *Against Epistemology: A Metacritique. Studies in Husserl and the Phenomenological Antinomies*, transl. Willis Domingo (Cambridge: Polity Press, 2013)

Adorno, Theodor W. 'Die Transzendenz des Dinglichen und Noematischen in Husserls Phänomenologie', in *Philosophische Frühschriften: Band 1*, red. Rolf Tiedemann (Frankfurt am Main: Suhrkamp, 1990)

Adorno, Theodor W. *The Jargon of Authenticity*, transl. Knut Tarnowski and Frederic Will (Evanston: Northwestern University Press, 1973)

Arendt, Hannah. *The Human Condition* (Chicago and London: The University of Chicago Press, 1998)

Benjamin, Walter. 'On the Image of Proust', in *Selected Writings: Volume 2. Part 1. 1927–1930*, ed. Michael Jennings, Howard Eiland and Gary Smith, transl. Rodney Livingstone et al. (Cambridge, MA and London: The Belknap Press of Harvard University Press, 2005)

Binswanger, Ludwig. 'Drei Formen missglückten Daseins', in *Ausgewählte Werke. Band 1: Formen mißglückten Daseins*, ed. Max Herzog (Heidelberg: Roland Asanger Verlag, 1992)

Binswanger, Ludwig. 'Lebensfunktion und innere Lebensgeschichte', in *Ausgewählte Werke. Band 3: Vorträge und Aufsätze*, ed. Max Herzog (Heidelberg: Roland Asanger Verlag, 1992)

30 Unworldliness in Twentieth Century German Thought

Binswanger, Ludwig. 'Traum und Existenz', in *Ausgewählte Werke. Band 3: Vorträge und Aufsätze*, ed. Max Herzog (Heidelberg: Roland Asanger Verlag, 1992)
Binswanger, Ludwig. 'Über Ideenflucht', in *Ausgewählte Werke. Band 1: Formen mißglückten Daseins*, ed. Max Herzog (Heidelberg: Roland Asanger Verlag, 1992)
Blumenberg, Hans. *Lebenszeit und Weltzeit* (Frankfurt am Main: Suhrkamp, 1986)
Blumenberg, Hans. *Phänomenologische Schriften: 1981–1988*, ed. Nicola Zambon (Frankfurt am Main: Suhrkamp, 2018)
Blumenberg, Hans. *Work on Myth*, transl. Robert M. Wallace (Cambridge, MA and London: The MIT Press, 1985)
Deleuze, Gilles. 'What Children Say', in *Essays Critical and Clinical*, transl. Daniel W. Smith and Michael A. Greco (Minneapolis: University of Minnesota Press, 1997)
Deleuze, Gilles and Guattari, Félix. *What Is Philosophy?* transl. Hugh Tomlinson and Graham Burchell (New York: Columbia University Press, 1994)
Didi-Huberman, Georges. *L'image survivante: Histoire de l'art et temps des fantômes selon Aby Warburg* (Paris: Les Éditions de Minuit, 2002)
Dreyfus, Hubert L. *Being-in-the-World: A Commentary of Heidegger's Being and Time, Division 1* (Cambridge, MA and London: The MIT Press, 1995)
Geroulanos, Stefanos. *Transparency in Post-War France: A Critical History of the Present* (Stanford: Stanford University Press, 2017)
Gordon, Peter Eli. *Adorno and Existence* (Cambridge, MA and London: Harvard University Press, 2016)
Gordon, Peter Eli. 'Realism, Science, and the Deworlding of the World', in *A Companion to Phenomenology and Existentialism*, ed. Hubert L. Dreyfus and Mark A. Wrathall (Oxford and Cambridge: Blackwell, 2006)
Heidegger, Martin. *The Basic Problems of Phenomenology*, transl. Albert Hofstadter (Bloomington and Indianapolis: Indiana University Press, 1988)
Heidegger, Martin. *Being and Time*, transl. Joan Stambaugh (Albany: SUNY Press, 1996)
Heidegger, Martin. *History of the Concept of Time*, transl. Theodore Kisiel (Bloomington: Indiana University Press, 1985)
Husserl, Edmund. *The Crisis of European Sciences and Transcendental Phenomenology*, transl. David Carr (Evanston: Northwestern University Press, 1970)
Husserl, Edmund. *Ideas Pertaining to a Pure Phenomenology and to a Phenomenological Philosophy. Second Book: Studies in the Phenomenology of Constitution*, transl. Richard Rojcewicz and André Schuwer (Dordrecht, Boston and London: Kluwer Academic Publishers, 1989)
Jay, Martin. 'The Lifeworld and Lived Experience', in *A Companion to Phenomenology and Existentialism*, ed. Hubert L. Dreyfus and Mark A. Wrathall (Oxford and Cambridge: Blackwell, 2006), 91–92
Kluge, Alexander. *Die Kunst, Unterschiede zu machen* (Frankfurt am Main: Suhrkamp, 2016)
Kluge, Alexander and Negt, Oskar. *History and Obstinacy*, ed. and intr. Devin Fore, transl. Richard Langston et al. (New York: Zone Books, 2014)
Levinas, Emmanuel. 'Heidegger, Gagarine et nous', in *Kainós* 3 (2003)
Miller, Jared A. 'Phenomenology's Negative Dialectic: Adorno's Critique of Husserl's Epistemological Foundationalism', in *Philosophical Forum* 40 (1) (2009)
Negt, Oskar and Kluge, Alexander. *Public Sphere and Experience: Towards an Analysis of the Bourgeois and Proletarian Public Sphere*, transl. Peter Labanyi,

Introduction 31

Jamie Owen Daniel and Assenka Oksiloff (Minneapolis and London: University of Minnesota Press, 1993)

Proust, Marcel. 'Chambres', in *Contre Sainte-Beuve* (Paris: Gallimard, Folio Essais, 1954)

Proust, Marcel. *In Search of Lost Time, Volume 1: Swann's Way*, transl. William C. Carter (New Haven and London: Yale University Press, 2013)

Proust, Marcel. *In Search of Lost Time, Volume 5: The Fugitive*, transl. and intr. Peter Collier (London: Penguin, 2003)

Proust, Marcel. *In Search of Lost Time, Volume 6: Time Regained*, transl. Andreas Mayor and Terence Kilmartin, rev. D. J. Enright (New York: The Modern Library, 2003)

Symons, Stéphane. *Ludwig Binswanger and Fernand Deligny on the Human Condition: Wandering Lines* (Cham: Palgrave Macmillan, 2024)

Symons, Stéphane. *The Work of Forgetting: Or, How Can We Make the Future Possible?* (London and New York: Rowman and Littlefield, 2019)

Vongehr, Thomas. 'Aus dem Schatzkästlein des Husserl-Archivs: Am Bodensee 1923. Husserl und die Psychiatrie. Husserl trifft Ludwig Binswanger und Aby Warburg', in *Husserl Archiv Mitteilungsblatt* 33 (2010)

Warburg, Aby. 'Dürer and Italian Antiquity', in *The Renewal of Pagan Antiquity*, intr. Kurt W. Forster, transl. David Britt (Los Angeles: The Getty Research Institute for the History of Arts and the Humanities, 1999)

Warburg, Aby. 'Reise-Erinnerungen aus dem Gebiet der Pueblo Indianer', in *Werke*, ed. Martin Treml, Sigrid Weigel and Perdita Ladwig with Susanne Hetzer, Herbert Kopp-Oberstebrink and Christina Oberstebrink (Frankfurt am Main: Suhrkamp, 2018)

Warburg, Aby. 'Sandro Botticelli's Birth of Venus and Spring: An Examination of Concepts of Antiquity in the Italian Renaissance' (1893), in *The Renewal of Pagan Antiquity*, intr. Kurt W. Forster, transl. David Britt (Los Angeles: The Getty Research Institute for the History of Arts and the Humanities, 1999)

Warburg, Aby. 'Symbolismus als Umfangsbestimmung', in *Werke*, ed. Martin Treml, Sigrid Weigel and Perdita Ladwig with Susanne Hetzer, Herbert Kopp-Oberstebrink and Christina Oberstebrink (Frankfurt am Main: Suhrkamp, 2018)

Zambon, Nicola. 'Die Phänomenologie Hans Blumenbergs', in *Rivista di Filosofia Neo-Scolastica* CXV (1) (2023)

1 Strange Bedfellows

The Young Georg Lukács and Ernst Jünger: Don Quixote, The Knight of Faith

I

When Germany announces the full mobilization of its military forces in preparation of World War I, on August 1, 1914, the 29-year-old Hungarian philosopher Georg Lukács is living in Heidelberg, working away on a systematic study of idealist aesthetics. In this unfinished book, which was only retrieved after his death in 1971 and is now known as *The Heidelberg Philosophy of Art*, Lukács sets up an inquiry into the conditions of art. In a letter to his friend and Heidelberg-colleague, Max Weber, he summarizes his research as follows: 'Works of art exist, how are they possible?'[1] Weber, for his part, deems Lukács' 'transformation of the Kantian question the first significant step forward in aesthetics since Immanuel Kant'.[2] In Kantian spirit, this research is indeed not directed to empirical variables but to the *legitimation* of an artwork and the determination of its *validity*. Lukács seeks to uncover the necessary conditions under which an artwork can present itself *as* an artwork, and which kind of truth it can thereby be believed to offer. But this Kantian influence ought not to be exaggerated. Lukács quite clearly moves beyond the Kantian framework since he rejects Kant's fundamental presupposition that aesthetics revolves around *subjective judgment*. For Lukács, aesthetics cannot do without an analysis of qualities that pertain to the *artwork*, and it is but these internal features that render it worthwhile. The first credo that underlies Lukács' early aesthetics is therefore not Kant's autonomy of the aesthetic judgment (i.e., it's being disinterested) but the autonomy of the artwork itself. This autonomy of the artwork is vouchsafed through purely *formal* qualities. Although these values originate in historical and empirical-social context, they pertain to the artwork itself and acquire timelessness.

> [A]esthetic value is only there when it is realized, . . . no process that leads to it and approaches it can claim any value . . . [O]nly in the achieved work, in the realized value, is that which is eternally and timelessly valid

DOI: 10.4324/9781003364009-2

present. The paradox that arises here is that something that stands in time in its innermost essence, for the categorical construction of which time is a priori indispensable, not only represents something timelessly valid, but is the timeless value itself.[3]

In the view of young Lukács, no genuine artwork derives its meaning from its connection with an empirical outside, be it a creating or perceiving subject or a represented and communal *world*. In art, contents become real to the extent that they are shaped and reshaped in aesthetic forms which, for their part, are constitutive of an unworldly, independent reality of their own.

Rather than Kant's *Critique of Judgment*, it is a particular blend of phenomenology and *Lebensphilosophie* that inspires Lukács in these early years. A first step to understand what makes an artwork *valid*, he argues, is a certain type of épochè, along the lines of Husserl's bracketing: for Lukács, the artwork's essence can only be gauged through a suspension of mere subjective components, that is, the perspective of both its creator and observer, because these are deemed a matter of sheer psychology. Like his friend Emil Lask and Husserl himself, Lukács embraces a distinct anti-psychologism since psychology cannot possibly come to terms with the reasons why a given artwork internally coheres.[4] An understanding of the psychological mechanisms that result in the creation of an artwork will not in any way illuminate the immanent lawfulness and truth of the artwork itself. According to Lukács, not even the artist (or rather: especially not the artist) can grasp the connections between underlying, psychological motivations and the artwork's internal, formal lawfulness. Even Shakespeare was unable to understand the artistic importance and genuine depth of Othello and Iago since he brought them into being only out of a creative urge, not being able to properly comprehend how this personae figure *within the play itself*. While the artist is well aware that she selects but one out of many possibilities when creating a work, the work itself is charged with a sense of necessity and internal perfection. 'For Shakespeare's artistic will, the meeting of Othello and Iago is merely a "fact", something common to ordinary reality: there are people like Othello and people like Iago, and when they meet, all the events of the tragedy necessarily follow from this fact. However, in this manner only a play of intrigue with a tragic outcome and with all the dramatic and lyrical beauties of tragedy is achieved, but not tragedy itself, the world of absolute, immanent, supra-empirical necessity'.[5] A true genius should, in the view of young Lukács, therefore take a step *back* from the artwork, enabling the latter to grow into an independent and incommensurable entity. Similarly, when an observer or reader approaches a work of art excessively from the point of view of their own emotional or psychological life, this does not, according to Lukács, increase the quality or intensity of the aesthetic experience.

34 Unworldliness in Twentieth Century German Thought

To the contrary, such excessive identification impedes the aesthetic experience since it amounts to a fragmentation of the artwork. For this reason, Lukács highlights that all aesthetic experience thrives on *mis*understanding. 'The process of self-discovery through the work, the experience of being affected by it at the innermost and most personal level – whose endless repeatability forms the basis of its eternal influence – precludes any possibility of a sharing of experience between creator and audience. The possibility of misunderstanding, which in empirical reality was only a *vérité de fait*, becomes here a *vérité éternelle*'.[6] For Lukács, there is no common ground between the emotional world of the artist and that of the observer, let alone that this relation could serve as an artwork's final legitimation.

To back up this argument Lukács presents a fundamental opposition between the notion of *Erlebnis*, that is, the lived experience of a shared world, on the one hand, and *Form*, on the other. While the former cannot be isolated from the contingencies of daily life (*Leben*), the latter is in essence a purified modification of our lived experiences, giving shape to a novel entity that surpasses the division between subject and object altogether. In itself, *Erlebnis* is no carrier of meaning since it is too much burdened by the unclarities and heterogeneity of daily life. *Erlebnis* at most carries within itself a strong *longing* for meaning, which can be realized only when it is reshaped into a *Form*.[7] The realities of *Erlebnisse* (*Erlebniswirklichkeiten*) are chaotic, unformed, and immediately given. These can only acquire meaning when they are reworked into *something else*. Lukács therefore strictly distinguishes the process of the creation and reception and art from the merely subjective perception of empirical reality. 'It is a self-deception to believe that, by "looking into" the "immanent flow of phenomena", and within the merely given psychic reality, which is the material and object of empirical psychology, one could retrieve forms or even indications of forms, subjective relationships to the supra-individual, attenuated premonitions and lived experiences of the objective'.[8] While an individual's perception of the shared world is marked by multiplicity and uncertainty, art evidences an act of making that transmutes this perception into a stable, homogeneous, and novel entity. At this level, the mere stuff of *Erlebnissein* is overcome into a realm of truth, *Erlebnissin*, with the expressions of an empirical individual ('the whole human') opening a multi-layered and fulfilling experience that speaks to the entirety of the human soul ('the human whole'). On account of this distance between the lived experiences of an empirical individual and the pure realm of the artwork, the latter is never merely *communicative*: 'This is the profound misery and the irrevocable isolation of the human being of experiential reality; every approach to something "universal" in expression makes [this expression] impossible from the outset and what is truly [the human being's] own gains, through the fact of expression, an effective factor independent of the expresser, his will and essence and in addition possesses an impenetrable immanence'.[9] But every true artwork simultaneously opens what Lukács calls a 'standpoint'. Once again, he does not have in mind a communicable subjective position, nor a perspective on an empirical, shared world. 'Standpoint', rather, is Lukács' term for the immanent cohesion and unity of the artwork, which renders it the singular strength to draw the observer in wholly on its (i.e., the artwork's) own terms: an artwork becomes real only on account of an internal necessity that invites the subject to relate to it. Standpoint is 'carrier and foundation of a totality that is shaped into a reality' and thus 'set[s] boundaries, clos[es] off, round[s] off'.[10] With this, Lukács so much as turns psychologism on its head: it is, in his view, not the subject (and her intentions and emotions) that bring forth the work of art but, vice versa, it is the object (i.e., the internal and formal unity of the artwork) that itself brings about genuine subjectivity as a relational attitude.[11]

A large part of this argument, and the jargon in which it is being developed, is clearly borrowed from the *Lebensphilosophen* of his time. The work of Georg Simmel, in particular, with whom Lukács was in close contact during his years in Berlin (1906–1907), is surely an important influence here. Simmel is undoubtedly a forerunner to Lukács in highlighting the autonomous nature of all artworks, describing them as a relational unity that stands on its own. In heated debates with naturalist and realist aesthetics, Simmel, like Lukács, dismisses the idea that an artwork derives its meaning from anything external. Naturalism and realism are *anti*-artistic evolutions since they reduce art to a mere instrument, seeking to reproduce what cannot possibly be reproduced: the experience that something truly *exists*. For Simmel, there is an inherent difference between artistic representation and 'actual existence'. The former is but 'a thing of the senses', whereas the latter is of metaphysical nature (actual existence is 'something abstract that lies beyond the surface of things'). Zooming in on artistic genres like the portrait or the landscape, Simmel considers an artwork first and foremost as a *re*-shaping of external, existing phenomena (a human face, natural elements). The latter do not as such *have* aesthetic meaning but *acquire* it. For this process to take place, these phenomena need to be released from their actual, worldly existence and fashioned anew in and as an artwork.[12]

Moreover, in an essay that Simmel would write a few years after Lukács' work on the *Heidelberg Philosophy of Art*, Simmel distinguishes between the notion of life and the concept 'more-than-life'. Like Lukács, Simmel argues that the former is not meaningful in its own right. As a mere natural given, life is but 'sheer physiological self-maintenance . . . involving continual regeneration'.[13] While life as such is marked by multiplicity, heterogeneity, and a continuous striving for change, it can only acquire meaning when it is shaped anew in and as something 'more': the constructs, images,

36 Unworldliness in Twentieth Century German Thought

and forms of *culture*. Only in this manner can the always 'more' life that is created grow into the vital driving force behind communal values that are 'more *than* life'. 'Culture in general', Simmel argues, 'arises where categories produced in life, and for life's sake, become autonomous shapers of intrinsically valued formations that are objective with respect to life'.[14] Simmel uses this distinction to identify a 'tragedy of culture' within modernity.[15] He diagnoses modernity with an incapacity to overcome life's mere flux of change and multiplicity. On account of a wide array of reasons, ranging from excessive individualism to money culture, modern man is no longer able to reshape the dynamic of life as such into meaning-giving and meaning-carrying constructs and forms. This brings with it, in Simmel's terms, a domination of 'objective' culture over 'subjective' culture, a distinction that was highly valued by Lukács.[16] In objective culture, the subject no longer recognizes her own constructs as an expression of lived beliefs and values since the latter have become ossified and obsolete. In Simmel's view, this opposition between life and form throws the modern subject back into a dangerous and paradoxical blend of dogmatism and relativism. A blind obedience to stale ideas and sterile values (forms without life) most often goes hand in hand with a widespread unwillingness (and inability) to hold any idea or value as deeply meaningful (life without forms).

In spite of obvious affinities, there is however a significant difference between the ideas of young Lukács and Simmel. From an early moment onward, Lukács' stance toward Simmel comes across as ambivalent. In a letter from 1910, Lukács already mentions that 'Simmel can give [him] very little': '[W]hatever I could learn from him, I have already learned a long time ago'.[17] And some years later Lukács publishes an essay in which he associates Simmel's theories with 'impressionism', arguing that they are no weapon against relativism but symptomatic of it.[18] Simmel does indeed emphasize that even the created constructs of culture ought to be considered worldly expressions of life itself. The images, shapes, and forms that are brought about as carriers of meaning derive their ultimate vitality from the dynamic of change and multiplicity that is built into the flux of life. Even the 'more-*than*-life' of culture is, in the last instance, a product of life's constant generation of 'more-life': 'On the level of the spirit, [life] begets something that is more-than-life: the objective, the construct, that which is significant and valid in itself'.[19] Simmel does describe how the constructs of culture entail an inevitable 'self-alienation' of life and are consequently bound to lose their expressive strengths after a while; but, given the inexhaustible nature of life itself, this interruption of its dynamic of self-renewal is part and parcel of a cycle of continual regeneration. '[L]ife cannot enter into form at all – beyond every attained structure it must at once seek out another one, in which the play – necessary structure,

Strange Bedfellows 37

and necessary dissatisfaction with the structure as such – is repeated'.[20] For this reason, an undisguised optimism underlies the majority of Simmel's writings despite his misgivings about the 'formless' condition of modernity. This optimism about life's inexhaustible potential for change will only be mitigated by somewhat wistful remarks in the final stages of Simmel's life (and of World War I), when he notes in his diary that he expects to 'die without spiritual heirs'.[21] Composed a few years before Simmel's death, Lukács' *Heidelberg Philosophy of Art* is indeed already much more radical than the former's *Lebensphilosophie*. Lukács highlights, not just a conceptual *distinction* but a downright *gap* between life/*Erlebnis* on the one hand and the forms of culture on the other. With this conceptual move, the forms of culture acquire according to Lukács an unworldliness that Simmel would reject. Vice versa, Simmel's suggestion that cultural forms are ultimately to be considered a product of the infinite dynamic of life itself would in Lukács' view jeopardize the entire argument about art's autonomy. For Lukács, this autonomy is a prerequisite for the expressive strength of all artworks, and it entails that true art lifts itself above the eternal instability of life.

Lukács' term 'totality', surely one of the most crucial terms in his entire oeuvre, plays a pivotal role in this regard. For Lukács, the artistic value of artworks is function of their being an incommensurable unity-on-their-own, having closed themselves off from the external world. He does therefore not hold back in calling artwork 'utopian' since it evidences a supra-individual ideality that cannot be confused with the empirical world.[22] Unlike empirical phenomena, which are but bits and pieces that are continually exposed to external forces, the artwork is marked by a wholeness that rests fully in itself. He argues that, in presenting a world that is independent from the outside world, the artwork should be considered a *created* form that is at peace and harmonious, devoid of the fears and anxieties of subjective, ordinary life. Art gives shape to 'a perfect world, which, in the immediacy of its physical reality, silences all pain and suffering . . . which exists in the here and now with undeniable concreteness and yet seems to have descended from regions far removed from the evanescence of the present. . . . Whatever the artists want to tell us in their works . . . comes to us in unbroken and authentic form, and when it reaches us, the world that surrounds us is freed of its frequently oppressive incoherence, of its tormenting silence: it becomes simple, clear, communicative, and self-evident'.[23] Shielded from the world's vicissitudes, the powers of an artwork to intervene directly in that world are inherently limited.

Nonetheless, Lukács endows such unworldly and 'utopian' art with the promise to redeem. While its wholesome effect cannot be mistaken for either a concrete depiction of a current state of events or a blueprint for a better world, the creation and perception of art render utopia a presence

38   Unworldliness in Twentieth Century German Thought

or reality of its own. Artworks may not prove that a longed-for world or desirable outcome can ever be brought into actual existence, let alone predict that it most certainly will, yet they set up the conditions for a *different* type of truth and reality. The internal fulfillment that is embodied by artworks has nothing to do with the mere being-there of phenomena and thus amounts to 'islands within the sea of fragmentation and struggle after unity'.[24] For Lukács, the realm of art is that of a utopian *presence* since it derives its strength from being proudly indifferent to the possibility of its being *empirically* real. Lukács is careful to distinguish his analysis of art from an all-encompassing and normative theory that would lay out ethical, political, and social ideals that can serve as a model for society, but he does admit that aesthetics plays a vital part in the quest for a communal and authentic existence.

II

The *Heidelberg Philosophy of Art* should be read as a further development of the criticism of modernity and modern art that Lukács had formulated prior to his move to Heidelberg, in texts such as *Soul and Form* (1908–1911) and the essay 'Aesthetic Culture' (1910). In these essays, Lukács endows art and art-criticism with the critical task to overcome individualism and relativism, unmasking values and norms that have lost their legitimacy. For the modern world is one of 'formlessness' where emotions and subjective sentiments have been given free reign. For this reason, the spiritual life of modern society, as manifested in its culture, art, politics, and ethics, is becoming worn-out and lifeless, unable to truly give meaning to modern man's existence. '[T]he undisciplined pantheism of feeling which is characteristic of our time . . . dissolved all form into a vague and formless lyricism of longing'.[25] Lukács describes how the randomness of a mere given (life) can be transmuted into an internally consistent and harmonious form. Anticipating the idealistic view of art that underlies his Heidelberg study, Lukács understands form as the result of an act of creation that dispels the seeming contingencies and uncertainties of ordinary existence. A form produces meaning because it 'springs from a symbolic contemplation of life-symbols', and it 'acquires a life of its own through the power of that experience'.[26] Although Lukács uses the word 'world-view', he does make sure to emphasize that form is in no way immanent to the shared, empirical world: it is 'a standpoint, an attitude vis-à-vis the life from which it sprang', but, in the first place, 'a possibility of reshaping it, of creating it anew'.[27] In *Soul and Form*, as well, Lukács builds on the opposition between life and form to render the latter as pure as possible. As such, form is endowed with an unworldly and timeless validity in spite of having grown from a historical and societal context.

Strange Bedfellows 39

A large part of these very early essays revolves around a criticism of aestheticism, which is taken to task for its inability to fashion life-giving and stable values. Caught up in mere 'atmosphere' or 'impressionism', the majority of modern artworks lack the formative capacity to conjure the totality and universality that animates any sense of genuine spirituality. Without this mediation of forms subjective experience is powerless against the arbitrariness and randomness of ordinary life and remains cut off from any sense of community. This 'tragedy of culture', for its part, introduces a nefarious gap between the individual and the collective and jeopardizes the feel for supra-individual norms and values. Lukács coins the notion of 'aesthetic culture' to attack this culture of mere inwardness. He rejects the idea that a shared and communal spiritual life can grow from the sentimental life of isolated individuals. Such individuals and their personal emotions lack the force to reinvigorate the stable, eternal values that are required for a lived and shared ethics. 'At the center of aesthetic culture stands the mood, the most frequent reaction to a work of art, if not the only response or the most profound and important one. Its essence is an accidental and unanalyzed connection (indeed, often a conscientiously non-analytical, circumstantial, and momentary one) between the spectator and the object of his gaze. Aesthetic culture was born the moment this psychic activity was extended to the totality of life, when the totality of life became the succession of continuously changing moods, when objects ceased to exist because everything became merely a potential inducement to a mood. It arose when all constancy disappeared from life, because moods do not tolerate permanence and repetition; when all values vanished from life, because value is ascribed only to possibilities that occasion the mood – hence to accidental circumstances disconnected from life'.[28] In a striking passage, moreover, Lukács criticizes *Lebensphilosophie* for having prepared the way for this dangerous relativism, instability, and subjectivism: 'Here is the eternal melody of Lebensphilosophie. "Nothing matters": only differences in the intensity of enjoyment are real differences'.[29]

Comparing these pre-Heidelberg essays, especially *Soul and Form*, to the *Heidelberg Philosophy of Art*, it is interesting to note that the concept of form, and the appeal for absolute and timeless values, is at this time still made dependent on the foundational notion of the *individual*.[30] While the *Heidelberg Philosophy of Art* identifies form with the (autonomous) *work of art*, these earliest essays focus on the singular power of great individuals, such as artists, to bring about the unworldly and timeless values that will strengthen the community. Such individuals are, in contrast to the aesthete, not fully cut off from society: unlike the latter, the form-shaping individual does not *escape* into her inwardness. Rather, she uses her solitariness to give shape to a truth that is made objectively and universally valid, in this way acquiring an authentic and soulful existence. For Lukács,

40   Unworldliness in Twentieth Century German Thought

such an authentic stance stems from the awareness that there is a distance between 'those who understand . . . but do not live' and 'those who live, but do not understand'.[31] Great individuals meet this very distance as the condition of an ethical attitude. In Nietzschean fashion, Lukács argues for a soulful life that revolves around an intensification of one's will and psychic energy. In this manner, the contingencies and impurities of daily life can be overcome in the embrace of a fated, unworldly necessity. It is no surprise that Lukács singles out the tragic hero as an exemplary of this authentic and self-legitimizing stance. In one of the key essays in *Soul and Form*, 'Metaphysics and Tragedy', the tragic hero is lauded for his proud indifference to the outside world, and his ability to transmute contingency into necessity – historicity into timelessness. 'Naked souls conduct a dialogue here with naked destinies. Both have been stripped of everything that is not of their innermost essence; all the relationships of life have been suppressed so that the relationship with destiny may be created; everything atmospheric between men and objects has vanished, in order that nothing should exist between them but the clear, harsh mountain air of ultimate questions and ultimate answers'.[32] The tragic hero is the clearest proof that 'only that which is individual, only something whose individuality is carried to the uttermost limit, is adequate to its idea – i.e., is really existent'.[33] From such pure realms, an ethical necessity radiates that is not made dependent on the possibility of becoming empirically real:

> The validity and strength of an ethic does not depend on whether or not the ethic is applied. Therefore only a form which has been purified until it has become ethical can, without becoming blind and poverty-stricken as a result of it, forget the existence of everything problematic and banish it forever from its realm.[34]

For this very reason, however, Lukács' pre-Heidelberg embrace of an unworldly individuality is, like the unworldly aesthetics he will develop in Heidelberg, both utopian *and* melancholic. Writing about Kierkegaard, Lukács highlights the 'tragedy [to] want to live what cannot be lived': Even '[a] poet's life is null and worthless because it is never absolute, never a thing in itself and for itself, because it is always there only *in relation to something*, and this relation is meaningless'.[35] The redemptive powers of the heroic individual cannot be systematized into an ethical framework that is accessible to all, but they do embody the peak of human powers. The ethical stance of the tragic hero is *inherently* non-shared and momentary, but it is nonetheless deemed exemplary for the path forward.

For Lukács, such tragic heroes are not just literary characters. The pure authenticity that they embody is proof of a *metaphysical* realm that has an intimate relation with 'death' and has never even been touched by the ailments of ordinary life. It is to this sphere of absolute, ethical values and mystical truths that he turns for redemption. In the pre-Heidelberg essay 'On Poverty of Spirit', therefore, the ethical and mystic soul of the heroic individual is quite clearly deemed more important than the forms of artworks: it is the hero who rejects social obligations and rationalist ethics as the foundation of true morality. As prime examples of modernity's lack of form, these stale conventions can never be fully *affirmed*.

> To be sure, most people live without life, but don't notice the difference. Their lives are *merely* social; you see: they could be satisfied with duties and their fulfilment. As a matter of fact, the fulfilment of duties is, for them, the only possible exaltation of their lives.[36]

To counter the obsolete values of conventional morality, Lukács argues for a sense of radical Goodness that is wholly external to the realm of history, refuting rather than completing the ethical norms of society. As a consequence, Lukács' concept of personal Goodness is clothed in metaphysical and mystical concepts: 'Goodness is madness, it is not mild, not refined, and not quietistic; it is wild, terrible, blind, and adventurous. The soul of the good man has become empty of all psychological content, of grounds and consequences; it has become a pure white slate upon which fate writes its absurd command, and this command will be followed blindly, rashly, and fiercely to the end. That this impossibility becomes fact, this blindness becomes clear-sightedness, this fierceness becomes Goodness – that is the miracle, the grace'.[37]

With the preparations for battle uprooting the entirety of German society at a staggering pace, Lukács' fascination with tragic heroes acquires a more than scholarly significance. His adopted home country, it seems, is crying out for the same renewed sense of duty and communal ethics that Lukács longs for. On August 12, 1914, the *Berliner Tageblatt und Handels-Zeitung* reports that no less than 1,200,000 young Germans have already presented themselves for voluntary service.[38] Still, contrary to what could perhaps be expected, these new recruits and conscripts are in Lukács' view no examples of the much-needed, heroic individuals who meet life as a fated 'totality'. The early days of World War I, rather, confirm to him that he has had it all too right for all too long. At the outset of the war Lukács already understands how the lifelessness, standardization, and anonymization that mark modern life would reach their apex in the first industrialized war in history. When Marianne Weber praises the moral values of the soldiers, his reply is very clear: 'The more heroic the deeds, the worse it is'.[39] The willingness to risk one's life for the nation is to him no proof of a true heroic sense of destiny or a 'radical Goodness' but a foremost illustration of stale and ossified ideals. A civilization that calls for blind obedience

42 *Unworldliness in Twentieth Century German Thought*

and the disavowal of all sense of individuality no longer speaks to our true spiritual needs. In the essay 'German Intellectuals and the War', he describes the 'general, spontaneous euphoria' about the war as 'lacking all clear and positive content'.[40] As a consequence, Lukács distances himself further from his former teacher Georg Simmel and even from his colleague and friend from Heidelberg, Max Weber, when the latter do embrace the war as the desired impetus behind a renewed sense of community. Lukács sharply rejects their assumption that the nationalism that is bringing war to all of them is proof that modern man has retained a lived feeling for supra-individual values and norms after all. To the contrary, the enthusiasm for the war is but the symptom of the formless culture that has caused the gap between the individual and community to arise in the first place.

Before long, Lukács' despair deepens to such a degree that he becomes more and more convinced that the tragedy of modern culture is not just symptomized by a gap between the spiritual needs of man and the formlessness of society's institutions but by a downright rift between meaning and reality. To the dismay of Max Weber, Lukács leaves behind his *Heidelberg Philosophy of Art* and starts work on an altogether different book. Less and less convinced by the need for an idealist aesthetics that conceptualizes 'utopian' art, Lukács analyzes modernity as a nihilistic universe in which people are not just estranged from each other but from any sense of objective truth. He will never finish the book that should have systematized this coupling of gnostic despair with metaphysical and mystical hope. Initially working on a study on Dostoyevsky, his bleak views during the first years of World War I will instead result in the broader themed *Theory of the Novel*. Lukács opposes the genre of the novel, as the expression of the 'transcendental homelessness' of modern man to the epic which, for its part, depicts a 'homogeneous world': in the epic 'the world of meaning can be grasped, it can be taken in at a glance'.[41] Lukács' observation that modernity is marked by a profound sense of meaninglessness clearly underlies his conception of the novel as the quintessential type of modern literature. The novel, it now appears to Lukács, resists the earlier promise of his idealist aesthetics: it does not reopen an isolated sphere of timeless values and pure essences ('the loss of all illusions'), nor can it be considered a form that adapts an individual's spiritual needs to the shared norms of society. In the novel, to the contrary, the modern conflict between reality and meaning is fully played out and remains immune to all efforts at sublation.

> The novel is the epic of a world that has been abandoned by God. The novel hero's psychology is demonic; the objectivity of the novel is the mature man's knowledge that meaning can never quite penetrate reality, but that, without meaning, reality would disintegrate into the nothingness of inessentiality.[42]

Strange Bedfellows 43

According to Lukács, one text in specific stands at the origin of the genre of the novel. It is a text, however, that brings the issues of utopianism and heroic unworldliness back to the center of the stage: *Don Quixote*.

Theory of the Novel includes Luckács' most elaborate discussion of Cervantes' novel. *Don Quixote* is believed to exemplify the genre of the novel because it exposes how the epic genre of the chivalry romance, along with its effortless mediation between absolute truths and reality, has lost its validity.[43] In showing up the estranged knight's vain efforts to retrieve a vestige of transcendence within the world, Cervantes is believed to have described the forlorn state of a modern world. Most symptomatic of this descent into disenchantment is the replacement of an all-powerful and well-meaning God by the 'evil demons' who do not cease to play tricks on poor Don Quixote. 'The God . . . actually becomes a demon, arrogating to himself the role of God, in a world forsaken by providence and lacking transcendental orientation'.[44] The universe that is depicted in *Don Quixote* can therefore be understood as a fairy-tale-gone-bad. It is 'the same one which God had previously transformed into a dangerous but wonderful magic garden; now, turned into prose by evil demons, this world yearns to be transformed back again into a magic garden by faithful heroes'.[45] In Lukács' reading, Cervantes is a sharp observer of the spiritual void that had characterized even the earliest stages of modernity. The cruelty with which Don Quixote's attachment to absolute values and ethical standards is met by all others symptomatizes a post-Christian, fallen world. 'The first great novel of world literature stands at the beginning of the time when the Christian God began to forsake the world; . . . when the world, released from its paradoxical anchorage in a beyond that is truly present, was abandoned to its immanent meaninglessness'.[46] As a consequence, *Don Quixote* is steeped in the sad awareness that even the greatest of goods and the most absolute of truths will at some point be mercilessly swept aside by the progress of time.

> The profound melancholy of the historical process, of the passing of time, speaks through this work, telling us that even a content and an attitude which are eternal must lose their meaning when their time is past: that time brushes aside even the eternal.[47]

If Cervantes' novel is believed to unmask the spiritual pains of a modern world, its protagonist serves Lukács as an illustration of the most powerful antidote: 'abstract idealism'. In line with his earlier fascination for a radical Goodness that needs to 'be followed blindly, rashly, and fiercely to the end', Don Quixote is endowed with the metaphysical and mystical power to counteract the state of overall meaninglessness that resonates elsewhere in the novel. According to Lukács, Don Quixote manages to withdraw

44 *Unworldliness in Twentieth Century German Thought*

from the world, thereby becoming wholly immune to its existential hollowness. For Don Quixote, it seems, there simply is no external universe anymore: here is a 'complete lack of any transcendental sense of space, i.e. of the ability to experience distances as realities'.[48] Having thus done away with any sense of outside, Don Quixote's ideals and values remain untested and uncontested by reality. In sharp opposition to modern man's restless seeking and never finding, Don Quixote is therefore presented as the zenith of mental calm and spiritual self-assurance:

> The soul is at rest in the transcendent existence it has achieved on the far side of all problems; no doubts, no search, no despair can arise within it so as to take it out of itself and set it in motion. Its grotesque, vain struggles to realise itself in the outside world will not really touch such a soul; nothing can shake it in its inner certitude, because it is imprisoned in its safe world – because it is incapable of experiencing anything.[49]

According to Lukács, Don Quixote's interiority is incapable of translating itself in purposeful behavior, but this lack of success is not perceived as a problem. His urge to act is unceasing, but it is in no way affected by the absence of any genuine impact on the world: 'Thus action and opposition have neither scope nor quality – neither reality nor orientation – in common. Their relationship to one another is not one of true struggle but only of a grotesque failure to meet, or an equally grotesque clash conditioned by reciprocal misunderstandings'.[50] Lukács is charmed by the knight's ability to meet the world wholly on his own terms. Unable to doubt the driving force behind his existence, Don Quixote divests the world of its potential to oppose man's projects and conceives of it, instead, as a playground for his adventures. 'The hero in his demonic search for adventure arbitrarily and disconnectedly selects those moments of this "reality" which he thinks most suitable for "proving himself"'.[51]

In the end, however, there is a crucial difference between Don Quixote's abstract idealism and the heroic individualism and 'radical Goodness' that Lukács longed for in his pre-Heidelberg years: Don Quixote's ethical values will not ever mediate between an individual and a community, let alone that they will ever bridge the gap between reality and meaning. To the contrary, Don Quixote's abstract idealism is fed by the drive to isolate himself from others and the world in such a way that the quest for supra-individual values ceases to matter all that much. This gives Don Quixote's life a tragic dimension but also an almost divine sense of autonomy: 'The hero's soul is at rest, rounded and complete within itself like a work of art or a divinity'.[52] For this reason, Lukács' verdict is in the end, rather ambiguous. On the one hand, he likens the erring knight to someone who is 'maniacally imprisoned in himself' and acknowledges that this

Strange Bedfellows 45

self-isolation carries within itself a kernel of redemption: '*Don Quixote* is the first great battle of interiority against the prosaic vulgarity of outward life, and the only battle in which interiority succeeded, not only to emerge unblemished from the fray, but even to transmit some of the radiance of its triumphant, though admittedly self-ironising, poetry to its victorious opponent'.[53] But, on the other hand, Lukács is very much aware that such a restoration of meaning cannot ever be translated back into the communal ethics that all healthy societies require. For Don Quixote, the sole means to overcome the emptiness of modern life rests in a merely *personal* morality that is based on unspoiled metaphysical and mystical values: he is driven by ideals that are 'subjectively clear' but 'lack any objective relationship'.[54]

III

When, in the final days of December 1918, 34-year-old Lukács joins the Hungarian Communist Party, this move comes to most friends as a surprise. Until then Lukács had rejected the revolutionary alternative to socio-democratic politics, deeming it too radical. And no more than a few weeks earlier he had published an essay with the title *Bolshevism as a Moral Problem*, leaving no unclarity either:

> I reject the view that it takes a deeper conviction to choose the "instant heroism" of Bolshevism than to accept the democratic way, which does not seem heroic at all but does require a sense of deep responsibility and commitment to an uphill battle that entails a long soul-wrenching process of teaching.[55]

Anna Leznai, one of his closest friends, therefore writes that 'from one Sunday to the next, he turned from Saul into Paul'.[56] Still, it seems exaggerated to speak of a deep discontinuity in Lukács' work and life. For it is surely partly on account of the aforementioned misgivings with excessive individualism, and the accompanying quest for a collectively embraced set of values that, after the war, Lukács ends up committing himself to a pronounced leftist, political agenda.[57] Much of Lukács' later *political* radicalism was in fact quite clearly prepared by the pre-Heidelberg plea for a radical *ethical* stance and the equally uncompromising convictions that underlay his Heidelberg *aesthetics*: 'Formation: the last judgement of things, which redeems everything redeemable and forces this redemption on everything with divine violence'.[58] Moreover, with this shift from a radical ethical mysticism and idealist aesthetics to a no less radical, political philosophy, some of Lukács' early concepts take on a very fascinating *Nachleben*: in his most important Marxist study, *History and Class Consciousness* (1923), they are not at all cast aside but, to the contrary,

46 *Unworldliness in Twentieth Century German Thought*

receive a sharpness that they initially lacked. For example, the flattening uniformization of our spiritual lives that was targeted by young Lukács is now no longer just a feature of a modern and 'formless' society, let alone the pain of a 'godforsaken', fallen universe, but, first and foremost, the symptom of a *capitalist* world: it will be termed 'reification' and is inserted into a critique of *commodity-production*.[59] Similarly, the collective ethics that, to the young Lukács, was so hard, if not impossible, to align with the heroic attitude of exemplary individuals will now be retrieved from within a consciousness of *socio-economic class*, and the revolutionary task of one class in specific: the proletariat. And the notion of 'totality', which, in Lukács' pre-Marxist work, refers to the internal unity and necessity of heroic values or autonomous artworks will from now on pertain to the set of relations that ties social phenomena together. 'Concrete analysis', writes Lukács in *History and Class Consciousness*, 'means then: the relation to society *as a whole*. For only when this relation is established does the consciousness of their existence that men have at any given time emerge in all its essential characteristics'.[60]

Nonetheless, one should neither underplay the shift that Lukács' work undergoes in 1918. While there is no steep divide between the pre-Marxist and the Marxist Lukács, it would be equally inaccurate to speak of a continuity.[61] One noteworthy difference has to do with the later Lukács' rejection of the mystical dimension in ethics, politics, and aesthetics. With the shift to Marxist philosophy the focus on *un*worldly truths and values is replaced with an emphasis on the importance of *societal* understanding and commitment. The notion of 'standpoint' for instance can therefore no longer refer to the internal coherence of an autonomous artwork. In *History and Class Consciousness*, this same notion refers to a specific view of the *world*. Standpoint, that is, now denotes the unique position of the proletariat within a capitalist society, and the vital epistemological and revolutionary task that rests on its shoulders. 'The historical knowledge of the proletariat begins with knowledge of the present, with the self-knowledge of its own social situation and with the elucidation of its necessity (i.e. its genesis)'.[62] In Lukács' view, the proletariat is singularly capable of perceiving the internal contradictions within capitalism, thereby shaping the indispensable perspective from which to develop both class consciousness and an emancipatory praxis. As such, standpoint is always, and ought forever to be, socially situated. This same emphasis on the necessity of societal commitment explains why the later Lukács becomes an adamant defender of realist aesthetics. In important texts such as *Historical Novel* (1936/7) and 'Realism in the Balance' (1938) he criticizes quite a few modernist artworks for their supposed decadence, subjectivism, irrationalism, or formalism. 'Realism in the Balance', for instance, builds on a polemic with Ernst Bloch whose own philosophical framework, as we will see in the next chapter, dismisses the idea of totality altogether, considering capitalist societies to be in the grip of fragmentation. On account of this affinity with phenomena of depersonalization, Bloch develops a marked interest in modernist art, primarily Expressionism. In Lukács' view, however,

> Bloch's mistake lies merely in the fact that he identifies this state of mind directly and unreservedly with reality itself. He equates the highly distorted image created in this state of mind with the thing itself, instead of objectively unravelling the essence, the origins and the mediations of the distortion comparing it with reality.[63]

The later Lukács' embrace of aesthetic realism rests on the distinction between 'appearance' (how a given society is perceived, e.g., as fragmented) and 'essence' (the objective 'totality' of a society, i.e., the internal unity of all social phenomena within one given society). While modernism fails to address, and contest, the objectively real, social world of capitalism, 'true realists' paint the picture of the dialectical relationship between the consciousness of human beings on the one hand (appearance), and the world in which they live on the other (essence). Somewhat remarkably, the later Lukács briefly returns to the novel of Cervantes to illustrate this argument. He suggests that even *Don Quixote* bears the traces of a realist aesthetics since it is 'concerned with the creation of types' and seeks out 'the lasting features in people, in their relations with each other and in the situations in which they have to act'.[64] Lukács' essay even starts with a quote from the Bulgarian politician Georgi Dimitrov that attributes a revolutionary power to Cervantes' novel. However, with this embrace of a realist aesthetics, the earlier fascination with *un*worldly, utopian ideals and tragic heroes has vanished almost entirely. The attempt to create values and forms that are autonomous from the empirical world is now deemed profoundly problematical rather than redemptive, because it is believed to open the door for a decontextualized and ultimately powerless stance. Twenty years after his conversion to communism, Lukács is even willing to disavow his own prewar framework in no uncertain terms: while his early 'subjective determination was a protest of a progressive sort, [t]he objective product, *The Theory of the Novel*, was a reactionary work in every respect, full of idealistic mysticism and false in all its assessments of the historical process'.[65]

IV

Let's take a step back. On August 1, 1914, Ernst Jünger, a 19-year-old high school student with lousy grades, is standing on a roof, helping to fix the damage after a fire destroyed part of the trade building in his home town of Rehburg, about 300 miles to the north of Heidelberg. Jünger's

48 *Unworldliness in Twentieth Century German Thought*

reaction to the news of the German mobilization is the polar opposite of Lukács'. While Lukács considers the call to arms a proof that modern politics pays no heed whatsoever to the existential needs of the individual, Jünger welcomes it with uninhibited enthusiasm. The nationalism that, in Lukács' view, increases the gap between individual and community, epitomizes for Jünger and his friends the very type of group mentality that will save modernity from its individualism and egotism. 'The roofer had just raised his hammer to strike a blow. Now he stopped in mid-motion and put it down again very gently. At that moment, another calendar came into effect. He was a man of service who had to report to his regiment in the next few days. . . . So all at once, as everywhere in Germany where men were together, our small peaceful community had become a military one'.[66] Lukács is relieved that he will be exempt from service; Jünger will sign up for voluntary service three days later.

Jünger's case poses a serious challenge to whoever might think that actual battle will instantly cure the war-enthused of their foolishness. The idea that the experience of war revitalizes a society and restores an authentic and communal sense of belonging will stay with him for the remainder of his long life. In essays like 'Battle as a Lived Experience' (1922, 1926) or the novel *Storms of Steel* (1920), moreover, Jünger does not hold back in romanticizing the experience of the trenches with the help of a metaphysical and mystical jargon. In spite of its having lost the war, Jünger argues, the shared experience of an entire generation has not only brought Germany the social cohesion that it desperately needed, it has even replenished a wellspring of meaning of an altogether different kind. For Jünger raises the soldier to the level of an ancient hero and describes his mental state and physical actions with unabashed religious terms. In Jünger's view, battle is the sole means of recuperating a 'primary relation' to the 'fated time' (*Schicksalszeit*) that is at work within history.[67] The soldier, that is to say, has come to terms with the fact that everything must irrevocably perish at some point: 'To live means to kill'.[68] When destruction and annihilation are thus taken to be the only features in life that are truly universal and eternal, the soldier who is doing the killing is believed to embrace nothing less than an ontological lawfulness: 'The hostile manifests itself as the unfolding of a gigantic, impersonal force, as fate that smashes its fists into the blind'.[69] The soldier who is being killed, for his part, is by this very token believed to rise above the transience of mortal existence since his death is in truth a type of 'sacrifice'. In other words, for Jünger, World War I is not at all the apex of an anonymous and standardized society that pushes the individual back into spiritual emptiness. To the contrary, armed battle is the greatest antidote to an overarching sense of randomness and futility. In Jünger's view, 'existence is in essence absolutely of a warlike nature'.[70] As an instantiation of an 'inner experience' the danger that comes with war enables the individual soldier to reestablish contact with the genuine core of his existence: instead of destabilizing the soldier's sense of identity, the confrontation with the possibility of a violent death is believed to enable him to finally say 'I' and become a true self. Jünger writes: 'Yes, the soldier in his relationship to death, in the abandonment of his personality for an idea, knows little of the philosophers and their values. But in him and his deeds, life expresses itself more movingly and deeply than any book could ever do. And again and again, despite all the absurdity and madness of external events, one radiant truth remains: death for a conviction is the highest achievement. It is confession, deed, fulfillment, faith, love, hope and goal; in this imperfect world it is perfection and perfection itself. The thing is nothing and the conviction is everything'.[71] According to Jünger, the fact that millions of people have fought and died during the war bestows onto the causes for war a supra-historical weight and mystical necessity rather than that it would make these causes seem ridiculous or vain.

Lukács and Jünger meet at least once in their lifetimes. In the winter of 1931–1932, Marxist intellectuals and members of the Communist party set up a 'Society for the study of Planned Economy' and seek the support of right-leaning authors. Together with Carl Schmitt, Jünger, as well, is solicited. These post-war attempts to draw Jünger away from his war-enthused rhetoric do not however bear much fruit.[72] As a consequence, in the 1950s, Lukács, who has by then fully embraced the Communist cause, will present a scathing rejection of Jünger's work. He takes Jünger to task for a 'reactionary . . . mission' and a 'romantically and mystically inflated nihilism' that foregoes class consciousness and historical awareness.[73] In fact, the later Lukács' criticism of Jünger has much in common with Adorno's charge of the pernicious 'inward turn' and 'jargon of authenticity' that burden the work of Husserl and Heidegger with an indefensible unworldliness. Jünger does indeed take explicit recourse to the Husserlian phenomenological jargon of lived experiences (*Erlebnisse*) and world-constituting, unspoiled selves to analyze the deep truth that is supposedly revealed through warfare. For the later Lukács, this jargon is intolerable since it conflates history with myth and conjures a false sense of inevitability and fatedness. Jünger's views rest on a 'radically anti-historical, mythicizing view of history'; they 'abolish history' and get stuck in a mere 'pretention to concreteness': 'With Junger, vitalism's radical subjectivism too was further heightened and given a politico-historical slant'.[74] However, this later Lukács has seemingly forgotten that, a few decades earlier, his own work revolved around a very similar adoption of unworldly religious and mythological concepts. Jünger's quest for a radical and personal morality is not at all irreconcilable with the young Lukács' plea for a 'wild, terrible, blind, and adventurous' morality. Both Jünger *and* the young Lukács seek

50 *Unworldliness in Twentieth Century German Thought*

to brush aside all pre-established social norms and rational ethics. Lukács' statement that the soul of moral man 'has become a pure white slate upon which fate writes its absurd command'[75] bears a striking resemblance with Jünger's claims about the moral superiority of the soldier. The later Lukács shoots his arrows primarily at Jünger's suggestion that unworldly 'forms' both originate in *and* surpass the realm of subjective, lived experience, but it is this precise argument that founded his own pre-war project as well. Indeed, some of the passages in Jünger's work that are singled out by the later Lukács could, before the war, have been written by him too. Let us, for instance, compare the young Lukács' statement that '[f]ormation [is] the last judgement of things, which redeems everything redeemable and forces this redemption on everything with divine violence'[76] with a statement by Jünger that is quoted *and* denounced by the later Lukács: 'The beholding of forms is a revolutionary act inasmuch as it perceives a being in the whole and unitary fullness of its life. It is the great advantage of this process that it takes place beyond the moral and aesthetic as well as the scientific law'.[77] As we have seen, the pre-war Lukács, as well, turned to *Lebensphilosophie* in a quest for the unspoiled totalities and forms of 'a perfect world, which, in the immediacy of its physical reality, silences all pain and suffering . . . which exists in the here and now with undeniable concreteness and yet seems to have descended from regions far removed from the evanescence of the present'.[78] Still, in the 1950s, Lukács will dismiss Jünger's work on account of the statement that '[a] form *is*, and no development can add to or detract from it. Hence evolutionary history is not a history of form. . . . Evolution knows beginning and end, birth and death, from which the form is removed. History does not produce any forms, but changes along with the form. History is that tradition which a victorious power bestows on itself'.[79]

In spite of the strong ideological oppositions, and a radically different perspective on World War I, the young Lukács and Jünger concur in connecting an unworldly and mystical inclination with a nihilistic and gnostic analysis of modernity. Jünger's notion of 'total mobilization', for instance, does not just refer to the deployment of all political, economic, and technological resources for the all-encompassing purpose of warfare. Beyond this societal dimension, total mobilization has become an 'event of cosmic significance' that brings to light the gap between meaning and reality that figures so prominently in the young Lukács' writings as well. In the eyes of Jünger the 'growing conversion of life into energy' and 'the increasingly fleeting content of all binding ties in deference of mobility' entail that modernity is characterized by a wholly novel sense of meaninglessness.[80] The outbreak of a fully industrialized war has derailed all previously held convictions, not in the least the belief that the world is on the path of progress. In other words, the war has not only made palpable that it is violence

Strange Bedfellows 51

and unreason, and not science or rationality that reign over history; it has also brought to light that the values of Enlightenment have estranged the human being from her intuitions, leaving her utterly unprepared to deal with such destructive powers. 'As sons of an age intoxicated by matter, progress seemed perfection, the machine of godlikeness seemed key, and the telescope and microscope seemed organs of knowledge. But beneath the ever shining polished shell, beneath all the garments with which we adorned ourselves like magicians, we remained naked and raw like the people of the forest and the steppe'.[81] In line with the early Lukács' rejection of relativism and his plea for a morality that is based on metaphysics and mysticism, Jünger's turn to a religious, mythological, and even apocalyptic jargon should therefore be understood as an endeavor to make visible the *distance* between reality and meaning, and not as a proof that this distance can be overcome through the embrace of a shared and unified *world*. It is for this reason that Jünger, in spite of his recourse to the phenomenological jargon, remains above all a thinker of *un*worldliness. In Jünger's view, the fragmentation of the world can and should be reckoned with *as such*. The destructiveness and meaninglessness of history cannot be neutralized through the interactions with a lifeworld or the retrieval of an ultimate *ground*. In the 1950s, this view will lead to an interesting discussion between Jünger and Heidegger. Heidegger criticizes Jünger's unwillingness to accept an ontological ground and argues that nihilism, as well, should be understood as a mode of Being: 'Above all, I would wish to ask whether . . . it is not a new turning of being that would first bring the moment for crossing the line [with nihilism]'.[82] Because it is itself a presentation of Being, even the most extreme type of nihilism cannot, according to Heidegger, fully undo the possibility that man will recover a foundational truth that resonates within the surrounding world. Jünger disagrees. While he does cling to absolute truths, these do not according to him offer an ultimate sublation of the world's state of overall meaninglessness. The necessity and lawfulness that Jünger encounters in the battlefields of World War I should not be confused with the foundational, worldly truths that phenomenologists are after: embracing the seeming *absurdity* of life itself is, in Jünger's view, the purest and, however paradoxical it may seem, *utopian* of ideals. The revelation of an essential and primordial force within the war entails, therefore, in the first place, the renunciation of all worldly norms and values. Rather than a shared horizon of meaning, Jünger seeks a 'magical point zero [at] which nothing and everything is at the same time'.[83]

It is with this mix of nihilism and utopianism in mind that the multiple references to Don Quixote in Jünger's work can gain depth and clarity. In the previously mentioned article 'Battle as a Lived Experience', Jünger describes the war-time experience of having stranded in a strange town where everything is 'hostile' and 'things waver in the fog, are like smoke,

52 Unworldliness in Twentieth Century German Thought

like spooky, unreal fluttering'. He feels 'as a tiny atom, restlessly whirled about by treacherous forces' and is 'so tired, so weary', that he wants 'to be dead'. It is at this exact moment that Don Quixote makes his first entry in Jünger's writings. In the midst of the madness of the war, Jünger identifies with 'a lansquenet, a knight errant, a Don Quixote who splinters many a lance and whose illusions dissolve into derisive laughter'.[84] Jünger's reading runs parallel to that of Lukács since, for Jünger, as well, Don Quixote is first and foremost an abstract idealist who refuses to reconcile himself to a universe that does not deserve being reconciled to. Jünger turns Don Quixote into the quintessential hero who does not doubt himself or his spiritual compass, even when it becomes clear that the purity of these values is no match for the plainness of one's immediate surroundings. In a universe that is emptied of meaning, Don Quixote's resolute refusal to let go of seemingly untenable ideals and absurd values grows into a redemptive force of its own. It is Don Quixote who makes Jünger realize with 'undoubted clarity that some strange meaning, some terrible significance lurks behind everything that happens'.[85] Five years later, in a letter, Jünger returns to Don Quixote to reiterate the same idea. The erring knight epitomizes 'a process of the highest metaphysical rank' that cannot simple be 'cancelled out' or 'understood'.[86] For this reason, Jünger is disappointed with Cervantes' decision to kill his protagonist after a supposed moment of rational illumination. Professing a clear preference for the protagonist of the novel over its creator, Jünger so to speak saves Don Quixote from Cervantes and takes the author to task for having forced the erring knight to 'betray his own ideals'. Rather than allowing him to die in the safety of his home, Don Quixote should have been granted the honor of being killed in the midst of the heroic fight for his own truths, however nonsensical they may have been.

> One thing I have always resented about Cervantes is that he lets his hero die in bed and in denial of his knighthood. It is so right and so necessary that a man must die when his idea leaves him burnt out. But in this case I didn't like it and I agreed with Sancho that it was stupid to die for nothing when you can have yourself killed.[87]

Another two years later, in the collection of his autobiographical writings *The Adventurous Heart*, Jünger claims that his fascination with Don Quixote predates the years he spent in combat. At the age of ten, he read Cervantes' novel with 'true Spanish earnestness' and, not discovering 'the merest trace of humor within it', became enamored with Don Quixote's unwavering heroism. From this moment onward, Jünger is convinced that the only compensation for the empty 'mechanical' time resides in an unshakeable 'faith in ideals'. For young Ernst, the clearest proof of this idealism can be found in the age of Don Quixote. The sustained presence of a faithful attitude in adulthood is a comfort to the young teenager since it convinces him that a more profound knowledge lies in wait, and that his own idealism will not just melt away with time. 'What I still like today as much as I did then is that this man was no longer a youth when he discovered the backbone that the world possesses'.[88]

Like the young Lukács, Jünger argues that Don Quixote's worldview is rooted in unworldly ideals and thus highlights that it is not a historical or empirical process that enables the human being to come to terms with the world's meaninglessness. Don Quixote is seeking the impossible: the realization of ideals that are nonetheless inherently abstract and absolute, or what was called above a utopian *presence*. For this reason, he does indeed deserve to be called 'mad'. However, in Jünger's view, as well, even a lost cause is worth fighting for. Don Quixote seems to experience no genuine doubt when time and again his attempts to realize his absurd ideals turn out to be unsuccessful. It is this refusal to be tested and contested by empirical reality that renders him, in both the interpretation of the young Lukács and that of Jünger, a heroic stature. For Jünger, Cervantes' novel is 'from the ground up a combative [*kriegerisch*] work, that was written by [an] old soldier and could only have been written by [an] old soldier'.[89] Both thinkers pit the idealism of Don Quixote against the endeavor to change society from within and thereby set an example for all. For the ideals of Don Quixote are no clear-cut universal model *for* the world but primarily an idiosyncratic inoculation *against* it. This becomes clear from Jünger's descriptions of the limit-experiences that brought Don Quixote to his mind. In such scenes, Jünger makes it seem as if a Don Quixote-like, unwavering faith in absolute ideals and truths at once exposes the senselessness of his actions *and* renders him immune to it. Such limit-experiences no longer revolve around the perception of a shared universe or an appeal to communal values. During the war, Jünger identifies with Don Quixote's ceaseless urge to realize unrealizable ideals because the blind commitment to these ideals offsets the meaninglessness of the experiences he is going through: metaphysical ideals and truths have here, so to speak, cast a veil over the world that surrounds us, and they remain untouched by the fact that they cannot be fully actualized within it. 'Here is a point where a magic line intersects with a real one'.[90] Don Quixote confirms Jünger's belief that the shortcomings of history can be both experienced and neutralized at the same time: 'But this is how I imagine the last moment of a knight errant, on the threshold between the divine error of life and the divine truth in which this error is meaningfully extinguished'.[91] Even the indifferent violence of industrial warfare can thus give way to the experience of a sense of necessity and unavoidability. Describing the moment when he is violently thrown on the ground during combat, for instance, Jünger notes how 'he felt that a wonderful significance had accompanied

54 *Unworldliness in Twentieth Century German Thought*

me up to this point, and that everything had to be as it was: more and more I lost faith in what is called chance; it was just a senseless piece of lead that cut through the chest – senseless as the windmill blade that knocked Don Quixote to the ground'.[92]

On account of this recourse to metaphysics and mysticism, the young Lukács' felicitous description of Don Quixote's 'grotesque failure' to meet reality is applicable to Jünger's reading as well. In taking recourse to an unwavering faith in absolute ideals and mythological truths, both the young Lukács and Jünger set up an impenetrable wall between meaning and *empirical* reality. With this gesture, truth and world become so antagonistic that there is no longer a chance that they can be truly reconciled. This is most palpable when Jünger connects his interpretation of Don Quixote with the metaphor of an alarm clock. For Jünger, the sound of an alarm clock going off does not indicate a moment of awakening, let alone the brutal confrontation with an empirical world. To the contrary, even this moment is divested of its interruptive potential when Jünger highlights that it is no match for the irrational powers of sleep: 'At the very moment when you realize that it was the alarm clock, but in which you are still just as strongly in the action of the dream, you feel in a flash, but with wonderful joy, an inkling of the great, resting harmony that is hidden behind the movement of the manifold'.[93]

Notes

1 Lukács, quoted in Richard Westerman, *Lukács's Phenomenology of Capitalism: Reification Revalued* (Cham, Germany: Palgrave Macmillan, 2019), 34. Together with Westerman's excellent analysis of *The Heidelberg Philosophy of Art*, the following sources were helpful: Tyrus Miller, 'Matthew, Mark, Lukács, and Bloch: From Aesthetic Utopianism to Religious Messianism', in *Georg Lukács and Critical Theory: Aesthetics, History, Utopia* (Edinburgh, UK: Edinburgh University Press, 2022), 31–54; Ferenc Fehèr, 'The Transformation of the Kantian Question in Lukács' *Heidelberg Philosophy of Art*' in *Graduate Faculty Philosophy Journal* 16 (2) (1993): 331–344; Mary Gluck, *Georg Lukács and His Generation, 1900–1918* (Cambridge and London: Harvard University Press, 1985), esp. Chapter 5. For historical context, see Bettina Szabados, 'Georg Lukács in Heidelberg: A Crossroad between the Academic and Political Career', in *Filozofia* 75 (2020): 51–64.
2 Weber, quoted in Fehèr, 'The Transformation of the Kantian Question in Lukács' *Heidelberg Philosophy of Art*', 331.
3 Georg Lukács, *Heidelberger Philosophie der Kunst*, ed. György Márkus and Frank Benseler (Darmstadt and Neuwied, Germany: Luchterhand Verlag, 1974), 153.
4 See Westerman, *Lukács's Phenomenology of Capitalism*, 37–41.
5 Lukács, *Heidelberger Philosophie der Kunst*, 135.
6 Lukács, *Heidelberger Philosophie der Kunst*, 56. Translation by Michael Clark, quoted in György Márkus, 'Life and the Soul: The Young Lukács and

the Problem of Culture', in *Lukács Revalued*, ed. Agnes Heller (Oxford: Basil Blackwell, 1983), 13.

7 Fehèr, 'The Transformation of the Kantian Question in Lukács' *Heidelberg Philosophy of Art*', 333–337.

8 Lukács, *Heidelberger Philosophie der Kunst*, 46.

9 Lukács, *Heidelberger Philosophie der Kunst*, 31–32.

10 Lukács, *Heidelberger Philosophie der Kunst*, 109.

11 See also Westerman, *Lukács's Phenomenology of Capitalism*, 36.

12 Georg Simmel, 'Vom Realismus in der Kunst', in *Gesamtausgabe 8. Aufsätze und Abhandlungen 1901–1908*, ed. Gregor Fitzi and Otthein Rammstedt (Frankfurt am Main, Germany: Suhrkamp, 2015), 407–411. For the following discussion of Simmel, see also my *More Than Life: Georg Simmel and Walter Benjamin on Art* (Evanston, IL: Northwestern University Press, 2017), esp. the Introduction and Chapter 2.

13 Georg Simmel, *The View of Life: Four Metaphysical Essays with Journal Aphorisms*, transl. Donald N. Levine and John A. Y. Andrews (Chicago: University of Chicago Press, 2011), 14.

14 Simmel, *The View of Life*, 33.

15 Georg Simmel, 'The Concept and Tragedy of Culture', in *Simmel on Culture*, ed. David Frisby and Mike Featherstone (London: Sage Publications, 2000), 55–75.

16 See the discussion of Lukács and Simmel in Gluck, *Georg Lukács and His Generation*, e.g. 22, 145–147.

17 Lukács, quoted in Gluck, *Georg Lukács and His Generation*, 146–147.

18 Georg Lukács, 'Georg Simmel', in *Theory, Culture & Society* 8 (3) (1991): 145–150.

19 Simmel, *View of Life*, 60.

20 Simmel, *View of Life*, 15.

21 Simmel, *View of Life*, 160.

22 For example, Lukács, *Heidelberger Philosophie der Kunst*, 161.

23 Lukács, quoted in Gluck, *Georg Lukács and His Generation*, 166 (translation by Gluck).

24 Lukács, *Heidelberger Philosophie der Kunst*, 16. See also Gluck, *Georg Lukács and His Generation*, 167.

25 Georg Lukács, *Soul and Form*, ed. John T. Sanders and Katie Terezakis (New York: Columbia University Press, 2010), 126.

26 Lukács, *Soul and Form*, 23.

27 Lukács, *Soul and Form*, 23.

28 Georg Lukács, 'Aesthetic Culture', transl. Rita Keresztesi-Treat, ed. Tyrus Miller, in *The Yale Journal of Criticism* 11 (2) (1998): 370–371.

29 Lukács, 'Aesthetic Culture', 375.

30 See also Tyrus Miller's introduction to Lukács, 'Aesthetic Culture', 366. This central position of the individual in *Soul and Form* will bring Lucien Goldmann to his existentialist interpretation of *Soul and Form*. See Martin Jay, 'Totality and Marxist Aesthetics: The Case of Lucien Goldmann', in *Marxism and Totality: The Adventures of a Concept from Lukács to Habermas* (Cambridge, UK: Polity Press, 1984), 300–330.

31 Lukács, quoted in Paul Browne, 'Philosophy as Exile from Life: Lukács' *Soul and Form*', in *Radical Philosophy* 53 (1989): 23.

32 Lukács, *Soul and Form*, 178–179.

33 Lukács, *Soul and Form*, 185.

56 *Unworldliness in Twentieth Century German Thought*

34 Lukács, *Soul and Form*, 198.
35 Lukács, *Soul and Form*, 56–57. See also Márkus, 'Life and the Soul', 14.
36 Georg Lukács, 'On Poverty of Spirit', in *Soul and Form*, ed. John T. Sanders and Katie Terezakis (New York: Columbia University Press, 2010), 203–204.
37 Lukács, 'On Poverty of Spirit', 207. For an excellent analysis of the romanticism of the early Lukács and the essays in *Soul and Form*, see the second chapter of Michael Löwy, *Georg Lukács: From Romanticism to Bolshevism*, transl. Patrick Camiller (London: NLB, 1979), 91–127.
38 See Alex Watson, '"For Kaiser and Reich": The Identity and Fate of the German Volunteers 1914–1918', in *War in History* 12 (1) (2005): 45.
39 Lukács, in an interview with István Eörsi and Erzsébet Vezérs, see www.versobooks.com/blogs/news/3283-georg-lukacs-during-war-and-revolution. This is reprinted in Georg Lukács, *Record of a Life: An Autobiography*, ed. István Eörsi, transl. Rodney Livingstone (London: Verso, 1985).
40 Georg Lukács, 'Die deutschen Intellektuellen und der Krieg', ed. Heinz Ludwig Arnold, in *Text + Kritik: Zeitschrift für Literatur* 39–40 (1973): 65. For the context of this standpoint, see Arpad Kadarkay, *Georg Lukács: Life, Thought, and Politics* (Cambridge, MA: Basil Blackwell, 1991), 154–160.
41 Georg Lukács, *The Theory of the Novel*, transl. Anna Bostock (Cambridge, MA: MIT Press, 1971), 32.
42 Lukács, *The Theory of the Novel*, 88.
43 For an overview of Lukács's reading of Cervantes, see Rachel Schmidt, *Forms of Modernity: Don Quixote and Modern Theories of the Novel* (Toronto: University of Toronto Press, 2021, 82–119). Interestingly, in his analysis of Lukács's *Theory of the Novel*, Jay Bernstein displaces Don Quixote as the founding novel and replaces it with Descartes's *Discourse on Method*. 'The novel, Lukács claims, is a product of a world in which all the models have disappeared, hence the sign of the novel is the productivity of spirit. The world of Cervantes, however, is one in which there is a superabundance of models, models which no longer inform or have a basis in the social "a prioris" governing institutional life and action'. In J. M. Bernstein, *The Philosophy of the Novel: Lukács, Marxism and the Dialectics of Form* (Minneapolis: University of Minnesota Press, 1984), 155.
44 Lukács, *Theory of the Novel*, 103.
45 Lukács, *Theory of the Novel*, 103.
46 Lukács, *Theory of the Novel*, 103.
47 Lukács, *Theory of the Novel*, 104.
48 Lukács, *Theory of the Novel*, 97.
49 Lukács, *Theory of the Novel*, 99.
50 Lukács, *Theory of the Novel*, 98.
51 Lukács, *Theory of the Novel*, 100–101.
52 Lukács, *Theory of the Novel*, 100.
53 Lukács, *Theory of the Novel*, 100, 104.
54 Lukács, *Theory of the Novel*, 103.
55 Georg Lukács, 'Bolshevism as a Moral Problem', transl. Judith Marcus Tar, in *Social Research* 44 (3) (1977): 424.
56 Leznai, quoted in Márkus, 'Life and the Soul', 1.
57 For an analysis of the early anti-capitalist strands in Lukács's thought, and the move toward communism, see Löwy, *Georg Lukács*, Chapters 1–2.
58 Lukács, 'Aesthetic Culture', 377.
59 For a good overview of the concept of reification, see Andrew Feenberg, 'Lukács's Theory of Reification: An Introduction', in *Confronting Reification: Revitalizing Georg Lukács's Thought in Late Capitalism*, ed. Gregory R. Smulewicz-Zucker (Leiden, Netherlands and Boston, MA: Brill, 2020), 13–24.

Strange Bedfellows 57

60 Georg Lukács, *History and Class Consciousness: Studies in Marxist Dialectics* (Cambridge, MA: The MIT Press, 1971), 50. See also Lukács's definition of 'totality' as 'the whole of society seen as process', 22. Cf. Westerman, *Lukács's Phenomenology of Capitalism*, 81: Lukács 'began to analyse society using a paradigm analogous to that which he applied to art: it is a realm in which the meaning of objects is determined in relation to the totality of all other such objects, according to a governing principle that simultaneously presupposes a definite intentional attitude on the part of the subject'.

61 See Márkus, 'Life and the Soul', 3.

62 Lukács, *History and Class Consciousness*, 159. For a discussion of this issue, see Titus Stahl, 'Social Structure and Epistemic Privilege: Reconstructing Lukács's Standpoint Theory', in *Análisis* 10 (2) (2023): 319–349.

63 Georg Lukács, 'Realism in the Balance', in *Ernst Bloch, Georg Lukács, Bertolt Brecht, Walter Benjamin, and Theodor Adorno, Aesthetics and Politics*, ed. and transl. Ronald Taylor (London: Verso, 1980), 34.

64 Lukács, 'Realism in the Balance', 47. For an interesting discussion of realism in Lukács and Adorno, see Peter Uwe Hohendahl, 'The Theory of the Novel and the Concept of Realism in Lukács and Adorno', in *Georg Lukács Reconsidered: Critical Essays in Politics, Philosophy and Aesthetics*, ed. Michael J. Thompson (New York: Continuum, 2011), 75–98. See also Rodney Livingstone, 'Introduction', in *Georg Lukács, Essays on Realism*, ed. Rodney Livingstone, transl. David Fernbach (London: Lawrence and Wishart, 1980), 1–22. As Livingstone writes, Lukács's 'commitment to realism is a commitment to the world in common of those who are awake. It is a sustained appeal to all progressive thinkers to abandon their residual private worlds. Realism is then not a substitute for political action: it is the structure of consciousness that accompanies it. It is this that constitutes the strength of Lukacs's position' (p. 21).

65 Lukács, 'Realism in the Balance', 49.

66 Jünger, quoted in Helmut Kiesel, *Ernst Jünger: Die Biographie* (Berlin: Pantheon, 2009), 87–88.

67 Ernst Jünger, 'Die Schicksalszeit', in *Politische Publizistik: 1919 bis 1933*, ed. Sven Olaf Berggötz (Stuttgart: Klett-Cotta, 2001), 275–280.

68 Ernst Jünger, 'Der Kampf als inneres Erlebnis', in *Betrachtungen zur Zeit: Sämtliche Werke, Band 9: Essays I* (Stuttgart, Germany: Klett-Cotta, 1995), 42.

69 Jünger, 'Der Kampf als inneres Erlebnis', 96.

70 Ernst Jünger, 'Krieg und Technik', in *Das Antlitz des Weltkrieges in Politische Publizistik: 1919 bis 1933*, ed. Sven Olaf Berggötz (Stuttgart, Germany: Klett-Cotta, 2001), 597.

71 Jünger, 'Der Kampf als inneres Erlebnis', 100.

72 Ernst Jünger, diary entry of May 10, 1945 in *Kirchhorster Blätter* in *Strahlungen II: Sämtliche Werke, Band 3. Tagebücher III* (Stuttgart, Germany: Klett-Cotta, 2015), 443. See also Kiesel, *Ernst Jünger*, 324.

73 Georg Lukács, *The Destruction of Reason*, transl. Peter Palmer (Atlantic Highlands, NJ: Humanities Press, 1980), 528, 844.

74 Lukács, *The Destruction of Reason*, 529–530.

75 Lukács, 'On Poverty of Spirit', 207.

76 Lukács, 'Aesthetic Culture', 377.

77 Jünger, quoted in Lukács, *The Destruction of Reason*, 529. The original quote can be retrieved in Ernst Jünger, *Der Arbeiter: Herrschaft und Gestalt* (Stuttgart, Germany: Klett-Cotta, 1982), 42.

78 Lukács, quoted in Gluck, *Georg Lukács and His Generation*, 166.

79 Jünger, quoted in Lukács, *The Destruction of Reason*, 530. The original quote can be retrieved from Jünger, *Der Arbeiter*, 82.

58 Unworldliness in Twentieth Century German Thought

80 Ernst Jünger, 'Total Mobilization', transl. Joel Golb and Richard Wolin, in *The Heidegger Controversy: A Critical Reader*, ed. Richard Wolin (Cambridge, MA and London: The MIT Press, 1992), 123–126.
81 Jünger, 'Der Kampf als inneres Erlebnis', 12.
82 See Martin Heidegger, 'On the Question of Being', in *Pathmarks*, ed. and transl. William McNeill (Cambridge, UK: Cambridge University Press, 2010), 307.
83 Ernst Jünger, 'Das Abenteuerliche Herz: Erste Fassung', in *Sämtliche Werke: Zweite Abteilung. Essays. Band 9. Essays III* (Stuttgart, Germany: Klett-Cotta, 1979), 162.
84 Jünger, 'Der Kampf als inneres Erlebnis', 67.
85 Jünger, 'Der Kampf als inneres Erlebnis', 67.
86 Ernst Jünger, quoted in Tom Kindt and Hans-Harald Müller, 'Zweimal Cervantes: Die Don Quijote-Lektüren von Ernst Jünger und Ernst Weiß. Ein Beitrag zur literarischen Anthropologie der zwanziger Jahre', in *Jahrbuch zur Literatur der Weimarer Republik: Band 1. 1995*, ed. Sabina Becker (St. Ingbert, Germany: Röhrig Universitätsverlag, 1995), 233.
87 Jünger, quoted in Kindt and Müller, 'Zweimal Cervantes', 233–234.
88 Jünger, *Das Abenteuerliche Herz*, 57.
89 Jünger, *Das Abenteuerliche Herz*, 54.
90 Jünger, quoted in Kindt and Müller, 'Zweimal Cervantes', 233.
91 Jünger, quoted in Kindt and Müller, 'Zweimal Cervantes', 234.
92 Jünger, quoted in Kindt and Müller, 'Zweimal Cervantes', 234.
93 Jünger, quoted in Kindt and Müller, 'Zweimal Cervantes', 233–234.

Bibliography

Bernstein, J. M. *The Philosophy of the Novel: Lukács Marxism and the Dialectics of Form* (Minneapolis: University of Minnesota Press, 1984)
Browne, Paul. 'Philosophy as Exile from Life: Lukács' Soul and Form', in *Radical Philosophy* 53 (1989)
Eörsi, István and Vezér, Erzsébet. 'Interview with Georg Lukács', www.versobooks.com/blogs/news/3283-georg-lukacs-during-war-and-revolution
Feenberg, Andrew. 'Lukács's Theory of Reification: An Introduction', in *Confronting Reification: Revitalizing Georg Lukács's Though in Late Capitalism*, ed. Gregory R. Smulewicz-Zucker (Leiden and Boston: Brill, 2020)
Fehèr, Ferenc. 'The Transformation of the Kantian Question in Lukács' Heidelberg Philosophy of Art', in *Graduate Faculty Philosophy Journal* 16 (2) (1993)
Gluck, Mary. *Georg Lukács and His Generation 1900–1918* (Cambridge and London: Harvard University Press, 1985)
Heidegger, Martin. 'On the Question of Being', in *Pathmarks*, ed. and transl. William McNeill (Cambridge: Cambridge University Press, 2010)
Hohendahl, Peter Uwe. 'The Theory of the Novel and the Concept of Realism in Lukács and Adorno', in *Georg Lukács Reconsidered: Critical Essays in Politics Philosophy and Aesthetics*, ed. Michael J. Thompson (New York: Continuum, 2011)
Jay, Martin. 'Totality and Marxist Aesthetics: The Case of Lucien Goldmann', in *Marxism and Totality: The Adventures of a Concept from Lukács to Habermas* (Cambridge: Polity Press, 1984)
Jünger, Ernst. 'Das Abenteuerliche Herz: Erste Fassung', in *Sämtliche Werke: Zweite Abteilung. Essays. Band 9. Essays III* (Stuttgart: Klett-Cotta, 1979)
Jünger, Ernst. *Der Arbeiter: Herrschaft und Gestalt* (Stuttgart: Klett-Cotta, 1982)

Strange Bedfellows 59

Jünger, Ernst. 'Der Kampf als inneres Erlebnis', in *Betrachtungen zur Zeit: Sämtliche Werke Band 9. Essays I* (Stuttgart: Klett-Cotta, 1995)

Jünger, Ernst. 'Die Schicksalszeit', in *Politische Publizistik: 1919 bis 1933*, ed. Sven Olaf Berggötz (Stuttgart: Klett-Cotta, 2001)

Jünger, Ernst. 'Kirchhorster Blätter', in *Strahlungen II: Sämtliche Werke Band 3. Tagebücher III* (Stuttgart: Klett-Cotta, 2015)

Jünger, Ernst. 'Krieg und Technik', in *Das Antlitz des Weltkrieges in Politische Publizistik: 1919 bis 1933*, ed. Sven Olaf Berggötz (Stuttgart: Klett-Cotta, 2001)

Jünger, Ernst. 'Total Mobilization' transl. Joel Golb and Richard Wolin, in *The Heidegger Controversy: A Critical Reader*, ed. Richard Wolin (Cambridge, MA and London: The MIT Press, 1992)

Kadarkay, Arpad. *Georg Lukács: Life Thought and Politics* (Cambridge: Basil Blackwell, 1991)

Kiesel, Helmut. *Ernst Jünger: Die Biographie* (Berlin: Pantheon, 2009)

Kindt, Tom and Müller, Hans-Harald. 'Zweimal Cervantes. Die Don Quijote-Lektüren von Ernst Jünger und Ernst Weiß. Ein Beitrag zur literarischen Anthropologie der zwanziger Jahre', in *Jahrbuch zur Literatur der Weimarer Republik. Band 1. 1995*, ed. Sabina Becker (St. Ingbert: Röhrig Universitätsverlag, 1995)

Livingstone, Rodney. 'Introduction', in *Georg Lukács Essays on Realism*, ed. Rodney Livingstone, transl. David Fernbach (London: Lawrence and Wishart, 1980)

Löwy, Michael. *Georg Lukács: From Romanticism to Bolshevism*, transl. Patrick Camiller (London: NLB, 1979)

Lukács, Georg. 'Aesthetic Culture' transl. Rita Keresztesi-Treat, ed. Tyrus Miller, in *The Yale Journal of Criticism* 11 (2) (1998)

Lukács, Georg. 'Bolshevism as a Moral Problem' transl. Judith Marcus Tar, in *Social Research* 44 (3) (1977)

Lukács, Georg. *The Destruction of Reason*, transl. Peter Palmer (Atlantic Highlands, NJ: Humanities Press, 1980)

Lukács, Georg. 'Die deutschen Intellektuellen und der Krieg' ed. Heinz Ludwig Arnold, in *Text + Kritik: Zeitschrift für Literatur* 39–40 (1973)

Lukács, Georg. 'Georg Simmel', in *Theory Culture & Society* 8 (3) (1991)

Lukács, Georg. *Heidelberger Philosophie der Kunst*, ed. György Márkus and Frank Benseler (Darmstadt and Neuwied: Luchterhand Verlag, 1974)

Lukács, Georg. *History and Class Consciousness: Studies in Marxist Dialectics* (Cambridge, MA: The MIT Press, 1971)

Lukács, Georg. 'Realism in the Balance', in *Ernst Bloch, Georg Lukács, Bertolt Brecht, Walter Benjamin, and Theodor Adorno, Aesthetics and Politics*, ed. and transl. Ronald Taylor (London: Verso, 1980)

Lukács, Georg. *Record of a Life: An Autobiography*, ed. István Eörsi, transl. Rodney Livingstone (London: Verso, 1985)

Lukács, Georg. *Soul and Form*, ed. John T. Sanders and Katie Terezakis (New York: Columbia University Press, 2010)

Lukács, Georg. *The Theory of the Novel*, transl. Anna Bostock (Cambridge, MA: MIT Press, 1971)

Márkus, György. 'Life and the Soul: The Young Lukács and the Problem of Culture', in *Lukács Revalued*, ed. Agnes Heller (Oxford: Basil Blackwell, 1983)

Miller, Tyrus. 'Matthew Mark Lukács and Bloch: From Aesthetic Utopianism to Religious Messianism', in *Georg Lukács and Critical Theory: Aesthetics History Utopia* (Edinburgh, UK: Edinburgh University Press, 2022)

60 *Unworldliness in Twentieth Century German Thought*

Schmidt, Rachel. *Forms of Modernity: Don Quixote and Modern Theories of the Novel* (Toronto: University of Toronto Press, 2021)

Simmel, Georg. 'The Concept and Tragedy of Culture', in *Simmel on Culture*, ed. David Frisby and Mike Featherstone (London: Sage Publications, 2000)

Simmel, Georg. *The View of Life: Four Metaphysical Essays with Journal Aphorisms*, transl. Donald N. Levine and John A. Y. Andrews (Chicago: University of Chicago Press, 2011)

Simmel, Georg. 'Vom Realismus in der Kunst', in *Gesamtausgabe 8: Aufsätze und Abhandlungen 1901–1908*, ed. Gregor Fitzi and Otthein Rammstedt (Frankfurt am Main: Suhrkamp, 2015)

Stahl, Titus. 'Social Structure and Epistemic Privilege: Reconstructing Lukács's Standpoint Theory', in *Análisis* 10 (2) (2023)

Symons, Stéphane. *More Than Life: Georg Simmel and Walter Benjamin on Art* (Evanston: Northwestern University Press, 2017)

Szabados, Bettina. 'Georg Lukács in Heidelberg: A Crossroad Between the Academic and Political Career', in *Filozofia* 75 (2020)

Watson, Alex. '"For Kaiser and Reich": The Identity and Fate of the German Volunteers 1914–1918', in *War in History* 12 (1) (2005)

Westerman, Richard. *Lukács's Phenomenology of Capitalism: Reification Revalued* (Cham: Palgrave Macmillan, 2019)

2 Ernst Bloch Meets Theodor Adorno

Don Quixote, or Hope in Dark Times

I

May 1964, a radio studio in Baden-Baden. The German novelist Horst Krüger is interviewing two elderly men about the importance of utopian thinking and imagination. Throughout their conversation, the two men refer to each other as 'old friends'.[1] Nothing indicates that Ernst Bloch and Theodor Adorno have, in fact, hardly been on speaking terms for a period of more than twenty years. Pointing out numerous times that they 'agree completely', it shall from now on be clear that this long interruption of their friendship, dating back from the dark years of World War II, has not been due to a philosophical clash. Looming behind Krüger's invitation to discuss the importance of utopia is a political system that will remain in power for another twenty-five years, with a reign of influence that stops a mere 200 miles to the North East from where the interview is presently being held. Adorno criticizes the state socialism of the German Democratic Republic for 'tend[ing] really to become a new ideology concerned with the domination of humankind'.[2] An important reason for this regression of state socialism into totalitarianism is its inability to develop a proper form of utopian thought: 'The horror that we are experiencing today in the East is partly connected to the fact that . . . the idea of utopia has actually disappeared completely from the conception of socialism'.[3] Even though he publicly denounced Soviet socialism only ten years earlier and waited until 1961 to settle in West Germany, Bloch has now converted to the same opinion. He, as well, is adamant in his critique of state socialism since it, after the example of Marx and Engels, rejects utopian imagination: 'The consequences that arise from this have been terrible, for people in a completely different situation have simply regurgitated Marx's statements in a literal sense'.[4]

In the Communist Manifesto, Marx and Engels did indeed cast aside utopianism on account of its supposed abstract and ahistorical nature, claiming that it therefore lacks 'all practical value and all theoretical

DOI: 10.4324/9781003364009-3

62   *Unworldliness in Twentieth Century German Thought*

justification'.[5] Bloch and Adorno's brand of utopianism is to be opposed firmly to such a type of abstract idealism. Bloch puts it as follows: 'I believe, Teddy, that we are certainly in agreement here: the essential function of utopia is a critique of what is present'.[6] Serving first and foremost as the contestation of a present situation, Bloch and Adorno's utopianism does not feed on ahistorical and eternal ideals but, paradoxically, on concrete shortcomings and injustice. This entails, first of all, that 'the contents of the Utopian changes according to the social situation' (Bloch) and that 'there is nothing like a single fixable Utopian content' (Adorno).[7] Bloch and Adorno argue that utopian thought receives its content from very concrete wishes and desires that, for their part, allow a firm grasp on what is most urgently lacking in a given situation. Utopian thought is for this reason always mediated by values and forces that are but characteristic to a specific society. These cannot ever be immobilized into quasi-religious 'pictures' or 'images' that are supposed to carry the eternal answers to all of our problems. '"Thou shalt not make a graven image!", states Adorno, 'was also the defense that was actually intended against the cheap utopia, the false utopia, *the* utopia that can be bought'.[8] For the same reason Bloch argues against the 'reification of ephemeral or non-ephemeral tendencies, as if it were already more than being-in-tendency, as if the day were already there'.[9] Moreover, utopian images are in their core historical features, rather than ahistorical and absolute values, because the contents they present are always and necessarily *possibilities*. Utopian thought is entwined with the physical world that surrounds us since the dreams and images that it conjures are never unrealistic figments of imagination. As situations that can at some point become actualized, they are 'objectively real' instead of merely 'subjective-reflective'.[10] Here, again, Bloch and Adorno speak with one voice. Utopia, says Bloch, 'is not something like nonsense or absolute fancy; rather it is not *yet* in the sense of a possibility'.[11] 'My thesis about this', Adorno immediately confirms, 'would be that all humans deep down, whether they admit this or not, know that it would be possible or it could be different'.[12] Bloch and Adorno put forward a conception of longing and action to mediate between the realization that a given situation is *flawed* and the belief that it can nonetheless be *improved*. For when the certainty of eternal and unchanging truths is deemed to be inaccessible to all human beings, what remains is man's desire for change and his capacity to intervene in the world: even more important than a clear grasp of *what* is needed in the world precisely is the belief '*that* it could be there if we could only do something for it'.[13] Both Bloch and Adorno, therefore, consider human longing and the will to act, and not a quasi-divine knowledge of truths and values, as the true foundation of utopianism. 'The content changes', says Bloch, 'but an invariant of the direction is there, psychologically expressed so to speak as longing, completely without consideration at all for the content – a longing that is the pervading and above all only honest quality of all human beings'.[14]

Fifty years set apart the idealism of Lukács and Jünger and that of Bloch and Adorno. In 1964, idealism comes with a face that has been radically altered by two world wars. The unshakeable trust in abstract ideals that is applauded by both Lukács and Jünger during the outbreak of World War I has now been replaced with an idealism that prides itself on its own doubts and hesitations. Neither Bloch's nor Adorno's utopianism ever boasts the certitude of firm convictions, and they do not at all consider reservations, not even despair, an obstacle for success. With Bloch and Adorno, *faith* gives way to *hope*: while the abstract idealism of Lukács and Jünger is nothing without the backing of ideals and truths, Bloch and Adorno's utopianism thrives on an awareness of both the possibilities *and* limitations of the life-world. Bloch puts it as follows: 'Hope is not confidence. If it could not be disappointed, it would not be hope. . . . Possibility is not hurray-patriotism. The opposite is also in the possible. The hindering element is also in the possible. The hindrance is implied in hope aside from the capacity to succeed'.[15] The unwavering confidence with which Lukács' and Jünger's idealists continue to cling to unrealizable goals is thus divested of its heroic grandeur. Since a sense for empirical opportunities *and* restrictions is an indispensable part of Bloch and Adorno's utopianism, idealism is no longer driven by the need to remain immune to, and *oppose*, a deeply flawed universe and the limitations of history. To the contrary, for Bloch and Adorno, hope remains dependent on a sustained interaction with an imperfect yet improvable universe. In 'Can Hope Be Disappointed?', his inaugural lecture at the University of Tübingen, in November 1961, Bloch had stated clearly that

> hope holds eo ipso the condition of defeat precariously within itself: it is not confidence. It stands too close to the indeterminacy of the historical process, of the world-process that, indeed, had not yet been defeated, but likewise has not yet won.[16]

Hope, as Adorno puts it, can only 'be said concretely'.[17]

According to Bloch and Adorno, it is only by virtue of 'objective possibilities' within our immediate surroundings that a meaningful connection to them can somehow be restored. Still, Bloch and Adorno's belief in a better world is not derived from a principle of *necessity*, let alone from a metaphysical and mystical power that would resonate *within* the empirical world, but from the awareness that this world is inherently *contingent*. In their view, the belief in a different world stems from nothing else than the realization that a current state of affairs is but one of many possible

64 Unworldliness in Twentieth Century German Thought

situations. Indeed, not even the most dire times can eradicate the potential to become different, but this is only the case because the realm of history at large defies all sense of predetermination. While, in the eyes of Lukács and Jünger, the discovery of absolute truths inoculates us to the apparent senselessness of these events, the conscious confrontation with such senselessness belongs to the core of Bloch and Adorno's thought. This explains why Bloch and Adorno substitute Lukács' and Jünger's outright *opposition* between meaning and reality with a 'determined *negation*' (Adorno).[18] The concept of negation does not stand for a heroic, Lukácian and Jüngerian rejection of the shortcomings of the surrounding world. Lukács and Jünger render the absence of meaning in the empirical world absolute but, in this manner precisely, they sublate this state of meaninglessness. By affirming the absence of meaning in the world as fated and unavoidable, it ultimately becomes the very source of existential and mystical *replenishment*. Bloch and Adorno's concept of negation, rather, yields a sustained, hopeful, and creative interaction with one's surroundings and it is for the very reason that they refuse to embrace the world's actual state as if it were the only one possible. Negating the world in its actual form entails voiding it of any sense of internal necessity or fatedness, and foreclosing the mystical heroism of Lukács and Jünger. An idealism that does not oppose but negate the world in which we live pushes the seeming meaninglessness of the world to the forefront of attention, but not without drawing from it the longing for something radically different. As Bloch puts it, 'Each and every criticism of imperfection, incompleteness, intolerance, and impatience already without a doubt presupposes the conception of, and longing for, a possible perfection'.[19] Likewise, Adorno emphasizes that 'Falsum – the false thing – index sui et veri': 'Insofar as we do not know what the correct thing would be, we know exactly, to be sure, what the false thing is'.[20]

II

Surprisingly so, the seeds of Bloch's 'concrete utopianism' can be traced back to the same time and place as Lukács' abstract idealism. After a meeting in 1910, Bloch and Lukács strike up a friendship and spend the years leading up to the Great War together in Heidelberg.[21] It is Simmel who sends Bloch to Lukács, sparking the latter's interest in what he calls 'a real philosopher in the Hegelian mold'. Bloch, similarly, confesses to the desire to 'become (Lukács') friend with all (his) might and to become so more and more deeply' and, in 1915, claims that 'there is no one with whom (he) feel(s) such an intellectual affinity . . . at a time when (he) feel(s) the past philosophers becoming as irrelevant as peas'.[22] This meeting sets off an intense philosophical conversation and a correspondence that will continue for many decades to come.[23] In the period when Lukács turns away

Ernst Bloch Meets Theodor Adorno 65

from his Kant-inspired aesthetics in favor of an irrational and radically personal morality, Bloch starts work on his own blend of religious and ethical elements. Written mostly in 1915–1916, a year later than Lukács' *Theory of the Novel*, Bloch's *The Spirit of Utopia* lays down the groundwork of his philosophical oeuvre. It is striking to see that, at this stage of their career, Bloch and Lukács do share quite a few fundamental insights. At some point Bloch even goes as far as claiming that 'this strange affinity took such a strong shape that there are parts in my book *Geist der Utopie*, which was written at that time, that are actually from Lukács and things in *The Theory of the Novel* that are from me. I don't know anymore who thought what. It didn't matter! It didn't matter at all!'[24] Under Bloch's influence, Lukács, for his part, develops an affinity with a type of messianic religiosity that his friends do not always find beneficial. The Hungarian philosopher Béla Balázs, for instance, described Bloch as an 'intellectual Condottiero who is only likeable because he is also a Don Quixote – and a child. He has a strongly hypnotic effect on Gyuri (Lukács), which makes me uneasy. He is bad for Gyuri – he is not to be relied upon. . . . The role of a prophet, a visionary, does not suit Gyuri's basically thorough and sober way of thinking, because he does not believe in it enough, because he hesitates a little and is anxious, as if he were in a strange house'.[25] The most remarkable parallel between Bloch's *The Spirit of Utopia* and Lukács' *Theory of the Novel* does indeed revolve around a singular blend of nihilism and utopianism. Bloch will later describe his study of utopianism as 'revolutionary gnosis', a formula that could just as well be used to describe Lukács' work of the same era. His *The Spirit of Utopia* is founded on the sentiment that the human species is forever bound to a given lack or absence. Bloch, like Lukács, sees a steep gap between the lives we lead and a 'genuine encounter' with the ethical and religious truths that are to support these lives. 'We live ourselves but do not "experience" ourselves'. 'We have no organ for the I or the We; rather we are located in our own blind spot, in the darkness of the lived moment, whose darkness is ultimately our own darkness, being-unfamiliar-to-ourselves, being-enfolded, being-missing'.[26] Like Lukács, Bloch takes recourse to a mystical jargon in order to clarify why human beings are at loss in the world, remaining incapable of truly grasping the norms and values that should serve as the moral and spiritual backbone of their existence. It is for this reason that Marianne Weber refers to both philosophers as 'messianic young men', while the philosopher Emil Lask jokes that the four evangelists ought to have been named 'Matthew, Mark, Lukács and Bloch'.[27] Moreover, alongside this mystical analysis of the failed encounter of man with himself, Bloch sets up a communist-inspired critique of capitalism that in some ways anticipates the post-war, Marxist phase of his friend Lukács. '[M]ost people around us, particularly since they have been entangled in a money economy, are so

66 *Unworldliness in Twentieth Century German Thought*

lethargically filthy that none of them, once they are scalded and marked, comes near any more difficult inner stirrings'.[28] The spiritual void that marks human existence is, according to both authors, exacerbated by processes of commodification that void the quest for shared standards.

Lukács and Bloch might, for these reasons, share certain assumptions when analyzing the problem of modern nihilism, but the solutions they offer run in opposite directions. At this early stage of his intellectual trajectory already, Bloch refuses to follow Lukács' turn to a realm that is seemingly *untouched* by the spiritual emptiness of day-to-day existence. The crux of their disagreement becomes visible in conflicting ideas about art and aesthetics. For the young Lukács, the work of art embodies an autonomous totality and internal unity that set itself proudly apart from the fragmented, empirical world. Even in the era of the novel, which no longer has recourse to the truths and meanings that resonate within the world at large, the artist is deemed capable of ultimately withstanding this 'transcendental homelessness'. For in the face of such spiritual challenges, the novel can, according to Lukács, still bring about the much-needed purity of thought and feeling.

> The novel is the epic of an age in which the extensive totality of life is no longer directly given, in which the immanence of meaning in life has become a problem, yet which still thinks in terms of totality.[29]

This autonomy of the artwork does entail that art can lay no claim to a *direct* impact on society, leaving its institutions unchanged and obfuscating a lived connection with the *future*. 'Art can never be the agent of such a transformation: . . . any attempt to depict the utopian as existent can only end in destroying the form, not in creating reality'.[30] Still, this absence of empirical or societal impact does not mitigate the meaning-giving powers of the artwork: to the contrary, it is this aesthetic autonomy itself which brings to the fore that no future validation is needed for the artwork to have a redemptive power within the *present*. With this complex argument, we have surely reached the pinnacle of the mystic intuitions that underlie the work of the early Lukács: by retreating from any direct interaction with the world, the artist makes palpable that modern society is forlorn while, *at the same time*, managing to reopen the space of a pure, non-empirical totality of meaning (i.e., that of the artwork itself). The deep suffering and 'absolute sinfulness' that is testified to by the novel thus become a token for the final possibility of a genuine and purely contemplative spirituality within the present world. According to the young Lukács, the artwork is therefore nothing less than the site of a *utopian presence*, however paradoxical such a combination of terms may seem.[31] The novelist is, above all, a form-giver who neutralizes the chaos of the surrounding world through

Ernst Bloch Meets Theodor Adorno   67

the productive dynamic of artistic creation and aesthetic form. Thus, meaning is restored at the precise moment when it seemed most out of reach.

> The immanence of meaning which the form of the novel requires lies in the hero's finding out through experience that a mere glimpse of meaning is the highest that life has to offer, and that this glimpse is the only thing worth the commitment of an entire life, the only thing by which the struggle will have been justified.[32]

In last instance, the artwork is marked by a unique plenitude and expressive strength that remains uncontaminated by the vicissitudes of modern life.

In Bloch's view, to the contrary, no artwork can fully raise itself above the fragmented universe from which it stems. The spiritual plenitude that Lukács endows on the artwork and the form-giving powers that he bestows on the artist are to him symptomatic to overly naïve beliefs regarding man's redemptive capacities. According to Bloch, all artworks are part and parcel to a flawed, empirical world and bear the traces of the finite creature that created them. In *The Spirit of Utopia* he attacks Lukács for thinking that

> the frenzy of external life has no power, that in other words the inhuman, or at least the slimy, gelatinous, unpredictable, arbitrarily stalling, falsely complex, moody, maliciously fortuitous and intermittent element within the external causal nexus could simply be overlooked as something simply and indiscriminately alogical.[33]

While Bloch agrees with Lukács about the 'nothingness of this godless world', he simultaneously suggests that this 'could very well become the actually coactive background' of our thoughts and actions.[34] The category of 'form' is therefore, along with Lukács' emphasis on the *supra*-subjective qualities of the artwork, to a large extent replaced by descriptions of artworks that stem from a subjective, lived interaction with the world.[35] In the 1930, this will lead to the aforesaid heated debate about expressionist art. In the view of the Marxist Lukács, expressionist art is overly formless, subjective, 'decadent', and incapable of attaining the 'objective' status of genuine art. Bloch to the contrary understands expressionist art as proof for the 'dialectical link between growth and decay' and takes seriously its critical powers. 'Perhaps Lukács' Reality, that of the endlessly mediated totality coherence, is not so – objective at all', Bloch asks himself, 'perhaps genuine reality is also – interruption. Because Lukács has an objectivistically closed concept of Reality, he therefore opposes, apropos of Expressionism, every artistic attempt to chop to pieces a world-picture (even if the world-picture is that of capitalism). He therefore sees in art which utilizes

68 Unworldliness in Twentieth Century German Thought

real underminings of the surface-coherence and attempts to discover something new in the hollow spaces, only subjectivistic undermining itself; he therefore equates the experiment of chopping to pieces with the condition of decline'.[36] Because Bloch rejects the young Lukács' sharp division between the purity of aesthetic forms and the formless contingencies of the empirical world, he also divests art of its status as a utopian *presence*. For him, the utopian dimension of art is inherently dependent to its being perceived as an *image* or *trace*, that is, as a *non*-totality. The artwork is at most the pre-figuration (*Vorschein*) of a desired situation: it refers forward to a future possibility but does not recover an unspoiled, past ideal. Having done away with the intuitive clarity and certainty of a beyond, Bloch puts all his money on the impenetrabilities and uncertainties of what is present at hand. 'Hope', writes Bloch, 'is in the darkness itself, partakes of its imperceptibility, just as darkness and mystery are always related; it threatens to disappear if it looms up too nearly, too abruptly in this darkness'.[37] '[T]he darkness of the lived moment, so near to us, therefore still contains the enigma of the beginning, the enigma of the existence of the world at maximum strength'.[38] For Bloch, indeed, despair and hope are but two sides of one and the same coin. This discovery of a hopeful element within man's spiritual poverty itself sets Bloch's 'revolutionary gnosis' apart from that of the young Lukács since it rejects the very opposition between a realm of abstract ideals and a 'godforsaken' universe. According to Bloch, the human failure to grasp his own spiritual self leads to anguish, but it simultaneously opens up a dynamic of 'not-yet-conscious' longing and striving. It is, in other words, precisely the failed encounter with his own essence, which gives impetus to man's sustained longing for a spiritual 'home'.

> [T]his is of decisive importance: the *future*, the *topos of the unknown within the future*, where alone we occur, where alone, novel and profound, the function of hope also flashes, without the bleak reprise of some anamnesis – is itself nothing but *our expanded darkness, than our darkness in the issue of its own womb, in the expansion of its latency*.[39]

Bloch is clearly waxing poetic when he describes the inseparability of hope and despair, but it does in his view amount to a rediscovery of one's immediate and concrete surroundings. In *The Spirit of Utopia*, he focuses on the 'amazement' that occurs when human beings discover that ordinary phenomena are animated with 'symbolic intentions' that cannot ever be made fully conscious. These intentions render a mysterious overtone onto the most common objects and retrieve an intimate sense of meaning. For this reason the opening pages of the first chapter of the book titled *Self-Encounter* are devoted to the description of an old pitcher that, in its seeming simplicity, 'speak[s] to us': '[M]ade . . . out of love and necessity, [it] leads a life of its own, leads into a strange new territory, and returns with us formed as we could not be in life, adorned with a certain, however weak sign, the seal of our self'.[40] Here as well, can be found a reason for Bloch's endorsement of expressionist art, because it projects an unexpected 'mystical gravity and a yet unknown, nameless mythology' onto an only apparently uninhabitable and deserted environment. 'For things have been different ever since Van Gogh: we are also present in the painting, and precisely this presence is what is being painted; true, there is still visible turmoil, sill railings, subways, girders, brick walls, but it suddenly, peculiarly undercuts itself, the rejected cornerstone strikes sparks all at once'.[41] When a blissful, mysterious and symbol-laden veil is cast over the most ordinary things, their very fragility and precariousness is brought to light. Objects are 'reborn to a different materiality than a mere thing's, reborn to its essence as the inmost principle of its potentiality, of all our potentiality'.[42] The most well-known thing can thus resonate with unentangled ambivalences and unexpected ambiguities:

> It is questioning in itself, an inmost, deepest amazement, which often moves toward nothing, and yet quiets the flux of what was just lived; lets one reflect oneself such that what is most deeply meant for us appears there, regards itself strangely.[43]

In Bloch's account, the sad emptiness of an overly conscious and rational outlook on the world is thus accompanied with a wealth of more profound experiences that give fuel to man's longing for spiritual unity. While such a process of reconciliation has not ever been realized within the realm of the empirical, it has, for this reason precisely, taken on the irreducibility of what is still 'possible' or, in Bloch's terms, has 'not yet become'. Because the process of spiritual completion has clearly not yet fully run its course, it can only be recovered in unfinished glimpses, fragile traces, and incomplete fragments. In other words, what carries hope can never fully crystallize into the stable unity of a *world*. Bloch is convinced that he has discovered a dimension of hope within history that, however precarious it may be, manages to outlast all of man's disappointments. Remaining beyond the grasp of consciousness, this dimension will at all times be the object of a 'dream' that, unlike the intoxicating and deeply irrational dream that is applauded by Jünger, wakes us up to the undepleted potential of our surroundings: such a 'waking dream' . . . 'brings about something real'.[44]

Bloch's philosophy of hope is rooted in both a metaphysical claim and a moral-political imperative: the presence of hope is ingrained within the contingent nature of history but, since it is confined to the 'not-yet-conscious' strata of our minds, one is bound by the duty to pay heed to the memories,

70   Unworldliness in Twentieth Century German Thought

dreams, and symbols that keep it afloat. 'Certainly the question how one imagines bliss is so far from forbidden that it is basically the only one permitted'.[45] This mixture of metaphysical and moral-political claims, as laid out in the early years of World War I, will remain the crux of Bloch's overall philosophy. In the 1930s it will result in two collections of literary essays and observations, *Traces* (1930) and *Heritage of Our Times* (1935). Both books revolve around a continuation of the quest for the mysterious presence of fragmented ideals within seemingly banal objects and events. In these literary collections, as well, the belief in change is fed by the undecidability of the realm of history at large. In *Heritage of Our Times*, Bloch introduces a new term to describe the inherent openness of all temporal phenomena: 'non-simultaneity'. Because the domain of history is disconnected from unshakable truths and ultimate determinations, it will be forever marked by seeming contradictions. 'Not all people exist in the same Now. They do so only externally, through the fact that they can be seen today. But they are thereby not yet living at the same time with the others'.[46] In Bloch's view, a large part of German society in the 1930s had failed to adapt to the urge for modernization and industrialization that capitalism brought with it. The peasantry, for instance, 'is harder to displace if only because [it] still has the means of production in his hands, and also uses agricultural machines merely as aids in the ancient framework of the farmyard and accompanying fields; no factory owner here introduces against economically weak craftsmen the mechanical loom and corresponding things which only the capitalist could possess'.[47] Bloch describes how social structures, cultural frameworks, and psychological mindsets from the past continue to live on in a society that is obsessed with innovation and standardization. In *Heritage of Our Times*, Bloch connects the rise of fascism to its uncanny ability to exploit this anachronistic presence of traditional beliefs and practices. Fascism uses the resentment of those who are threatened by an industrialized society as the engine for a backward-looking mythology of the chosen people and reactionary politics. This explains the large popularity of fascism among members of the peasantry, and even within the middle class. Like the peasantry, the middle class does 'not take part in (capitalist) production directly at all, but enter[s] into it only with intermediate activities, with such a distance from social causality that an illogical space can develop, in an increasingly undisturbed way, in which wishes and romanticisms, primeval drives and mythicisms revive'.[48] The middle class consists primarily of white-collar workers or, in the terms of Bloch's friend Siegfried Kracauer, 'salaried employees' (*Angestellten*) who remain unaware of their social position: while they still cling to imaginary ideals like individual agency and aspire the consumer habits of a bourgeois lifestyle, their professional lives are dehumanized by excessive bureaucratization and rationalization.[49] Because neither the

Ernst Bloch Meets Theodor Adorno   71

peasantry nor the middle class can cast off their archaic self-image, they are vulnerable to the self-aggrandizing rhetoric of fascism and fail to grasp the genuine political, economic, and social challenges of a capitalist society. Once again, however, Bloch retrieves a space for hope within the very same dimension that had apparently been hollowed out by despair. For the elements that breed fascism can equally well give birth to its most radical antidote: revolutionary politics. Bloch takes the progressive politicians of his time to task for dismissing the anachronistic tendencies within German society as *merely* reactionary. Marxism has 'undernourished the imagination of the masses' and 'almost surrendered the world of imagination'. 'Nazi's speak deceitfully, but to people, the Communists quite truly, but only of things'.[50] Rather than adopting capitalism's future-oriented ideology for its own purposes, left-wing politics should turn to the maladapted urges, wishes, and dreams of the peasantry and the middle class. It is from these wish-images that the age-old quest for a just and equal society receives its impetus, precisely because they are so out of tune in a capitalist society, so *un-worldly*.

III

The rise of fascism that is central to *Heritage of Our Times* is not just an intellectual concern for Bloch. When his works are banned from publication and circulation, he soon finds himself forced to emigrate together with his wife and son. After fleeing to Zurich, Vienna, and Paris, he boards a ship to New York in 1938, where he will stay until 1949. It is there that he will continue his philosophical exploration of the perennial force of hope and connect it to an in-depth analysis of Cervantes' novel. In his magnum opus, *The Principle of Hope* (1938–1947), he picks up the intellectual project that was started with *Spirit of Utopia*. In three thick volumes Bloch gives us an encyclopedia of the various historical forces and literary examples that should confirm the argument that hope remains ingrained within the very course of history, even in those times when it seems most out of reach. Bloch's reading of Cervantes is much more layered than that of Lukács and Jünger. To begin with, Bloch refuses to endow Don Quixote with the heroic traits that are so important to the earlier interpretations. Cervantes' story, that is, comes together with a clear 'warning' to the reader.[51] Bloch follows Lukács and Jünger's lead in maintaining that Don Quixote 'is not troubled by the slightest doubt about his vocation'.[52] He, as well, associates Don Quixote with 'abstract idealism' and an unwavering faith in absolute norms and values. But Bloch clearly holds back in wholeheartedly embracing such a stance. Since Bloch's own concept of utopianism revolves around its critical function and the need to mediate wishes and dreams through *concrete* experiences, longing, and action, it runs counter to Don

72   Unworldliness in Twentieth Century German Thought

Quixote's 'unconditioned dreaming' and his 'unworldly', 'undistracted', and 'unmediated' attitude. 'Mediated-balanced action is capable of also being *objective-moral* and thus truly venturing beyond the limits, not into what is empty or expired. It is less heroic in its stance but more manly in its thrust; it has less blossom, but more fruit'.[53] Bloch is adamant in criticizing Don Quixote's 'travesty of a utopian' and denounces the 'craziest and most battered abstractions the world has ever known' because they remain blind to both society's injustices and opportunities. Such abstract ideals can no longer serve to unmask the shortcomings of a concrete world, nor open a path forward. 'Quixotry is a bearing which learns nothing and acknowledges nothing changed, which is never mediated, which fails to see that medieval times have shifted, even in Spain and especially in its healthy people who are so fond of laughter and alive to irony, and therefore because of its abstract idealism it is the caricature of a phantasma bene fundatum and of its constitutive content'.[54] In Bloch's view, Don Quixote refuses to heed the distance between an ideal and the 'concrete possibility' of its realization because, for his troubled mind, the ideal *is* already a reality. Taking the content of the chivalric romances he is infatuated with as empirical realities, Don Quixote does not so much *strive* toward the actualization of his dreams and wishes as that he 'hallucinate[s] the intended as already fulfilled'.[55] Bloch gives the example of Don Quixote's love for the splendid and inaccessible Dulcinea. He argues that it would be wrong to think that Don Quixote has entangled himself in a ceaseless quest for a non-existent ideal since this ideal is never believed to be outside of reach in the first place:

> Dulcinea, la femme introuvable, does not need to be sought, let alone wooed, she does not even need to be discovered; only the obstacle must be removed that has come between the loveliest Here and Now and its knight. The perfectly achieved is available.[56]

Because the ideal is met as a concrete reality, the relation between Don Quixote and the factual world is marked by antagonism. Acting out hallucinations that are in no way related to possibilities in the world, Don Quixote meets with nothing but suffering and disappointment. But Bloch follows Lukács and Jünger's suggestion that Don Quixote's abstract idealism is at once the cause of pain *and* its most powerful anesthetic. According to Bloch, as well, the unshakeable trust in abstract ideals does indeed immunize Don Quixote to the very suffering that it produces. In his reading, Don Quixote is a 'ghost' or 'specter' who is never really affected by the failed interaction with his surroundings.

> Confronted with the onset of this utopia, the real, in so far as it was commonplace or even banal, could not survive, could not even be

Ernst Bloch Meets Theodor Adorno   73

perceived: sheep become soldiers, clouds castles, windmill-sails giants, half a barber's basin glinting in the sun becomes Mambrino's helmet.[57]

This is most palpable, argues Bloch, each time Don Quixote invokes the sudden intervention by a wicked sorcerer and thus explains away the conflict between his dream-world and the possibilities of the actual world. Don Quixote's (non-)relation to the world is therefore characterized by a strange paradox: the violent encounter with an indifferent and unresponsive world does not result in doubt, let alone that it would cure him from his belief in unrealistic ideals, since it can at times even reinvigorate these ideals. Bloch mentions the example of the scene when Don Quixote, resting in the attic of an inn, is visited by a cow-girl who had expected to find her secret lover, a mule driver. Upon finding out that Don Quixote has become smitten with his mistress because he mistakes her for a princess, the mule driver delivers him such a forceful blow to the mouth that it fills with blood. Instead of bringing Don Quixote to his senses, this confrontation increases the depths of his insanity since, for him, it only confirms that the mule driver is in fact an enchanted 'Moor' under whose protection the princess stands. 'The damaged delusion is not replaced for example by empirical reality, on the contrary it is repaired by a new, far greater delusion'.[58] For this reason, Bloch argues that Don Quixote not only mistakes figments of the imagination for empirical realities but, vice versa, also mistakes these empirical realities for merely imaginary and irreal entities.

While this ability to inoculate himself to the empirical world is to Lukács and Jünger a distinctly positive and heroic feat, Bloch is much more skeptical about it. His main argument rests on the observation that the abstract norms and values of Don Quixote have so far risen above the world that they can no longer be *judged*. While Bloch's own 'concrete utopianism' is dependent on 'objective possibilities' that enable the evaluation of our beliefs, norms, and values, Don Quixote's idealism prides itself of its unworldly position. This self-proclaimed purity renders these norms and values *un-negatable*: such ideals have done away with the possibility to be critically assessed and can only result in blind obedience and passive following: 'abstract utopia, world-blind hope, has no limit, nor does it have any means of correcting its fantastic notions'.[59] In Bloch's view, the problem with Don Quixote's imaginary universe is not that it is wholly illusionary but that he leaves us no way to argue for why, and when, some of its beliefs might in fact be the ones we need. This renders his abstract idealism vulnerable to all kinds of intellectual and political abuse. Bloch interprets Don Quixote's beliefs as the root of a dangerous 'political romanticism' that clings to all the right values, such as 'loyalty, honour, leader, allegiance', but exploits them for 'reactionary-terrible' purposes. In Bloch's view, it seems, Don Quixote is the very antithesis of the revolutionary radical

74 Unworldliness in Twentieth Century German Thought

that Lukács and Jünger make him out to be: the moral framework that is embraced by Don Quixote is incapable of unmasking, let alone overturning the status quo because it fails to ever question *itself*. Bloch therefore follows Marx' assessment that Don Quixote belongs to the category of the 'honest-abstract social idealists' whose dream-universe of an equal and just society might seem praiseworthy but nonetheless remains powerless in the face of the crises of capitalism. 'What Don Quixote intended with the background of his dreams: the realm of justice, has never been furthered but often discredited by abstract heart-thumping for the good of humanity; for ignorant magnanimity is no stalwart fighter in this realm'.[60] Don Quixote's refusal to use money, for this reason, is no counter-capitalistic stance but the mark of dogmatism, bad faith, and false consciousness.

Three quarters into his interpretation of Don Quixote, Bloch's text suddenly takes a turn that only makes sense if you consider the background of his philosophy of hope at large. Without preparing for it, Bloch introduces an 'other' Don Quixote who deserves to be seen in a 'very serious light' and presents us with a 'hearty reminder, something not to be forgotten' and even an 'obligation'.[61] While this 'other' Don Quixote has not sobered up completely, he is nonetheless deemed capable of gauging the distance between his dream-world and the empirical world. The second Don Quixote is reconstructed from the scene of his passing, when he brushes aside Sancho Panza's call to return to the earlier adventures and utters a warning against such excessive idealism: 'Steady on, gentlemen, it's no good looking for birds in last year's nests'.[62] This brings Bloch to the suggestion that, behind all of Don Quixote's mad adventures, there were, after all, 'patches of light' and 'sober judgements, almost as if the delusion was only feigned'.[63] Bloch refers to the interpretations of Dostoyevsky, Suarez, and Kant to highlight that Don Quixote's 'defenselessness' in the face of the world's violence should be met with melancholy and empathy rather than with laughter or cold indifference.[64] Endowing Don Quixote with Christ-like features, Bloch maintains that his apparent aloofness harbors in fact a moral condemnation of the world's injustices and wrongdoings. 'There is an ecce homo in the knight's derided purity, a kind of reflection of Christ even in this debased caricature'.[65] In these final pages on Don Quixote, Bloch casts a redemptive light on the knight's dream-universe. His norms and values are now no longer reduced to symptoms of an overly abstract idealism but endorsed as the seeds of a politically driven and much-needed 'dream of a *Golden Age*'.[66] In line with his early suggestion, laid out in *Spirit of Utopia*, that 'symbolic intentions' and a specific type of 'amazement' can cast a blissful and magical, but simultaneously critical and accusing, veil over the most dire circumstances, Don Quixote is assumed to restore hope by re-enchanting the world. His fantasy-world no longer stands for dogmatism, false consciousness, and bad faith but

Ernst Bloch Meets Theodor Adorno 75

for a much-needed unmasking of the world's problems. Bloch refers to the performance in which the devil, Merlin, and a maiden, pretending to be Dulcinea, trick Don Quixote and Sancho Panza into thinking that the spell on Dulcinea can be lifted if Sancho Panza whips himself 3,300 times.[67] The overblown and grandiose nature of this performance is meant to mock Don Quixote's and Sancho Panza's naivete. Be that as it may, Bloch highlights that its ultimate meaning resides in a denunciation of the cynicism and fraudulence of the duke and duchess because it strengthens Don Quixote's confirmation that the world is not devoid of hope and wonder. 'In fact the theatrical performance at the court is utterly cynical, a bathing in froth and fraud; Don Quixote, on the other hand, who does not need this kind of theatre at all, sees even here nothing but the embodiment of the wishful dreams in which he believes'.[68] According to Bloch, therefore, it would be wrong to think that Don Quixote's set of moral values needs only to be saved *from* his abstract idealism since it is just as likely that there is a very concrete and saving power at work *within* this abstraction itself: like the 'mystical gravity and nameless mythology' that is endorsed in the *Spirit of Utopia* as a means to revitalize the perennial force of hope in dire times, Don Quixote's 'hallucinatory thinking' deserves at times to be considered a 'faithful ideality' instead of being reduced to a 'terrifying unreality'.[69]

Crucial to this ultimate endorsement of Don Quixote is that his chivalric values are not just derived from novels and fiction but from a *historical* era, the Middle Ages. According to Bloch, seemingly abstract values are thus rendered the immanent and 'concrete' quality of an 'objective possibility'. This puts them at odds with the types of utopianism that Bloch takes issues with. In Bloch's view, Cervantes presents the supposedly dark and irrational era of the Middle Ages as an antidote to the emergent, bourgeois society in which the novel is set. 'Don Quixote did not extract from the feudal age the holy tithe and its ideology as political romanticism did, he saw the knight-errantry of yore as nonetheless a nobler guiding image than the budding bourgeoisie'.[70] With this assessment, the final part of Bloch's interpretation of Don Quixote has moved far away from his earlier critique that Don Quixote is an anti-revolutionary who has paved the way for a reactionary exploitation of values such as loyalty, leadership, and allegiance. Bloch now distinguishes alienating and escapist quixotry from a 'correctly understood quixotry' that inserts the indispensable 'dash of unconditionalness in the shrewdness of the conditional' and thus enables us 'to avoid being defaitist'. Instead of denouncing him as a 'doer without deeds', Don Quixote has now become a 'martyr' who is 'never utterly refuted'.[71] Bloch pits Don Quixote's purity of heart against the spiritual emptiness of the ducal couple and considers him the proof that no present situation can ever eradicate the possibility of genuine change. In marked

76   *Unworldliness in Twentieth Century German Thought*

contrast with Lukács and Jünger, who endow Don Quixote with the ability to embrace the most unexpected and uncalled for events as fated and governed by an internal necessity, Bloch reads Don Quixote as the embodiment of the realization that one should never 'mak[e] peace with the merely existing world which parades as complete'.[72] In other words, in this positive reading of Don Quixote, he no longer embraces the non-negatability of abstract ideals, but the negatability of the world at large: the dimension of hope that is retrieved in Don Quixote's concrete idealism rests not on an unshakeable trust in infallible virtues, but on the awareness that one should 'never take things as they are'. 'In the transportable dream-cell he lives in, Don Quixote sees no really existing world, yet he is also far from a belief in fate, a belief in a naturally given or divinely imposed necessity. Quixotry, when combined with worldly-wisdom, certainly can make the lion of fate blink very hard indeed'.[73]

IV

Fast rewind to the dark years of World War I. A few years after its publication, seventeen-year-old Theodor Adorno reads Bloch's *The Spirit of Utopia* and is smitten with its revolutionary agenda. Adorno endows the book with epic qualities that will have a lasting effect on his own intellectual trajectory: 'Dark as a gateway, with a muffled blare like a trumpet blast, it aroused the expectation of something vast, an expectation that quickly rendered the philosophy with which I had become acquainted as a student suspect as shallow and unworthy of its own concept'.[74] When he finally meets Bloch in Berlin in 1928, it is the start of a complicated relationship. On the one hand, Adorno will leave no ambiguity in confessing to Bloch's profound philosophical influence, going as far as to claim that he does 'not believe [to] have ever written anything without reference to [Bloch's motif of anti-renunciation], either implicit or explicit'.[75] On the other hand, both in writing and behind Bloch's back, Adorno will continue to mock Bloch's mystical tendencies, describing him as a 'Buber without a beard'.[76] In 1958, he refuses to endorse the republication of *The Principle of Hope*, deeming it 'simply poor in spiritual content'.[77] But the relationship between Adorno and Bloch will clearly suffer from both political and personal tensions as well, which come to a climax when both authors are stranded in New York in the early days of World War II. On account of his continuing endorsement of Stalinist politics, Bloch's plea for support is rejected by the relocated Institute of Social Research. When Adorno starts a public campaign in support of his colleague, Bloch takes issue with Adorno's paternalism, and the initiative explodes in his face. 'I am old enough for experience to have taught me that nothing damages a person's loyalty more than the help one grants them', Adorno will write to his parents in

Ernst Bloch Meets Theodor Adorno 77

explanation of 'the Bloch affair'.[78] The relation between Adorno and Bloch will indeed remain stone-cold until the late 1950s.

In an essay written on the occasion of Bloch's eightieth birthday in 1965, Adorno singles out the aforementioned 'rebellion against renunciation' as the most important feature of his 'old friend's' philosophy. It is Bloch who, in the earliest days of his intellectual trajectory, teaches Adorno that the first task of philosophical thought consists of unmasking that a given situation is always but one of a series of possible states of affairs. *Spirit of Utopia*, writes Adorno, 'protests the nonsensical state of affairs, frozenly taken for granted'.[79] In a review of the revised edition of Bloch's collection *Traces*, Adorno gives us the material to flesh out this fundamental resonance between their thinking. Bloch and Adorno's philosophies come together in, as Adorno puts it, 'the feeling that what exists here and now cannot be all there is'.[80] Adorno's embrace of Bloch's philosophy revolves around a concept that plays a pivotal role in his own thinking as well: non-identity. Adorno distinguishes 'two aspects of . . . non-identity' in Bloch's thought, a 'materialist' one and a 'mystical' one, therewith pointing to the idea that the genuine core of an individual can never be identified with their current position in a capitalist society nor their lived, psychological sense of self.[81] In both Bloch and Adorno's thought, this awareness of a fundamental self-estrangement keeps alive the promise of a more genuine self and, in extension, a more truthful reality that are *yet to come*.[82] Adorno applauds Bloch's search for the 'truly different' that can never be 'captured by that philistine concept of pure identity with the self'.[83] Adorno thus joins forces with Bloch in denouncing the quest for an unspoiled present totality, casting aside both the possibility and desirability of a set of absolute truths that can be wholeheartedly embraced by heroic individuals in the face of a godforsaken world. In his *Negative Dialectics*, published one year before the radio-interview in Baden-Baden, he will define utopia as the 'consciousness of possibility' and, like Bloch, makes it inseparable from the concreteness of *history*: utopia 'sticks to the concrete, the undisfigured. Utopia is blocked off by possibility, never by immediate reality'.[84] For this reason, the non-identical cannot even be fully grasped in conceptual thought. It is bound to escape the (universal) concepts that are mobilized to think it but, by that very token, the non-identical marks the moral obligation to bring it to expression.[85] On account of this inseparability with the particular, or, in Adorno's words, their being *mediated*, the dreams and wishes that feed utopian thought cannot be deemed ahistorical. To the contrary, utopian desires thrive on the contingencies of history and are motivated by the cracks and fissures within it. It is only because history cannot ever be reduced to what it currently is or deemed to be (i.e., because it testifies to the 'non-identical') that it has a chance of changing and being changed.

78 Unworldliness in Twentieth Century German Thought

It is therefore no surprise that Adorno, like Bloch, explicitly rejects the overblown jargon of Lukács and Jünger. In *Negative Dialectics* he takes the young Lukács to task for clinging to a 'romantic tradition that survived all romanticism'. Lukács is believed to hold on to the possibility that the gap between the empirical world on the one hand and its underlying meaning on the other can be mitigated by way of collectively held truths and values. In Adorno's view,

[T]he truth of (such) metaphysical views is not assured by their collective obligatoriness, by the power they exert over life in closed cultures. Rather, the possibility of metaphysical experience is akin to the possibility of freedom, and it takes an unfolded subject, one that has torn the bonds advertised as salutary, to be capable of freedom.[86]

A few years earlier, in a critical review of Lukács' late book *Realism in Our Time* (1958), Adorno had deepened this criticism of Lukács' romanticism and the inability to think through genuine freedom. Adorno there distinguishes between a young and a later Lukács, identifying a *Kehre* of some sort ('It was probably in his *The Destruction of Reason* that the destruction of Lukács' own reason manifested itself most crassly'[87]), but it is clear that the entire oeuvre of the Hungarian philosopher is being rejected on account of having missed the essentially *negative, critical, utopian*, or, in short, non-identical moment in dialectical thinking. The crux of the disagreement between both thinkers revolves around Adorno's dismissal of a key presupposition in Lukács' philosophy: '[T]he postulate of a reality that must be represented without a breach between subject and object and which must be "reflected" . . . for the sake of that lack of breach'.[88] In Adorno's view, this assumption is symptomatic of a naïve notion of 'reconciliation' that Lukács inherits from the overly *positive* dialectical method of Hegelian idealism. According to Adorno, this naivete inevitably results in Lukács' reactionary acceptance of the status quo as something inalienable. For the postulate that thought can penetrate to the core of reality and uncover its hidden truths and meanings 'implies that that reconciliation has been achieved, that society has been set right, that the subject has come into its own and is at home in its world. . . . But the division, the antagonism, continues'.[89] Adorno's famous reply to Lukács' quest for recovered totalities and absolute truths is a quip: 'The whole is the false'.[90] Lukács' notion of totality and his paradoxical defense of a spiritual restitution-through-opposition are famously cast aside as dangerous illusions. Philosophy, that is, ought not to seek to make an undeniable truth *present* since it originates from the sustained awareness of a fundamental 'breach'. As is stated in the first sentence of *Negative Dialectics*, 'Philosophy . . . lives on because the moment to realize it was missed'.[91] Infallible, internally coherent truths deserve a position in philosophical thought only to the extent that they are highlighted as still *missing*.

Adorno's rejection of Jünger's philosophy is less developed but no less fundamental. It runs along the same lines as the dismissal of Lukács' romanticism-after-romanticism. Jünger is denounced in a letter to Thomas Mann from 1949: he is 'a wretchedly meretricious writer who has mutated from his appalling quondam steeliness into an, if possible, even more appalling second-hand George complete with gleaming fronds, iridescent scales, and a mass of false concretion, and upon whom those representatives of "youth" who are pleased to describe themselves as such would now appear to dote'.[92] Indeed, from Adorno's perspective, Jünger paints the soldier's existence as a prerequisite for true selfhood, supposedly unearthed in the chaos and camaraderie of battle. This warped sense of authenticity is deeply regressive, celebrating the very oppression and brutality that enlightened thought strives to eradicate. Jünger's almost mythical reverence for war is not a pathway to real identity but a plunge into barbaric delusion.

When Adorno accepts a position at the University of Frankfurt in May 1931, his inaugural address, 'The Actuality of Philosophy', already zooms in on this same argument. In his opening statement, Adorno rejects the idea that 'the power of thought is sufficient to grasp the totality of the real'. 'The fullness of the real, as totality, does not let itself be subsumed under the idea of being which might allocate meaning to it'.[93] Adorno takes the most important schools of thought of that time, the Marburg school, *Lebensphilosophie*, and phenomenology, to task for failing to address the concrete and material nature of reality. While these thinkers had, in the wake of Kant, reduced the world to a correlate of the allegedly universal concepts of subjective cognition, Adorno seeks to liberate reality from the clutches of meaning: 'Philosophy . . . which no longer believes reality to be grounded in the *ratio*, but instead assumes always and forever that the law-giving of autonomous reason pierces through a being which is not adequate to it and cannot be laid out rationally as a totality – such a philosophy will not go the entire path to the rational presuppositions, but instead will stop there where irreducible reality breaks in upon it'.[94] Adorno and Bloch concur in thinking that this breaking-in of 'irreducible reality' shatters the internal unity of a phenomenological world as supposedly posited by a conscious and stable self. '[T]he mind is indeed not capable of producing or grasping the totality of the real, but it may be possible to penetrate the detail, to explode in miniature the mass of merely existing reality'.[95] In Bloch, Adorno discovers the same 'affinity with the concrete, beginning with material strata devoid of meaning'.[96] Both thinkers, in short, argue that the concreteness of the object destabilizes human consciousness, rendering the latter incapable of positing a unified world. And both thinkers consider the particular to, for this reason precisely, open up a space for the radically new.

80 *Unworldliness in Twentieth Century German Thought*

In Bloch's work, Adorno encounters the same 'primacy of the object' that will underlie his own metaphysical framework until the latest stages. He connects Bloch's project with 'the need to disappear into the object' and understands his utopianism as an attempt to conceptualize a 'nature' that is 'pacified . . . and free of domination'.[97] In a lecture on 'natural history' that is presented at the Kant-Gesellschaft in Frankfurt in July 1932, Adorno goes into details about what such a project could consist of. Like Bloch, Adorno shares Lukács' analysis that history has become drained of its meaning. In Adorno's view, the reification and commodification that are part and parcel of a capitalist society have resulted in the petrification of historical constructs. Quoting extensively from *Theory of the Novel*, Adorno describes how the products of human action have been modified into what Lukács has termed 'second nature'.[98] No longer visible as the outcome of a historical, and therefore changeable, process the realm of history takes on the seeming immutability and timelessness of nature. 'From the perspective of the philosophy of history the problem of natural history presents itself in the first place as the question of how it is possible to know and interpret this alienated, reified, dead world'.[99] However, once more in line with Bloch's most foundational intuitions, Adorno rejects Lukács' ultimate suggestion that such meaninglessness can solely be countered by abstract and ahistorical truths: 'Lukács can only think of this charnel-house in terms of a theological resurrection, in an eschatological context'.[100] Adorno thus explicitly shares Bloch's plea for a completely novel sense of metaphysics, allowing for the recovery *and* creation of truths and values that can only be retrieved by way of our interaction with concrete 'particulars' and the specificity of certain historical events. For, in the minds of Adorno and Bloch, the awareness that our world lacks the ontological support of unspoiled transcendent and absolute truths and meanings does not at all cancel out the importance of morality and metaphysics. It is precisely the retrieval of moral values and metaphysical truths *as* fragments and from *within* the realm of history itself which endows them with the critical and contesting power of philosophical thought. 'It just is not the task of philosophy to present . . . meaning positively, to portray reality as "meaningful" and thereby justify it. Every such justification of that which exists is prohibited by the fragmentation in being itself'.[101] In important passages in his review of *Traces*, Adorno pulls Bloch's project to his own side: Bloch's metaphysics 'cannot be reduced to questions of being, of the true essence of things, of God, freedom and immortality, even though those questions reverberate through it everywhere. Rather, it wants to describe, or . . . "construct" that other space: metaphysics as the phenomenology of the imaginary'.[102] With Bloch, Adorno dismisses the idea of a utopian *presence* that both Lukács and Jünger build upon, substituting it with an emphasis on the *imagistic* nature of all utopian thinking. His dialectics and, as we will see, his aesthetics revolve around the suggestion that only 'semblance' enables a truthful revisiting of our world. Only utopian *non*-realities can serve as a redemptive perspective onto a concrete society because they reveal that the latter is at present *removed* from the desired state of affairs. In his lecture on natural history, likewise, Adorno dismisses the quest for the 'substance in history' and rejects the concept of nature as 'what has always been, what as fatefully arranged predetermined being underlies history and appears in history'.[103] History is the realm of 'constellations', 'products', and 'constructs' in which meaning is never a mere given, let alone an 'archaic presence' but at most a highly contingent and changeable creation.

V

In spite of these fundamental resonances, at least two elements set Adorno's intellectual project apart from Bloch's utopianism. The first one revolves around the concept of 'myth'. In his early talk on 'natural history', Adorno introduces this term to describe the seeming timelessness and changelessness of nature: 'The concept of nature that is to be dissolved is one that, if I translated it into standard philosophical terminology, would come closest to the concept of myth'.[104] Remaining one of Adorno's most crucial concepts throughout his entire work, it is this concept of myth which, ten years after his talk in Frankfurt, will trigger the well-known analysis of instrumental reason that underlies *Dialectics of Enlightenment*. When nature is deemed immutable and utterly foreign to man's own projects, it can only provoke anxiety and fear. The emancipatory potential of reason, however, goes lost when it is thus reduced to an instrument to combat nature. For Horkheimer and Adorno, it is such instrumental rationality that has caused Enlightenment to flip back on itself and miss out on its promise of progress and freedom. For an instrumental use of human reason no longer creates the mental distance that is needed to reflect on and interact with nature and should itself be called 'mythic'.[105] Rooted as it is in the drive to control and manipulate, it is one with non-reason and only deepens the sentiment that sparked it: external nature is now but an anxiety-provoking object to be mastered and possessed. Moreover, the antagonism between external nature and man that feeds instrumental reason is bound to result in a similar antagonism with the nature *within* man (his passions) and, ultimately, with other human beings. Adorno criticizes Bloch's propensity to endow only desires, wishes, and dreams with

82 *Unworldliness in Twentieth Century German Thought*

an emancipatory potential because, rather than battling myth, these forces of *un*reason risk increasing it even further. '[A]t times Bloch's philosophy fails to measure up to culture and falls flat on its face. . . . The *Spuren* are most suspect when they tend to the occult: once forays into intelligible worlds become established as a principle there is not antidote to the dreams of a spirit-seer'.[106] For this reason, Bloch's insistence, in *Heritage of Our Time*, that the dark powers of fascism should be overcome by revisiting man's 'primeval drives and mythicisms' can only meet with Adorno's skepticism. Far from being the answer to fascism, the perennial forces of myth are what make up the cult of the 'authoritarian personality' that allows such a pernicious ideology to do its work in the first place. Adorno's overall project revolves, not around a return to myth or unreason, but around the recovery of the emancipatory potential of Enlightenment and the conceptualization of a non-instrumental use of reason. Rooted in a Hegelian notion of self-reflective reason, Adorno pledges loyalty to the project in which man does not seek to close itself off from the sphere of nature altogether, let alone that he would meet it as a merely antagonistic presence.[107] Through a non-instrumental use of reason man learns how to engage with nature in ever new ways and, moreover, is taught how to cope with the limits of reason: what sets such a type of reason apart from instrumental reason is precisely its capacity to testify to the radical alterity of what cannot be properly grasped and therefore retains a fundamental sense of meaninglessness. It is this active embrace of its own limitations that differentiates Adorno's project from that of Bloch. In Bloch's work 'the boundary between finite and infinite, between phenomenal and noumenal, the intellect with its limitations and faith with its lack of logic, is not respected'.[108] In the end, Bloch's project falls into the trap of transcendental illusion, being too much wedded to the supposed powers of unfettered imagination, rather than limiting itself to the scope of self-reflective reason.

Works of art are of vital importance to Adorno's exploration of such a self-reflective and non-instrumental use of reason, and it is here that Adorno's interpretation of Cervantes' novel becomes relevant. If Bloch's *The Principle of Hope* can be read as an encyclopedia of the eternal and 'mythic' force of imagination that underlies the realm of history, Adorno's posthumously published *Aesthetic Theory* needs to be read as an analysis of the highly divergent uses of self-reflective and non-instrumental reason that result from that same realm.[109] Unlike instrumental reason, the use of reason that culminates in artistic creation and perception is not motivated by the need to merely oppose nature. Rather, the artwork is the prime site in which man finds ever new ways to negotiate the intricate connection between his faculty of thought and a reality that will not ever be fully made rational. 'By its difference from empirical reality the artwork necessarily constitutes itself in relation to what it is not, and to what makes it an artwork in the first place'.[110] Because artworks result from a fruitful interaction with external reality, and not from a mere antagonism to it, they escape from the clutches of fear and anxiety: resisting the pull of 'mythic' and archaic imagination, artistic creation plays a crucial role in the establishment of a true Enlightenment. Such an emancipatory use of reason is, in Adorno's view, the starting point of the bourgeois era that comes after the Middle Ages, and it is exemplified by the work of Cervantes. Bloch turns to the *character* Don Quixote as a spiritual heir of the Middle Ages and the proof that the irreducible force of 'myth' can go against a disenchanted and hopeless universe. Adorno, for his part, is fascinated with the *novel Don Quixote* and reconstructs the historical moment when modern man's self-reflective powers strike a blow at such dark and irrational forces: 'The object of bourgeois art is the relation of itself as artifact to empirical society; Don Quixote stands at the beginning of this development'.[111] Adorno's mentioning of the self-reflective elements in *Don Quixote* is particularly relevant with regard to the second book, which includes intertextual references to the first book and hence initiates a discussion of the status of all works of fiction. Indeed, a key insight in Adorno's aesthetic theory is the connection between artworks and 'semblance'. With this notion, Adorno emphasizes that artworks derive their expressive powers from a created, inner unity that cannot be confused with the supposedly given, external world. On account of this alleged 'irreality', artworks are the prime site from which to criticize the instrumental use of reason and its ambition to grasp the totality of being with universal and allegedly infallible concepts. 'Aesthetic identity seeks to aid the nonidentical, which in reality is repressed by reality's compulsion to identity'.[112] For Adorno, it is this self-reflective dimension or, put differently, its 'irreal' autonomy from the merely existent, which endows the artwork with a social and political dimension.[113] Artworks do not contain any clear-cut lessons, nor do they provide us with a univocal compass for the lives we lead or the societies we build.[114] For Adorno, the isolated locus of the work of art enables us to experience the very *absence* of such absolute truths and meanings. For this reason precisely Adorno charges artworks with social and political capacities. In their stubborn clinging to ambiguities and ambivalences that cannot ever be made fully rational, they insist on their own limitations and thereby warn us against an overbearing quest of ultimate answers. This explains why Adorno reads *Don Quixote*, as well, in the context of an analysis of social and political art. Unlike Bloch, who applauds Don Quixote for showing us the ongoing importance of values such as 'loyalty, honour, leader, allegiance', Adorno

84 Unworldliness in Twentieth Century German Thought

does not however derive the social and political dimension of Cervantes' novel from the idealism of its protagonist. In Adorno's reading, Cervantes' novel does not revolve around Don Quixote's attempt to realize the non-realizable: to the contrary, what matters most in *Don Quixote* is the sustained endeavor to shield the 'semblance' of the *artwork* from all claims of determinate meaning. 'The antagonism of literary genres in which Cervantes' work originated was transformed, in his hands, into an antagonism of historical eras of, ultimately, metaphysical dimension: the authentic expression of the crisis of immanent meaning in the demystified world'.[115] In this way Adorno suggests that it is not the content of the novel so much as its idiosyncratic play with fiction, its formal openness, and its polyphonous structure that make it socially and politically relevant. '[A]rt becomes social by its opposition to society, and it occupies this position only as autonomous art. By crystallizing in itself as something unique to itself, rather than complying with existing social norms and qualifying as "socially useful", it criticizes society by merely existing, for which puritans of all stripes condemn it'.[116]

The depths of this argument can be gauged only if we take into account a second, and equally fundamental, difference between Adorno and Bloch's philosophies. Adorno agrees with Bloch that everything that takes place could just as well take place *differently* or *not at all*, but this statement is rooted in a *moral* obligation, that is, in a 'new categorical imperative that has been imposed by Hitler upon free mankind: to arrange their thoughts and actions so that Auschwitz will not repeat itself, so that nothing similar will happen'.[117] In Adorno's own blend of metaphysics and morality, it is morality that ultimately grounds metaphysics rather than the other way around, as it is the case with Bloch. In Adorno's work, it is in the last instance not the world's overall contingency that legitimizes hope but, vice versa, an unsuspected moment of hope (a 'hope against hope') that reinvigorates the realization that no given situation is fated. In other words, while Adorno does indeed follow Bloch's lead in replacing Lukács' and Jünger's non-negatable ideals by an insistence on the negatability of reality, this gesture is above all of a *moral* nature. In his *Negative Dialectics*, for instance, he describes the negatability of reality as follows: 'If thought it not measured by the extremity that eludes the concept, it is from the outset in the nature of the musical accompaniment with which the SS liked to drown out the screams of its victims'.[118] A consequence of this ultimate primacy of morality over metaphysics is that, as Adorno quips, 'hope is not a principle'.[119] In the end, even Bloch's philosophy is deemed too Lukácsian because it considers hope to be a metaphysical presence that is always readily at hand. For Adorno hope is no presence ingrained within reality, no perennial part of being. Rather,

Ernst Bloch Meets Theodor Adorno 85

such a view lacks critical depth and moral sharpness, taking the conditions of reconciliation and justice to always already have been realized. Hope, in Adorno's view, is an eternally unstable construct that will forever need to be fought for in the struggle for a just world. In other words, Adorno rejects Bloch's ontologization of hope and the concomitant suggestion that all hope is legitimate because, even in those cases when it is ultimately disappointed, it had been sparked by the world's irreducible contingency. Bloch's 'speculative thought wants to take root in the air, to be *ultima philosophia*, and yet its structure is that of *prima philosophia* and its ambition is the grand totality'.[120] In Adorno's view, statements about *the* real, history *in general*, or life *as such* suffer from what he calls a 'lack of mediation': concepts like reality, history, or life do not refer to a mere 'given' since they are always tainted by the social and economic specificities through which they were introduced. Speculations about the allegedly genuine structure and eternal features of reality at large are for this reason guilty of ideological abuse, selling off particular interests as universal truths. As a consequence, Bloch is wrong when he builds on '[t]he general concept, which washes away the trace and cannot plausibly genuinely sublate it, [but] nevertheless by its very intention has to speak as though the trace were present within it'. '[T]he trace itself is involuntary, spontaneous, inconspicuous, intentionless'.[121] In the final paragraph of his *Minima Moralia*, therefore, Adorno describes 'redemption' not as an event in the future or a continuous dynamic in the past or present but as a specific 'light that is shed on the world'. Redemption is no un-uprootable presence in history but the precarious force behind a 'philosophy that can responsibly be practiced in the face of despair'.[122] Hope cannot be derived from an ontological quality that is supposedly ever-present and inherent to the realm of history as such.

This complex view of the relation between metaphysics and morality casts light on the second important reference to *Don Quixote* in Adorno's work. In the essay 'Is Art Lighthearted?', written two years before his death, Adorno first presents the already mentioned argument that 'art frees itself of myth' and connects this to the issue of lightheartedness. For him, lightheartedness exemplifies the self-reflective and non-instrumental use of reason that marks artistic creation: 'It is in the lightheartedness of art that subjectivity first comes to know and become conscious of itself. Through lightheartedness it escapes from entanglement and returns to itself'.[123] However, with this essay Adorno's attention shifts to the reader's *response*, which is deemed of even greater importance than the structure of Cervantes' novel itself. For *Don Quixote* is introduced as a prime expression of 'bourgeois personal freedom' on account of the reader's ability to be carried away by events that are so clearly unreal.[124] This

86 Unworldliness in Twentieth Century German Thought

play with semblance is epitomized in the laughter provoked by the novel. For Adorno, it is this humoristic effect on the reader, rather than the actual novel itself, which creates the moral space to negotiate the limits of human understanding and overcome the quest for ultimate answers and infallible knowledge. Moreover, Adorno now highlights that the emancipatory powers of this humoristic effect are, on account of their historical determination, precarious and easily canceled out, instead of perennial and un-uprootable. For, he asks himself, 'Who could still laugh at *Don Quixote* and its sadistic mockery of the man who breaks down in the face of the bourgeois reality principle?'[125] Because it is dependent on a specific response and has no roots beyond the contingencies of historical events, hope is but a temporary gain that can always be taken away, and no asset that is possessed ad infinitum. While Don Quixote was once a figure of hope, exposing the pitfalls of the mythic and irrational worldview of the Middle Ages, he also 'shares in the historical fate of the bourgeoisie': 'In the end, (the humor in *Don Quixote*) becomes intolerable'.[126] Because the non-instrumental and self-reflective use of reason that underlies Cervantes' artistic creation has, in the centuries after him, given way to an instrumental and 'mythic' type of reason, the response to his novel's hero should undergo a drastic change. From a pioneer of the sphere of subjective freedom, Don Quixote has come to stand for the unwanted madman whose worldview can in no way be squared with the modern search for efficiency, rationalization, and standardization. With this shift, the moral effect of Cervantes' humor has worn out. The reader who is still inclined to meet Don Quixote's fate with laughter is now no longer part and parcel of the spirit of Enlightenment but 'complicit'. 'The more profoundly society fails to deliver the reconciliation that the bourgeois spirit promised as the enlightenment of myth, the more irresistibly humor is pulled down into the netherworld and laughter, once the image of humanness, becomes a regression into inhumanity'.[127]

Notes

1 Stefan Müller-Doohm, *Adorno: Eine Biographie* (Frankfurt am Main, Germany: Suhrkamp, 2003), 637. For a transcription of the debate, see Ernst Bloch and Theodor W. Adorno, 'Something's Missing: A Discussion between Ernst Bloch and Theodor W. Adorno on the Contradictions of Utopian Longing', in *Ernst Bloch, the Utopian Function of Art and Literature: Selected Essays*, transl. Jack Zipes and Frank Mecklenburg (Cambridge and London: The MIT Press, 1988), 1–17.
2 Bloch and Adorno, 'Something's Missing', 13.
3 Bloch and Adorno, 'Something's Missing', 12.
4 Bloch and Adorno, 'Something's Missing', 14.
5 Karl Marx and Friedrich Engels, *Manifesto of the Communist Party: A Modern Edition*, intr. Tariq Ali (London: Verso, 2016), 93 (epub).

6 Bloch and Adorno, 'Something's Missing', 12.
7 Bloch and Adorno, 'Something's Missing', resp. 5–6.
8 Bloch and Adorno, 'Something's Missing', 11.
9 Bloch and Adorno, 'Something's Missing', 11.
10 Bloch and Adorno, 'Something's Missing', 6.
11 Bloch and Adorno, 'Something's Missing', 3.
12 Bloch and Adorno, 'Something's Missing', 4.
13 Bloch and Adorno, 'Something's Missing', 3.
14 Bloch and Adorno, 'Something's Missing', 5.
15 Bloch and Adorno, 'Something's Missing', 16–17.
16 Ernst Bloch, 'Can Hope Be Disappointed?', in *Literary Essays*, ed. and transl. Andrew Joron et al. (Stanford, CA: Stanford University Press, 1998), 340. See also Gerhard Richter, 'Can Hope Be Disappointed? Contextualizing a Blochian Question', in *Symploke* 14 (1–2) (2006): 42–54.
17 Bloch and Adorno, 'Something's Missing', 13. See also Timo Jütten, 'Adorno on Hope', in *Philosophy & Social Criticism* 45 (3) (2019): 284–306.
18 Bloch and Adorno, 'Something's Missing', 10 (italics added).
19 Bloch and Adorno, 'Something's Missing', 10 (italics added), 16.
20 Bloch and Adorno, 'Something's Missing', 10 (italics added), 12.
21 Arno Münster, *Ernst Bloch: Eine politische Biographie* (Berlin and Vienne, France: Philo, 2004), 49.
22 Lukács and Bloch, quoted in Werner Jung, 'The Early Aesthetic Theories of Bloch and Lukács', in *New German Critique* 45 (1988): 41–42. Much has been written about the relation between Bloch and the early Lukács, see, e.g. Richard Wolin, 'Notes on the Early Aesthetics of Lukács, Bloch, and Benjamin', in *Berkeley Journal of Sociology* 26 (1981): 89–109; Lilian Weissberg, 'Utopian Visions: Bloch, Lukács, Pontoppidan', in *The German Quarterly* 67 (2) (1994): 197–210; Michael Löwy, *Redemption and Utopia: Jewish Libertarian Thought in Central Europe*, transl. Hope Heaney (London: Verso Books, 2007); Frederic Jameson, *Marxism and Form* (Princeton, NJ: Princeton University Press, 1977); Tyrus Miller, 'Matthew, Mark, Lukács, and Bloch: From Aesthetic Utopianism to Religious Messianism', in *Georg Lukács and Critical Theory: Aesthetics, History, Utopia* (Edinburgh, UK: Edinburgh University Press, 2022), 31–54.
23 For an excellent overview, see Miklós Mesterházi and György Mezei, eds., *Ernst Bloch und Georg Lukács: Dokumente Zum 100. Geburtstag* (Lukács Archivum: MTA Filozófiai Intézet, 1984), see https://core.ac.uk/download/pdf/35134735.pdf
24 Bloch, quoted in Mesterházi and Mezei, *Ernst Bloch und Georg Lukács*, 45.
25 Balazs, quoted in Éva Karàdi, 'Ernst Bloch and Georg Lukács in Max Weber's Heidelberg', in *Max Weber and His Contemporaries*, ed. Wolfgang J. Mommsen and Jurgen Osterhammel (London and New York: Routledge, 1987), 500.
26 Ernst Bloch, *The Spirit of Utopia*, transl. Anthony A. Nassar (Stanford, CA: Stanford University Press, 2000), 191, 200.
27 Weber and Lask, quoted in Miller, 'Matthew, Mark, Lukács, and Bloch', 34.
28 Bloch, *The Spirit of Utopia*, 165.
29 Lukács, *Theory of the Novel*, 56.
30 Lukács, *Theory of the Novel*, 152.
31 See also Miller, 'Matthew, Mark, Lukács, and Bloch', 42.
32 See also Miller, 'Matthew, Mark, Lukács, and Bloch', 80. See also Wolin, 'Notes on the Early Aesthetics of Lukács, Bloch, and Benjamin', 95–96.

88 *Unworldliness in Twentieth Century German Thought*

33 Bloch, *The Spirit of Utopia*, 222.
34 Bloch, *The Spirit of Utopia*, 223.
35 For an analysis of the role of 'objectifications' and 'subjectivity' in resp. Lukács and Bloch, see Sándor Radnóti, 'Lukács and Bloch', in *Lukács Revalued*, ed. Agnes Heller (Oxford: Basil Blackwell, 1983), 63–74, esp. 68–71. Radnóti's opposition between the 'ethical' Lukács and the 'religious' Bloch does however overlook the mystical elements that I highlight.
36 Ernst Bloch, 'Discussions of Expressionism' (1938), in *Heritage of Our Times*, transl. Neville and Stephen Plaice (Berkeley and Los Angeles: University of California Press, 1991), 246–247.
37 Bloch, *The Spirit of Utopia*, 201.
38 Bloch, *The Spirit of Utopia*, 227.
39 Bloch, *The Spirit of Utopia*, 201 (emphasis in original).
40 Bloch, *The Spirit of Utopia*, 8–9.
41 Bloch, *The Spirit of Utopia*, 31.
42 Bloch, *The Spirit of Utopia*, 32.
43 Bloch, *The Spirit of Utopia*, 193.
44 Bloch, *The Spirit of Utopia*, 171.
45 Bloch, *The Spirit of Utopia*, 196.
46 Bloch, *Heritage of Our Times*, 97.
47 Bloch, *Heritage of Our Times*, 99.
48 Bloch, *Heritage of Our Times*, 102.
49 See Siegfried Kracauer, *The Salaried Masses: Duty and Distraction in Weimar Germany*, transl. Quintin Hoare (London: Verso, 1998).
50 Bloch, *Heritage of Our Times*, 135, 138.
51 Ernst Bloch, *The Principle of Hope, Part 3*, transl. Neville Plaice, Stephen Plaice and Paul Knight (Cambridge, MA: The MIT Press, 1986), 1035.
52 Bloch, *The Principle of Hope*, 1036.
53 Bloch, *The Principle of Hope*, 1035.
54 Bloch, *The Principle of Hope*, 1042.
55 Bloch, *The Principle of Hope*, 1041.
56 Bloch, *The Principle of Hope*, 1042.
57 Bloch, *The Principle of Hope*, 1037–1038.
58 Bloch, *The Principle of Hope*, 1039.
59 Bloch, *The Principle of Hope*, 1039.
60 Bloch, *The Principle of Hope*, 1045, see also Bloch, *The Principle of Hope*, 1043–1044: 'Even if the revolutionary work must always bear in mind the whole and the highest ideal of its goal in order to be more than reform, the better society does not come about through fanaticism or ideal propaganda from above. Not through a pure soul without habitation in the movements of the world and without knowledge of the less pure interests which move the world'.
61 Bloch, *The Principle of Hope*, 1047–1051.
62 Cervantes, quoted in Bloch, *The Principle of Hope*, 1046. The quote is taken from Part II, Chapter 74.
63 Bloch, *The Principle of Hope*, 1046.
64 Bloch, *The Principle of Hope*, 1048.
65 Bloch, *The Principle of Hope*, 1048.
66 Bloch, *The Principle of Hope*, 1049.
67 See Part II, Chapters 34–35.
68 Bloch, *The Principle of Hope*, 1049.

69 Bloch, *The Principle of Hope*, 1049.
70 Bloch, *The Principle of Hope*, 1046.
71 Bloch, *The Principle of Hope*, 1049–1050.
72 Bloch, *The Principle of Hope*, 1051.
73 Bloch, *The Principle of Hope*, 1035, 1050.
74 Theodor W. Adorno, 'The Handle, the Pot, and Early Experience', in *Notes to Literature: Volume 2*, ed. Rolf Tiedemann, transl. Shierry Weber Nicholsen (New York: Columbia University Press, 1992), 211. For the relation between Bloch and Adorno, see e.g. Gunzelin Schmid-Noerr, 'Bloch und Adorno: Bildhafte und bilderlose Utopie', in *Zeitschrift für Kritische Theorie* 13 (2001): 25–55; Arno Münster, 'De l'amitié à la polémique: À propos de correspondence Adorno-Bloch (1928–1968)', in *Europe* (2008): 15–35; Inge Münz-Koenen, *Konstruktion des Nirgendwo: Die Diskursivität utopischen Denkens bei Bloch, Adorno, Habermas* (Berlin: Akademie, 1997); Jonathan Roessler, 'Utopianism in Pianissimo: Adorno and Bloch on Utopia and Critique', *Critical Horizons* 23 (3) (2022): 227–246; Hent de Vries, 'The Antinomy of Death: Ernst Bloch and Theodor W. Adorno on Utopia and Hope', *Angelaki* 27 (1) (2022): 110–127; Ivan Boldyrev, 'The Void of Utopia and the Violence of the System: Bloch Contra Adorno', in *Ernst Bloch and His Contemporaries* (London and Oxford: Bloomsbury Academic, 2014), 167–178.
75 Adorno, 'The Handle, the Pot, and Early Experience', 211.
76 Adorno, quoted in Ivan Boldyrev, *Ernst Bloch and His Contemporaries* (London and Oxford: Bloomsbury Academic, 2014), 167.
77 Adorno, quoted in de Vries, 'The Antinomy of Death', 124.
78 Theodor W. Adorno, letter to his parents on December 21, 1942, in Theodor W. Adorno, *Letters to His Parents: 1939–1951*, ed. Christoph Gödde and Henri Lonitz, transl. Wieland Hoban (Cambridge, UK: Polity Press, 2006), 119. For the context, see Münster, *Ernst Bloch*, 227–232.
79 Adorno, 'The Handle, the Pot, and Early Experience', 212.
80 Theodor W. Adorno, 'Ernst Bloch's *Spuren*: On the Revised Edition of 1959', in *Notes to Literature: Volume 1*, ed. Rolf Tiedemann, transl. Shierry Weber Nicholson (New York: Columbia University Press, 1991), 201.
81 Adorno, 'Ernst Bloch's *Spuren*', 205.
82 For an illuminating discussion of the notion 'not yet' in Adorno, and the influence of Bloch, see Max Blechman, 'Not Yet: Adorno and the Utopia of Conscience', in *Cultural Critique* 70 (2008): 177–198. See, for instance, the claim that 'Adorno wants to highlight the inexpungible grounds of subjective freedom, the inexpugnability of human negativity that tends towards self-transformation and resistance' (p. 192).
83 Adorno, 'Ernst Bloch's *Spuren*', 203.
84 Theodor W. Adorno, *Negative Dialectics*, transl. E. B. Ashton (London and New York: Routledge, 2004), 56–57.
85 For a very clear discussion of the notion of the non-identical, within an analysis of Adorno's philosophy of history, see Iain MacDonald, 'Philosophy of History', in *A Companion to Adorno*, ed. Peter E. Gordon, Espen Hammer and Max Pensky (Hoboken, NJ: Wiley Blackwell, 2020), esp. 200–202. See also the subchapters 'Ontology as Wish Fulfillment', 'Into the Looking Glass', and 'Disenchanting the Concept' in Peter Gordon, *Adorno and Existence* (Cambridge and London: Harvard University Press, 2006), 149–157; Oshrat T. Silberbusch, *Adorno's Philosophy of the Nonidentical: Thinking as Resistance* (Cham, Germany: Palgrave Macmillan, 2008), esp. 217–222.

90 Unworldliness in Twentieth Century German Thought

86 Adorno, *Negative Dialectics*, 396–397.

87 Theodor W. Adorno, 'Extorted Reconciliation: On Georg Lukács' *Realism in Our Time*', in *Notes on Literature: Volume 1*, ed. Rolf Tiedemann, transl. Shierry Weber Nicholson (New York: Columbia University Press, 1991), 217. For a discussion of Adorno's criticism of Lukács, including his rejection of social realism and his comments on the concept of reification, see Michael J. Thompson, 'Adorno's Reception of Weber and Lukács', in *A Companion to Adorno*, ed. Peter E. Gordon, Espen Hammer and Max Pensky (Hoboken, NJ: Wiley Blackwell, 2020), 221–236.

88 Adorno, 'Extorted Reconciliation: On Georg Lukács' *Realism in Our Time*,' 240.

89 Adorno, 'Extorted Reconciliation: On Georg Lukács' *Realism in Our Time*,' 240.

90 Theodor W. Adorno, *Minima Moralia: Reflections on a Damaged Life*, transl. E. F. N. Jephcott (London and New York: Verso, 2005), 50.

91 Adorno, *Negative Dialectics*, 3. For an analysis of Adorno's concept of totality and its relation to Lukács, see Martin Jay, 'Theodor W. Adorno and the Collapse of the Lukácsian Concept of Totality', in *Marxism and Totality: The Adventures of a Concept from Lukács to Habermas* (Cambridge, UK: Polity Press, 1984), 241–275. As Jay puts it, '[W]hat is clear is that Adorno's attitude towards normative totality manifested a certain ability that resulted from his distaste for perfect consistency. Although . . . he sometimes saw the organic wholeness of great works of art as promises of future happiness, he generally tended to deny that it would appear in the form of a fully integrated community without alienation' (p. 266).

92 Theodor W. Adorno, letter to Thomas Mann on December 28, 1949, in Theodor W. Adorno and Thomas Mann, *Correspondence 1943–1955*, ed. Christoph Gödde and Thomas Sprecher, transl. Nicholas Walker (Cambridge, UK: Polity Press, 2006), 35.

93 Theodor W. Adorno, 'The Actuality of Philosophy', transl. Benjamin Snow, in *Telos* 31 (1977): 120.

94 Adorno, 'The Actuality of Philosophy', 132.

95 Adorno, 'The Actuality of Philosophy', 133.

96 Adorno, 'Ernst Bloch's *Spuren*', 202.

97 Adorno, 'The Handle, the Pot, and Early Experience', 215; Adorno, 'Ernst Bloch's *Spuren*', 205.

98 Theodor W. Adorno, 'The Idea of Natural History', transl. Bob Hullot-Kentor, in *Telos* 60 (1984): 111–124.

99 Adorno, 'The Idea of Natural History', 118.

100 Adorno, 'The Idea of Natural History', 118.

101 Adorno, 'The Actuality of Philosophy', 126.

102 Adorno, 'Ernst Bloch's *Spuren*', 211.

103 Adorno, 'The Idea of Natural History', 111.

104 Adorno, 'The Idea of Natural History', 111.

105 See, for instance, the 'The Concept of Enlightenment' and 'Excursus I: Odysseus or Myth and Enlightenment', in Max Horkheimer and Theodor W. Adorno, *Dialectic of Enlightenment*, ed. Gunzelin Schmid-Noerr, transl. Edmund Jephcott (Stanford, CA: Stanford University Press, 2002), 1–62.

106 Adorno, 'Ernst Bloch's *Spuren*', 210.

107 See also Martin Jay's discussion of the concept of (non-)instrumental reason in Marcuse, Horkheimer and Adorno, in 'The Critique of Instrumental Reason. Horkheimer, Marcuse, and Adorno', in *Reason after Its Eclipse* (Madison: University of Wisconsin Press, 2016), 97–113, esp. 104.
108 Adorno, 'Ernst Bloch's *Spuren*', 206.
109 See, for instance, Lambert Zuidervaart's discussion of Adorno's *Aesthetic Theory* in his *Adorno's Aesthetic Theory: The Redemption of an Illusion* (Cambridge, MA, and London: The MIT Press, 1991), esp. 159–169.
110 Theodor W. Adorno, *Aesthetic Theory*, transl. and ed. Robert Hullot-Kentor (London and New York: Continuum, 1997), 9. For an interesting, almost analytic discussion of Adorno's notion of aesthetic autonomy, leading to an emphasis on the cognitivist and judgmental significance of aesthetic experience in Adorno, see Owan Hulatt, 'Aesthetic Autonomy', in *A Companion to Adorno*, ed. Peter E. Gordon, Espen Hammer and Max Pensky (Hoboken, NJ: Wiley Blackwell, 2020), 351–364.
111 Adorno, *Aesthetic Theory*, 296.
112 Adorno, *Aesthetic Theory*, 5.
113 See also Peter Uwe Hohendahl, 'Aesthetic Theory as Social Theory', in *A Companion to Adorno*, ed. Peter E. Gordon, Espen Hammer and Max Pensky (Hoboken, NJ: Wiley Blackwell, 2020), esp. 423–426.
114 Once more, this marks a crucial difference between Adorno and Lukács. Adorno is, like Lukács, wedded to a view of autonomous art, but this is to him no realm of a utopian *presence*, that is, a fulfilled totality and a 'breachless' encounter of subject and object.
115 Adorno, *Aesthetic Theory*, 322.
116 Adorno, *Aesthetic Theory*, 296.
117 Adorno, *Negative Dialectics*, 365.
118 Adorno, *Negative Dialectics*, 365.
119 Adorno, 'Ernst Bloch's *Spuren*', 213.
120 Adorno, 'Ernst Bloch's *Spuren*', 212.
121 Adorno, 'Ernst Bloch's *Spuren*', 213.
122 Adorno, *Minima Moralia*, 247.
123 Theodor W. Adorno, 'Is Art Lighthearted?' in *Notes to Literature: Volume 2*, ed. Rolf Tiedemann, transl. Shierrry Weber Nicholsen (New York: Columbia University Press, 1992), 250.
124 Adorno, 'Is Art Lighthearted?', 250.
125 Adorno, 'Is Art Lighthearted?', 250.
126 Adorno, 'Is Art Lighthearted?', 250.
127 Adorno, 'Is Art Lighthearted?', 251.

Bibliography

Adorno, Theodor W. 'The Actuality of Philosophy' transl. Benjamin Snow, in *Telos* 31 (1977)
Adorno, Theodor W. *Aesthetic Theory*, ed. and transl. Robert Hullot-Kentor (London and New York: Continuum, 1997)
Adorno, Theodor W. 'Ernst Bloch's Spuren: On the Revised Edition of 1959', in *Notes to Literature: Volume 1*, ed. Rolf Tiedemann, transl. Shierry Weber Nicholson (New York: Columbia University Press, 1991)

92 *Unworldliness in Twentieth Century German Thought*

Adorno, Theodor W. 'Extorted Reconciliation: On Georg Lukács' Realism in Our Time', in *Notes on Literature: Volume* 1, ed. Rolf Tiedemann, transl. Shierry Weber Nicholson (New York: Columbia University Press, 1991)

Adorno, Theodor W. 'The Handle, the Pot, and Early Experience', in *Notes to Literature: Volume* 2, ed. Rolf Tiedemann, transl. Shierry Weber Nicholsen (New York: Columbia University Press, 1992)

Adorno, Theodor W. 'The Idea of Natural History' transl. Bob Hullot-Kentor, in *Telos* 60 (1984)

Adorno, Theodor W. 'Is Art Lighthearted?' in *Notes to Literature: Volume* 2, ed. Rolf Tiedemann, transl. Shierry Weber Nicholsen (New York: Columbia University Press, 1992)

Adorno, Theodor W. *Letters to His Parents. 1939–1951*, ed. Christoph Gödde and Henri Lonitz, transl. Wieland Hoban (Cambridge: Polity Press, 2006)

Adorno, Theodor W. *Minima Moralia: Reflections on a Damaged Life*, transl. E. F. N. Jephcott (London and New York: Verso, 2005)

Adorno, Theodor W. *Negative Dialectics*, transl. E. B. Ashton (London and New York: Routledge, 2004)

Adorno, Theodor W. and Mann, Thomas. *Correspondence 1943–1955*, ed. Christoph Gödde and Thomas Sprecher, transl. Nicholas Walker (Cambridge: Polity, 2006)

Blechman, Max. 'Not Yet: Adorno and the Utopia of Conscience', in *Cultural Critique* 70 (2008)

Bloch, Ernst. 'Can Hope Be Disappointed?' in *Literary Essays*, ed. and transl. Andrew Joron et al. (Stanford: Stanford University Press, 1998)

Bloch, Ernst. 'Discussions of Expressionism' (1938), in *Heritage of Our Times*, transl. Neville and Stephen Plaice (Berkeley and Los Angeles: University of California Press, 1991)

Bloch, Ernst. *Heritage of Our Times*, transl. Neville and Stephen Plaice (Berkeley and Los Angeles: University of California Press, 1991)

Bloch, Ernst. *The Principle of Hope*, transl. Neville Plaice, Stephen Plaice and Paul Knight (Cambridge, MA: The MIT Press, 1986)

Bloch, Ernst. *The Spirit of Utopia*, transl. Anthony A. Nassar (Stanford: Stanford University Press, 2000)

Bloch, Ernst and Adorno, Theodor W. 'Something's Missing: A Discussion Between Ernst Bloch and Theodor W. Adorno on the Contradictions of Utopian Longing', in *Ernst Bloch, the Utopian Function of Art and Literature: Selected Essays*, transl. Jack Zipes and Frank Mecklenburg (Cambridge and London: The MIT Press, 1988)

Boldyrev, Ivan. 'The Void of Utopia and the Violence of the System: Bloch Contra Adorno', in *Ernst Bloch and His Contemporaries* (London and Oxford: Bloomsbury Academic, 2014)

de Vries, Hent. 'The Antinomy of Death: Ernst Bloch and Theodor W. Adorno on Utopia and Hope', in *Angelaki* 27 (1) (2022)

Gordon, Peter Eli. *Adorno and Existence* (Cambridge and London: Harvard University Press, 2006)

Hohendahl, Peter Uwe. 'Aesthetic Theory as Social Theory', in *A Companion to Adorno*, ed. Peter E. Gordon, Espen Hammer and Max Pensky (Hoboken: Wiley Blackwell, 2020)

Horkheimer, Max and Adorno, Theodor W. *Dialectic of Enlightenment*, ed. Gunzelin Schmid-Noerr, transl. Edmund Jephcott (Stanford: Stanford University Press, 2002)

Ernst Bloch Meets Theodor Adorno 93

Hulatt, Owan. 'Aesthetic Autonomy', in *A Companion to Adorno*, ed. Peter E. Gordon, Espen Hammer and Max Pensky (Hoboken: Wiley Blackwell, 2020)

Jameson, Frederic. *Marxism and Form* (Princeton: Princeton University Press, 1977)

Jay, Martin. 'The Critique of Instrumental Reason: Horkheimer, Marcuse, and Adorno', in *Reason After Its Eclipse* (Madison: University of Wisconsin Press, 2016)

Jay, Martin. 'Theodor W. Adorno and the Collapse of the Lukácsian Concept of Totality', in *The Adventures of a Concept from Lukács to Habermas* (Cambridge: Polity Press, 1984)

Jung, Werner. 'The Early Aesthetic Theories of Bloch and Lukács', in *New German Critique* 45 (1988)

Jütten, Timo. 'Adorno on Hope', in *Philosophy & Social Criticism* 45 (3) (2019)

Karàdi, Éva. 'Ernst Bloch and Georg Lukács in Max Weber's Heidelberg', in *Max Weber and His Contemporaries*, ed. Wolfgang J. Mommsen and Jurgen Osterhammel (London and New York: Routledge, 1987)

Kracauer, Siegfried. *The Salaried Masses: Duty and Distraction in Weimar Germany*, transl. Quintin Hoare (London: Verso, 1998)

Löwy, Michael. *Redemption and Utopia: Jewish Libertarian Thought in Central Europe*, transl. Hope Heaney (London: Verso Books, 2007)

MacDonald, Iain. 'Philosophy of History', in *A Companion to Adorno*, ed. Peter E. Gordon, Espen Hammer and Max Pensky (Hoboken: Wiley Blackwell, 2020)

Marx, Karl and Engels, Friedrich. *Manifesto of the Communist Party: A Modern Edition*, intr. Tariq Ali (London: Verso, 2016, epub)

Mesterházi, Miklós and Mezei, György, eds. *Ernst Bloch und Georg Lukács: Dokumente Zum 100. Geburtstag* (Lukács Archivum: MTA Filozófiai Intézet, 1984), https://core.ac.uk/download/pdf/35134735.pdf

Müller-Doohm, Stefan. *Adorno: Eine Biographie* (Frankfurt am Main: Suhrkamp, 2003)

Münster, Arno. 'De l'amitié à la polémique: À propos de correspondence Adorno-Bloch (1928–1968)', in *Europe* 86 (2008)

Münster, Arno. *Ernst Bloch: Eine politische Biographie* (Berlin and Vienne: Philo, 2004)

Münz-Koenen, Inge. *Konstruktion des Nirgendwo: Die Diskursivität utopischen Denkens bei Bloch, Adorno, Habermas* (Berlin: Akademie, 1997)

Radnóti, Sándor. 'Lukács and Bloch', in *Lukács Revalued*, ed. Agnes Heller (Oxford: Basil Blackwell, 1983)

Richter, Gerhard. 'Can Hope Be Disappointed? Contextualizing a Blochian Question', in *Symploke* 14 (1–2) (2006)

Roessler, Jonathan. 'Utopianism in Pianissimo: Adorno and Bloch on Utopia and Critique', in *Critical Horizons* 23 (3) (2022)

Schmid-Noerr, Gunzelin. 'Bloch und Adorno: Bildhafte und bilderlose Utopie', in *Zeitschrift für Kritische Theorie* 13 (2001)

Silberbusch, Oshrat T. *Adorno's Philosophy of the Nonidentical: Thinking as Resistance* (Cham: Palgrave Macmillan, 2008)

Thompson, Michael J. 'Adorno's Reception of Weber and Lukács', in *A Companion to Adorno*, ed. Peter E. Gordon, Espen Hammer and Max Pensky (Hoboken: Wiley Blackwell, 2020)

94 Unworldliness in Twentieth Century German Thought

Weissberg, Lilian. 'Utopian Visions: Bloch, Lukács, Pontoppidan', in *The German Quarterly* 67 (2) (1994)

Wolin, Richard. 'Notes on the Early Aesthetics of Lukács, Bloch, and Benjamin', in *Berkeley Journal of Sociology* 26 (1981)

Zuidervaart, Lambert. *Adorno's Aesthetic Theory: The Redemption of an Illusion* (Cambridge, MA and London: The MIT Press, 1991)

3 The Missed Conversation Between Max Kommerell and Siegfried Kracauer

Sancho Panza, The Man Without Convictions

I

While in the process of finishing his *Habilitationsschrift* on Kierkegaard, Adorno is crossing paths with two men who have most likely never met but will end up sharing more than they would have ever cared to admit: Siegfried Kracauer (1889–1966) and Max Kommerell (1902–1944). In 1930, Kracauer has just published his earlier-mentioned sociological study *Die Angestellten* ('The Salaried Masses'), in which he develops a Marx-influenced framework to diagnose the proletarization of the lower middle class. In hindsight, this analysis of the estranged condition of the 'white collar workers' will prove a most useful tool in understanding the rise of Nazism. Kracauer will already have left Frankfurt by the time Adorno defends his thesis in February 1931, but he and Adorno strike up a friendship, be it a complicated one, when meeting each other near the end of World War I.[1] Kommerell, for his part, arrives in Frankfurt only in 1929, but he will already defend his own *Habilitationsschrift* a few months later and ends up staying in the city until 1941, when Kracauer and Adorno will both have crossed the Atlantic. In spite of sharing Kracauer's (very) early affinity with *Lebensphilosophie* and Adorno's fascination with authors such as Goethe, Hölderlin, and von Hofmannsthal, Kommerell is not exactly on the same ideological page as his two left-leaning colleagues, to put it mildly. While Kommerell's sympathetic response to the rise of Nazism is most likely at least partly driven by careerist motivations, he does describe Hitler's *Mein Kampf* as 'in the instincts many times healthy and right' and will join the NSDAP (National Socialist German Workers' Party) as late as 1939.[2] Moreover, this is how he, in a letter from July 1932, describes the recent visit of a Nazi mob to the department that at the time also houses Adorno:

> The Nazis – good boys, by the way – paid a violent visit to us the other day. Perhaps they were annoyed that Goethe University is a

DOI: 10.4324/9781003364009-4

96 *Unworldliness in Twentieth Century German Thought*

hotbed of Marxist microbes, at least in its philosophical and sociological stock. . . . It's a pity that the intellectual household of the Nazis still smells so much like a makeshift.[3]

It's little surprise that Adorno mainly remembers Kommerell as the 'fascist' who 'once said that men like me should be put against the wall'.[4]

In the first part of this chapter, a juxtaposition of some of Kommerell and Kracauer's writings from the 1920s indicates how puzzling it is that both thinkers will defend similar philosophical positions near the end of their lives. The early Kommerell's work originates in a political and intellectual context that, motivated by the Stefan George-group, strongly defends the importance of lived interactions with an internally unified and shared culture. The early Kracauer's analysis of Weimar culture, however, revolves around the critical and positive potential of negation, fragmentation, and *un*-worldliness. In the second part of this chapter, I analyze the evolution in the work of Kommerell that pushes him in the direction of a more moderate and humanistic version of *Lebensphilosophie*. I reconstruct how this underlies his interpretation of Cervantes' novel. In the final part, building on Kracauer's own interpretation of *Don Quixote*, I outline how the post-war Kracauer slowly but certainly sheds his pre-war fascination with the critical potential of negation and unworldliness. Embracing the notion of 'lifeworld', he even adopts the jargon of phenomenology and *Lebensphilosophie* and thereby shows affinities with the thought of the later Kommerell.

II

One year before coming to Frankfurt, in 1928, Kommerell publishes *Der Dichter als Führer in der deutschen Klassik*, a voluminous study that seeks to re-introduce the major writers of the German classic age to a young audience. In the years of its conception, Kommerell belongs to the inner circle of the German poet and all-round spiritual leader Stefan George (1868–1933), and at some point becomes his personal secretary and traveling companion. Apart from his symbolist poetry and translations, George is known for his circle of devoted followers and the literary salon that hosts guests such as Rainer Maria Rilke, Georg Simmel, Ernst Kantorowicz, Hugo von Hofmannsthal, and Lou Andreas-Salomé. Inspired by the Nietzschean project to bridge the gap between art and life, it is George's ambition to counter the modern threat of spiritual poverty and individualism through the creation of an intellectual and artistic elite.[5] Kommerell's *Der Dichter als Führer* is one of three so-called *Geistesbücher* that are published to celebrate the sixtieth birthday of the Master. These *Geistesbücher* are most often biographies in which the jargon of *Lebensphilosophie*

The Missed Conversation   97

is deployed for an espousal of the unique value and merits of the German nation. Focusing on the likes of emperor Frederick II, Goethe and Nietzsche, the men that figure most prominently in the *Geistesbücher* of the George circle, are considered the embodiment of an eternal and absolute wellspring of creativity and renewal, thereby lighting the path for a spiritual community of great minds. Rejecting the rigorous methodology of academic research, these books modify the 'scientists of art into scientific artists' (*Kunstwissenschaftler zum Wissenschaftskünstler*).[6]

Kommerell's study revolves around the thesis that the significance of Klopstock, Herder, Goethe, Schiller, Jean Paul, and Hölderlin is not of a merely artistic nature since, together, these authors make up the sole force that can overcome the fragmentary state of the nation. It begins with the statement that he wants 'to let the poets appear as role models of a community (*Vorbilder einer Gemeinschaft*)', and thus follows George's dictum that the *Geistesbücher* are primarily a form of 'politics'.[7] Kommerell, that is, builds on the idea that Germany is characterized by 'one of the incomprehensibilities that only occur in *our* history: other peoples blossom and fall in a determined unbroken succession (*gesetzlich undurchbrochener Abfolge*) . . . for us, against all possibility, several times a creative will and a new beginning came out of nothing'.[8] *Der Dichter als Führer in der deutschen Klassik* follows the familiar trope that the German poet is the true heir of the Greek spirit. At the same time, it goes beyond such clichés in highlighting that the German poet, in opposition to his ancient ancestor, cannot be considered the spokesman of a rich and unified community for the simple reason that, in Germany, such a 'maturity of the people' (*völkischen Reife*) is as yet 'lacking'.[9] In Kommerell's view, however, there is an *Ersatz* for, and even a true 'ground in life' (*Lebensgrund*) of the rich spiritual community that Germany is in need of: the friendships that are set up between the great poets and their disciples, or between the Greats among themselves. 'Equal to Klopstock's poetic achievement is another: he instinctively [*triebmäßig*] discovered the only sphere of activity that allowed for the creation of a substitute for the lacking maturity of the people [*völkische Reife*]: the circle of friends. This was . . . *his* state concentrated into the poetic circle. Without this ground in life [*Lebensgrund*], as small as this sliver was, the new song would have been idle play. Antiquity and friendship stand at the cradle of German literature as the eternal and the present, from whose encounter emerges the miracle'.[10]

The importance of friendship for the creation of a spiritual and political community is most extensively argued for in the chapter on Schiller. According to Kommerell, Schiller's early plays center around the issue of conspiracy and the rebellion against the state. From Don Carlos onward, the theme of friendship is introduced to endow such political maneuvers with a spiritual weight: it is only by virtue of friendship that a conspiracy

98   Unworldliness in Twentieth Century German Thought

can become more than a blind force and result in noble and concerted action.[11] Still, in Kommerell's reading, Schiller grows unsatisfied with this early view because the concept of conspiracy is deemed an overly narrow foundation for the rich force of friendship. When it is tied together too closely with the issue of rebellion and conspiracy, the true wealth and profundity of friendship are reduced to a mere means for political purposes. Such a type of instrumentalized friendship remains 'almost without the appearance or succession of significant experiences'.[12] Kommerell interprets the later stages of Schiller's oeuvre as the quest for a much more substantial and reflexive concept of friendship. Schiller's attempt to properly think through the issue of friendship brings him to the idea that it is, above all, a love of perfection. Friendship is not rooted in a mere rebellion against the state since, within friendship, 'the sensations that belong to one and those that belong to the other flow into each other'.[13] At the heart of such an 'exchange of essentialities' (*Wesenstausch*) lies the appropriation of the loved one's virtues and merits, which leads to a genuine knowledge of the good and the subsequent self-improvement. Schiller's 'concept of love' is 'derived' from the idea that 'through love the lover takes possession of the higher qualities of the beloved. This harbors within itself an almost violent will to self-perfection (*ein fast gewaltsamer Wille zur Selbstvollendung*)'. Schiller 'always loved upwards (*Schiller liebte immernachoben*)'.[14]

This new account of friendship and love comes with its own set of challenges since it, too, runs the risk of becoming stale and lifeless. When friendship is first and foremost driven by a longing for knowledge and perfection, it jeopardizes its own creative dynamic. 'How quickly the love of who is being guided (*die Liebe des Geführten*) shoots out beyond the person of the leader (*die Person des Führers*) into a perfection of thought, which the Schiller of the time considered as much to be the highest fulfillment as we consider it empty (*eine Volkommenheit des Gedankes, die dem damaligen Schiller ebenso höchste Fülle bedeutete wie sie uns Leere dünkt*)'.[15] In an argument that will remain crucial to the entirety of his oeuvre, Kommerell pits the faculties of thought and rationality against an *intuitive* and *emotive* recuperation of life's supposed infinite capacities. Only *non*-rational feelings and *lived* interactions set up a genuine connection with the surrounding world, enabling an encounter with the world's internal unity and meaning-giving ground. In Kommerell's view, friendship and love are deprived of their 'vital substance' (*Lebenstoff*) when they are made dependent on the need to *understand*. Such a 'joyful devotion' is but 'the earthly fuel for the bodiless flame of knowledge' and misses out on life's irrational powers of regeneration and rejuvenation.[16] Like the *Lebensphilosophen* that he meets in the George circle, Kommerell deems man's passions and feelings a much more vital and dynamic source of existential meaning than his quest for knowledge and understanding. Therefore, in

The Missed Conversation 99

Kommerell's reading there is only one reason why Schiller ultimately manages to see through the deficiencies of an overly epistemological concept of friendship: the real-life and vital friendship that he develops with Goethe after 1794. Schiller finds in Goethe the 'complete opposite of his I' because he embodies a 'sensuality' and 'soul' that share in the absolute wellspring of life and pre-exists 'mind' (*Verstand*) and 'understanding' (*Begriff*). The famed relationship between Schiller and Goethe is the ideal type of Kommerell's concept of friendship and the backbone of his study of the German classic authors. For it is the intuitive and emotive connection with 'a Greek under a Nordic sky', which saves Schiller from his obsession with thought, encourages him to distance himself from Kantian philosophy and, ultimately, inspires his plea for an *aesthetic* education. 'His solution was Goethe and the way of being given in him: the formative-formed (*das Gestaltend-Gestaltete*), which shows how material and spirit are inseparably interpenetrated and which stands up in tremendous simplicity against the modern age'.[17]

When Kracauer meets Stefan George's friend Georg Simmel in the winter of 1907 in Berlin, he briefly falls under the influence of a type of *Lebensphilosophie* as well. Until the end of World War I, when Simmel dies, Kracauer remains quite taken with the idea that the products of culture need to be first and foremost analyzed as an expression and remodeling of the flux of life and the surrounding world's internal coherence. In Kracauer's view, Simmel's philosophy and sociology revolve around a 'metaphysics of life' that brings *unity* to man's many constructs and projects. It is Simmel's task to 'grasp the manifold as a totality and to somehow master this totality, experience its essence, and express it'. 'One of Simmel's fundamental aims is to rid every spiritual/intellectual phenomenon of its false being-unto-itself and show how it is embedded in the larger contexts of life'.[18] Kracauer's own, first, essay on the topic of friendship (1917/1918) offers a convincing illustration of his interest in *Lebensphilosophie* and the early affinities with Kommerell's views. According to Kracauer, as well, friendship counts among the most profound relationships two individuals can potentially build up. While any individual is characterized by a unique and irreplaceable 'soul', true friendship refers to a lived 'interconnection' (*Zusammenhang*) between two souls. Friendship brings with it an internal 'completion' (*Ergänzung*) of an individual's soul since it allows him to truly recognize his own deepest strivings and passions in those of someone else: 'Ideal friendship is . . . two people finding each other according to their whole being, which is united in the I-consciousness'.[19] This lived connection does not only cure the friend of any sense of social or psychological isolation but comes together with a distinct metaphysical and political weight. Like Kommerell, Kracauer opposes true friendship to social relationships that have either a merely instrumental value (e.g., camaraderie

100   *Unworldliness in Twentieth Century German Thought*

[*Kameradschaft*]) or do not reach into the deeper layers of one's psyche (e.g., collegial relationship [*Fachgenossenschaft*] or acquaintanceship [*Bekanntschaft*]). Like Kommerell, moreover, Kracauer insists that friendship denotes a genuine 'community of values and ideals' (*Gesinnungs- und Idealgemeinschaft*) in which our souls are 'expanded' (*erweitet*) and ultimately 'sublated' (*aufgehoben*) in a supra-individual unity: friendship is 'the expansion of being' through a 'realisation of one's innate approaches'. 'Everyone lives two souls'.[20]

This influence of the *Lebensphilosophen* on Kracauer's early writings does not initially last very long, launching him on a path that, for the next twenty years, will set his thinking apart from that of Kommerell. In Kracauer's view, World War I does not leave the optimistic assumption of an underlying principle of vitality and the internal unity of the surrounding world unscathed. By the early 1920s Kracauer criticizes Simmel's naive belief in 'life as the last absolute' and connects it to a pernicious type of relativism.

> (T)his doctrine recognized life-transcending norms and values only for the time being, so to speak, and destroyed the absolute in the very act of making the ebb and flow that is indifferent to value – in other words, the process of life – into an absolute.[21]

'This wandering from relation to relation . . . gets lost in the infinite'.[22] Kracauer's *second* essay on friendship, published in 1921, is a case-in-point of this growing discomfort with the main presuppositions of *Lebensphilosophie*. While not explicitly rejecting his earlier (Kommerell-like) ideas on the topic, Kracauer does move away from an analysis of the ideal friendship as an expression of shared vitality and the retrieval of a lived connection. Instead, he focuses on the '*mittlerer Freundschaft*' ('in between friendship') that remains on the surface of one's psyche. In the early 1920s, Kracauer is less fascinated with the lived 'interconnection' between two souls than with the fact that, in the '*mittlerer Freundschafte*' 'a good part of one's being, whole stretches of one's life lie outside the relationship'.[23] Moreover, Kracauer seeks above all to understand what happens to a friendship when two friends are *separated*. This, he argues, should not be considered a merely harmful event. 'Even if friendship, like every human connection, ultimately draws its strength from direct verbal intercourse, the periods of separation also play a significant and by no means negative role in it'.[24] In Kracauer's view, friends retain 'an image' (*Bild*) of each other that lives on during the time of separation. Because this image evolves together with the mental and psychological processes that an individual undergoes, it steadily loosens up its connection with the person it originally was an image of: friends 'carry an image of each other, of which it is uncertain whether it still

The Missed Conversation 101

corresponds to reality'.[25] For this reason, Kracauer suggests that friendship is ultimately not so much a relation of fusion between individuals as one of internal *division*. Friends who separate from each other continue a mental and emotional dialogue with the image they have preserved from each other, but they are inevitably haunted by the inaccessibility of the real person behind that image: there is no way to find out for sure whether the feelings and opinions that are projected onto a friend's internalized image are an accurate reflection of his real disposition. 'In the first place, one is closer to the image of the friend than to the friend himself'.[26] The awareness that one's most profound relations are marked by an inherent lack of immediacy and transparency comes with profound consequences for the metaphysical and political weight that Kracauer had earlier attached to friendship. Unlike Kommerell, Kracauer highlights the difference between love and friendship. Referring to a genuine 'merging' (*Verschmelzung*) of two souls, love is described as a deep longing to withstand the flow of time by way of an unshakeable unity, a common trajectory, and shared experiences. 'In love, this is understood to mean the course of life as it is and spreads out in time, with its good and repulsive sides and all that it brings day after day of happiness and suffering'.[27] Friendship, to the contrary, is not connected to the retrieval of an uninterrupted continuity but to an anticipation, and even acceptance, of transience and contingency. According to Kracauer, the confrontation with the possibility of separation and, in the last instance, death of one's friends belongs to the inner core of all true friendships.

> The dawning realisation of the end of the bond makes both friends self-conscious and closes their mouths. While they are still together, they already feel separated in reality. Their condition is like that of a person who has already packed all his bags for departure and is forced to remain in the empty, bare flat for a long time.[28]

In opposition to Kommerell, therefore, Kracauer now no longer regards friendship as a metaphysical ground for a *Volk* that builds on shared ancestors and a fated future. The community that is founded in friendship is at all times a historical one, mediated by the impermanence and openness of all historical events.

When, in 1922, Kracauer is made responsible for the feuilleton section of the *Frankfurter Zeitung*, he further turns away from the sweeping claims and heavy-handed jargon of thinkers like Simmel, George, and Kommerell.[29] With regard to both style and content, a large part of his output in the 1920s can be read as a rejection of the framework that underlies Kommerell's writings of that same era.[30] In this period, Kracauer embraces the positive and critical value of processes of fragmentation, negation, and

102 Unworldliness in Twentieth Century German Thought

de-selfing. In sharp and short essays that are written for a broad audience, Kracauer introduces his own alternative to the *Geistesbücher*. Kracauer rejects two of the main categories that underlie the work of the George circle and Kommerell in specific: that of a unique, unified, and spiritual community, and that of the great individual who is deemed capable of growing into a historical force that lights the path ahead for everyone else. In his essay 'The Group as Bearer of Ideas' (1922) Kracauer rejects the suggestion that a specific group of people can incarnate a spiritual life that surpasses the psychological limitations of each of its members. According to Kracauer, a group organizes itself on the basis of traits that are shared by all of its members and, as a consequence, retain a fundamental 'coarseness'. For this singling out of specific characteristics that are shared by all members of the group comes at the cost of denying the complexity and psychological wealth of each of the individuals: 'The people united in the group are no longer fully individuals, but only fragments of individuals whose very right to exist is exclusively a function of the group's goal'.[31] Kracauer's suggestion that individuals are inhibited to express the profundities of their personality when they join in a specific community is at odds with Kommerell's belief that the literary Greats can be deemed forerunners to an enriched, new German people: 'When a number of people are welded together into a group, it is utterly impossible for them to enter into this relationship with the full range of their souls. . . . In terms of features and aspirations, the latter (group individuality) is impoverished compared with the former (solitary self), lacking the fruitful and creative spiritual foundation that emits a rationally incomprehensible abundance of contents'.[32]

In a short article in the *Frankfurter Zeitung* from June 29, 1930, Kracauer goes a step further and even casts aside the very concept of a spiritually enriched 'solitary self'. His critique of this concept is introduced in the context of an analysis of the popularity of literary and scholarly biographies. Such biographies are, in his view, symptomatic of a dangerous type of 'evasion'.[33] While Kracauer does not explicitly refer to the *Geistesbücher* or Kommerell's work, the main literary format of the George-circle is here recast as a 'cult of hero worship'.[34] Biographies are deemed unable to capture the true conditions, let alone the possible resolutions, of the deep social, political, and historical conflict that destabilizes the world. The main reason of this flaw is that, in modern societies, individuals are but members of an anonymous mass and no soulful, internally unified 'selves'. Since the modern individual is plagued by feelings of worthlessness and the inadequacy of human action, the exploration of a protagonist's inner strivings and convictions can now no longer regarded as a convincing source of existential meaning or societal commitment: 'In the most recent past, people have been forced to experience their own insignificance – as well as that of others – all too persistently for them to still

The Missed Conversation 103

believe in the sovereign power of any one individual. It is precisely this sovereign power, however, which is the premise of the bourgeois literature produced during the years preceding the war'.[35] For Kracauer, the format of the biography is most often the expression of a reactionary attitude because it is motivated by a pseudo-mystical longing for a 'redemption'.[36] Instead of looking at the disempowerment of the individual squarely in the eye, biographies tend to sketch the conflict between man and the world as a type of *Bildung* in which the individual ultimately overcomes external obstacles. In such biographies, the awareness that modern man is reduced to a powerless state of anonymity 'do(es) not lead (the bourgeoisie) to draw any conclusions capable of illuminating the current situation. In the interest of self-preservation, the bourgeoisie shies away from confronting that situation'.[37]

In the most influential essay from this period, *The Mass Ornament* (1927), Kracauer elaborates on the underlying causes of this bourgeois 'evasion'. He connects the widespread 'retreat . . . into mythological structures of meaning' and the embrace of an 'irreality' to the structure of a capitalist society.[38] Anticipating Adorno and Horkheimer's later argument about the 'dialectics of enlightenment', Kracauer maintains that the quest for ceaseless rationalization, functionalism, and utilitarianism that underlies capitalism is itself a blind spot that is never reasonably questioned. For this reason, there is an inherent link between the *Ratio* of modern societies and the *un*-reason that numbs our critical faculties: capitalism 'rationalizes not too much but rather *too little*. . . . The prevailing abstractness reveals that the process of demythologization has not come to an end'.[39] The main symptom of this lack of reason is the creation of a culture that no longer '*encompasses man*'.[40] The 'mass ornament' is Kracauer's concept to describe a realm of culture that is no longer expressive of a people's spirit, self-identity, and core values. In capitalism, the cultural artifacts that are produced by man are not the lived result of his inner strivings or ambitions, but they stand over against him as external and alien entities. 'Although the masses give rise to the ornament, they are not involved in thinking it through. . . . The ornament resembles *aerial photographs* of landscapes and cities in that it does not emerge out of the interior of the given conditions, but rather appears above them'.[41] Kracauer's main example of such a mass ornament is the popular dance troupe Tiller Girls, a group of dancers who were drilled in military fashion to move and dance flawlessly together. Their choreographies result in nearly disembodied, mathematically perfect figures that break up the organic and natural unity of the individual dancer's body. 'The Tiller Girls can no longer be reassembled into human beings after the fact. Their mass gymnastics are never performed by the fully preserved bodies, whose contortions defy rational understanding. Arms, thighs, and other segments are the smallest component part of the

104 *Unworldliness in Twentieth Century German Thought*

composition'.[42] For Kracauer, this mass ornament is governed by the same type of functionalist and abstract *Ratio* that underlies the division of labor in mass industrialization and assembly-line production. No longer expressive of any spiritual or moral value, it is an *'end in itself'* that takes place in a 'vacuum'.[43] By the end of the 1920s, Kracauer has sufficiently moved away from the jargon of *Lebensphilosophie* to no longer merely deplore this loss of a soulful, lived, and shared world: '(T)he *aesthetic* pleasure gained from ornamental mass movements is *legitimate'*.[44] In spite of its inner emptiness, the mass ornament is of great importance because it at least reflects the real, *de*-worlded conditions of the working class, and the increased sense of replaceability that resonates in the minds of its members. As a consequence, Kracauer's main scorn is not directed toward mass ornament as such but toward the bourgeois appeal to worn-out ideals that, one should add, the products of the George-circle are a foremost illustration of. These need to be considered as hollow and far more dangerous than the mass ornament.

> Enterprises that ignore our historical context and attempt to reconstruct a form of state, a community, a mode of artistic creation that depends upon a type of man who has already been impugned by contemporary thinking – a type of man who by all rights no longer exists – such enterprises do not transcend the mass ornament's empty and superficial shallowness but flee from its reality.[45]

III

With these oppositions between Kommerell and Kracauer's writings of the 1920s in the back of our mind, it comes as a big surprise that their reading of Cervantes will run in a parallel direction. These unexpected commonalities can only be brought to light when we first understand how the thoughts of both authors are gradually bending toward each other from the 1930s onward. Kommerell's rupture with Stefan George is a major event in this regard.[46] In the years after the publication of *Der Dichter als Führer*, Kommerell becomes uncomfortable with the mystical and eschatological assumptions of George's project and takes issue with some of the overblown claims that underlie his mixture of aesthetics, religion, and politics. The George circle is now no longer considered an intellectual vanguard but an authoritarian milieu that stifles individual liberty and intellectual freedom. In June 1930, when Kommerell refuses to become a member of the Foundation that would be tasked with the care over Stefan George's heritage and archive, a clash can no longer be averted. The members of the circle, bound by a code of secrecy, are forced to break off all contact with Kommerell. Kommerell, for his part, notes in his diary: 'I was

28 years old and the decision not to let anyone, no matter how great, touch my self-respect overcame all inhibitions'.[47] Kommerell leaves for Frankfurt to finish his *Habilitationsschrift* and dedicates his inaugural speech of November 1, 1930 to another apostate of the George circle: Hugo von Hofmannstahl. The lecture amounts to a downright patricide since von Hofmanstahl is described as the antithesis of the German *Führer* that was so central to Kommerell's early work: 'To be a leader (*Führer*) means to solve the tasks of the time in such a way that the solution is also valid for others. . . . The opposite is poignant in (von Hofmannstahl's) work, (and) has become permanent in his work: the soul that calls into the air and to which no answer is given'.[48]

The rupture with George will have a profound impact on the final phase of Kommerell's intellectual trajectory, that is, the years between the early 1930s and his premature death in 1944. Kommerell's book-length study of the German humorous writer Jean Paul (1763–1825) (1933) can be read as the confirmation of this shift since it no longer focuses on the powers of classical art but on the crisis of art in modernity. Throughout the book, Kommerell plays Goethe and Jean Paul off against each other: while Goethe is firmly anchored in the social stratifications of a bourgeois world, Jean Paul exemplifies the type of writer who is perplexed by the upheavals of his time.[49] 'Both Goethe and Jean Paul are poets of the bourgeoisie . . . – but in Goethe bourgeoisie is still a class (*Stand*), while in Jean Paul it is only deplorable (*mißstand*)'.[50] In Kommerell's reading, Goethe is a physiognomic writer who describes the myriad ways in which a rich emotional life can express itself in an external medium such as the human body, nature, or language.[51] Jean Paul, to the contrary, is believed to have cut through this stable connection between an internal, immaterial world and an external, material one. In Jean Paul's work the soul is at once driven by the impulse to express itself and haunted by the incapacity of doing so. By allocating a central position to 'gestures of the soul', Jean Paul diagnoses the breakdown of the main dispositions that, in Goethe's work, could still function as a stable manifestation of man's mental and emotional life. The human body, first of all, is for Jean Paul a merely material substratum and confronts man with an uncanny presence deep within his most intimate self. In Jean Paul's work, the human body is never fully *lived* by or *expressive* of the ego since it cannot shed a lifeless mechanicity. This clash between soul and body drowns out the voice of an internally unified and authentic ego, burdening the individual with unmistakable feelings of fragmentation and fakery. 'The beginning is a sentiment of self that experiences in every possible gesture and especially in every personal gesture something false, a disfiguration of the inner (*Verunstaltung des Inneren*), according to which it is precisely the truest presentation that appears to blaspheme spirit. Looking in the mirror, the I discerns a pamphlet attached to it and, indeed

106 *Unworldliness in Twentieth Century German Thought*

incorporated by it'.[52] Second, Jean Paul is no more inclined to meet nature as an unspoiled reflection of the human passions. While, in Goethe's work 'nature appears like a beloved in the eye of the lover: not with an imposed self, but with its own', Jean Paul's 'gestures of nature' describe the loss of the mysterious beauty of nature.[53] The human soul does seem inclined to project its inner strivings onto nature, but not without thereby dislodging nature from any contents that could properly be called its own. When, in Jean Paul's work, human beings perceive natural phenomena as mirrors of their own selves, this experience yields no sense of meaningful recognition or fulfillment. Instead, it dissolves both the intimacy of the human psyche and the unalloyed autonomy of nature. 'Nature is so much, is so much everything and allows for so much interpretation that Jean Paul's thought is also not entirely alien to it, that a sound sleeps in its vaults for him too'.[54] Third, Kommerell takes Jean Paul to have deprived even the medium of language of some of its expressive powers. Jean Paul's 'pure gestures' (*reine Gebärde*) point toward a language that communicates nothing but *itself*, having more or less suspended the reference to an extra-linguistic content or meaning. Jean Paul thus pushes language beyond its limits as a means of signification. For such a language of 'pure' gestures, or 'overproze', opens to no more than a disjointed 'overworld' (*Überwelt*) of troubled and chaotic, dreamlike associations and no longer conjures a stable, shared, and external lifeworld of things and events. With language thus being brought to 'sing', the difference between poetry and prose all but gives way. Such non-signifying 'pure' gestures remain self-referential and suspended in a state of mere 'potentiality', thereby capturing all the better the sense of helplessness, seclusion, and *de*-worldedness that marks the modern soul:

> The linguistic inspirations in which the soul expresses itself here . . . are the pure possibility of speaking itself and, taken together with the gestures of the soul and of nature, point to their extra-worldly origin. These 'pure gestures' have surrendered every claim to reality . . . consumingly turned inward, the soul paints itself with its own luminous colours.[55]

With his references to the 'disfiguration of the inner' in Jean Paul's writings, Kommerell rejects the main presupposition of his earlier study: there is now no longer any talk of the *Vorbild* of a shared culture and internally coherent world that fulfills the souls of its individual members. Modern man is on his own and remains cut off from any communal *Volk* or 'Lebensgrund'. However, one should not exaggerate the conceptual changes that Kommerell's writings undergo after his rupture with the George circle. Unlike the Kracauer of the 1920s, the Kommerell of the 1930s does clearly continue to deplore the loss of the promise of a shared culture and

The Missed Conversation 107

lifeworld. Rather than doing away completely with the *Lebensphilosophie* that once enthused him, Kommerell remains driven by the quest to make some of its intuitions serviceable for modern man, however unworldly his existence may have become. From the 1930s onward Kommerell's philosophy may have shed most of its eschatological assumptions and political ambitions, but it remains founded in the idea that man, even in his isolated state, can and should encounter the lifeworld as animated by a mysterious beauty and truth.[56] What continues to matter most to Kommerell is to combat the forlornness and mechanicity of the modern world through a type of re-enchantment. Unlike the early Kracauer, Kommerell will in no way be inclined to embrace the lifeless forms of mass entertainment, such as the Tiller Girls, as the sole 'legitimate' art for a modern society. It is, then, hardly a surprise that Kommerell does not in fact applaud the deworldedness that he so succinctly describes in Jean Paul's literary work. Though he is noticeably taken with the creative genius of Jean Paul, it is clear whose side he is on in his standoff with Goethe. Throughout the book, Kommerell takes Jean Paul to task for conjuring a pernicious unworldliness in which the ties with the lifeworld are annihilated. In Kommerell's view, the humor in Jean Paul's work is of a very dangerous type since it cannot break through the confines of interiority, thereby showing itself an heir to the romantic use of irony: 'Everything (aims) at boundless internalisation (*grenzenlose Verinnerlichung*)'.[57] Jean Paul's 'gestures' of the soul, nature, and language can therefore in no way be considered a laudable response to the challenges of modernity. His appeal to a 'pure' language that no longer communicates a content and ought to make language 'sing' does not result in true poetry, but in an unsuccessful mixture of poetry and prose. This shatters the unity of his novels and burdens them with an inescapable heterogeneity: Jean Paul is 'the born enemy of rhythm'.[58] In fact, Jean Paul's gestures do not for this reason even deserve to be called 'gestures' at all. 'As long as "external" life can be seen as beautiful, or, in so far as it has melody, can be heard as beautiful, spirit is not limitlessly free to reject it. . . . The fully freed spirit (in Jean Paul's work) is a consequence of a bourgeoisie that has lost its gestures'.[59] In other words, Jean Paul's work does not just isolate the individual from his peers (a move that will also underlie Kommerell's own work from the 1930s onward), but it estranges him from the universe at large since it brings down all that can still yield unity, beauty, and truth. This is, according to Kommerell, no less dangerous than depriving the human soul of its 'earthly fuel' (*irdischen Brennstoff*).[60]

'Von Wesen des Lyrischen Gedichts', the introduction to the volume *Gedanken über Gedichte* (1943) can be read as a programmatic text for this final stage of Kommerell's intellectual project, marking the conceptual distance that has been covered since the publication of *Der Dichter als Führer* in 1928. On account of an 'ontological alienation' (*Seinsentfremdung*)

108 *Unworldliness in Twentieth Century German Thought*

the individual can no longer be believed to experience the lived ties with a spiritual community as the wellspring of existential meaning.[61] This affects the fate of modern poetry as well, since, in opposition to the 'convivial life' (*geselligen Leben*) of yore, modern art is no longer governed by the social, religious, and political rituals and practices that once brought unity and coherence to a *Volk*.[62] Instead, modern poetry stems from the 'soul' of the individual artist himself. This cannot but deflate the quasi-mystical claims that motivated Kommerell's early study: modern poetry, it is now affirmed, has 'lost its connection with destiny' (*die Bindung mit Schicksal*) and become 'spontaneous'.[63] No longer resting on the recovery of shared and supposedly trans-historical truths, poetry is now a thing of 'pure form' (*reine Formlichkeit*) and 'free rhythms' (*freie Rhythmen*).[64] However, this modern condition of individualization does not at all take away the poet's meaning-giving capacities. To the contrary, Kommerell insists that the modern poet's forms and rhythms continue to illuminate the path ahead. As the trustee of an 'ethical heritage' (*Sittenerbe*) it is he who is capable of 'outliving the crisis' and should be regarded as someone who 'sets right the confused traits of life' and 'founds laws of a secular-spiritual kind (*Gesetzgeber weltlich-geistiger Art*)'.[65] This trust in the capacities of the poet is underpinned by Kommerell's ambition to adapt some of the main assumptions of *Lebensphilosophie* for modern use. Though shedding the political-religious hyperboles of the late 1920s, Kommerell's later claims about the moral capabilities of the modern poet rest on the very same opposition between the intuitive recuperation of the powers of life on the one hand and the distrusted faculties of abstract thought and understanding on the other. The modern poet's creative powers are supposed to grow from his soul's intuitive interactions with the world. The poet, that is, perceives his surroundings as somehow 'human'[66] and 'enchanted' (*bezaubert*).[67] Though sanitized into a humanistic intellectual framework, *Lebensphilosophie* continues to illuminate Kommerell's path in the final years of his life. It is only by accepting its opposition between rational understanding and intuition, and by heeding its promise of a restored immediacy of life, that a non-alienated, properly human life is deemed retrievable. The most important categories for modern poetry, therefore, are 'being-affected' (*Betroffenheit*) and 'mood' (*Stimmung*): to the modern poet, the world is no external and alien outside that needs to be *known*, but a rich and expressive unity that gives itself freely to man and needs to be *responded to*. 'To the extent that an outside "tunes" (*stimmt*) the soul, or is "tuned" (*gestimmt*) by it, the manifoldness in (this outside) becomes univocal in itself. *Betroffenheit* is, to use an expression of Goethe's, the shock that has to precede solidescence'.[68] Even though this intuitive connection between the poet's inner world and his surroundings is 'unique' (*einmalig*) and cannot for this reason be 'handed down' (*überliefert*), art is capable of restoring the deep sensation that the world shares in the 'rhythm of the soul' and the 'feeling for life'.[69]

In the final years of his life, Kommerell develops this opposition between life (soul) and mind (thought) by differentiating between two different 'forces' (*Kräfte*) in language. On a first level, language serves as a means for 'communication' (*Mitteilung*) and 'understanding' (*Verständigung*).[70] Poetic language, however, shares in a much more originary and rich 'language of gestures' (*Gebärdesprache*) that does not so much communicate *something* as that it draws attention to its own expressive capacities. By making creative use of the acoustic qualities of certain words, the poet's language both suspends and surpasses the human need for knowledge and understanding. According to Kommerell, poetic language is a fulfillment (*Ergänzung*) since it is one with the spontaneous, revelatory dynamic of the world's unity, truth, and beauty.[71] In other words, unlike the language of non-signifying 'pure' gestures that characterizes Jean Paul's work, the *Gebärdensprache* of genuine poetry does not just open to an 'unrhythmic', fragmentary and chaotic 'overworld' but to the soulful immediacy and rhythm of life as such. In Kommerell's view, such poetry can counter the modern condition of spiritual isolation by bringing out the unspeakable mysteries of a world that is immediately present and does not cease to give itself to man. The poet's language thus points to a deeper 'silence' (*Schweigen*) or 'unsaid' (*Ungesagten*), and even a wholesome 'incapacity' (*Unvermögen*) that lies hidden within language.[72] It is this second level of language that manages to express man's intuitive *Betroffenheit* by a '*gestimmte*' world: 'So there is also something in words through which man responds to something that affects him (*auf irgend ihn Treffendes antwortet*), a gesture of the affected soul. (W)hile the virtuosity of language (as means for) conceptual designation has appeared as (language's) suitability and purpose in more recent times and reveals but little of its earlier stages, this other, repressed operation of language (as) a gesture and express(ion of) the soul's *Betroffenheit* perhaps points to its origin'.[73]

In this final stage of his life, Kommerell credits the poet with the capacity to combat spiritual isolation by restoring the lived veneration for the world's mysteries. By allowing a foundational 'language of gestures' to ring through his words, the poet is believed to tap into a simplicity of truth and beauty that is much more primary than the stale constructions of society. 'Two qualities will never be lacking in the poetic individual who is called to write a lyric poem: a loving openness to life and a capacity for fulfilment that saves the undivided simplicity of human existence in the midst of one-sided activities and dispositions'.[74] As a consequence, the same authors who, in the 1920s, were deemed the pioneers of a new political community, Goethe and Schiller, are now returning in a very different guise: as masters of 'pure forms' and 'free rhythms', they now provide proof for

110 *Unworldliness in Twentieth Century German Thought*

art's *autonomy* vis-à-vis the vicissitudes of the public and political domain. Around this time, and from the same perspective, Kommerell also turns to the counter-tradition of authors such as Kleist and Rilke. Rilke's *Dueno Elegies*, for instance, are analyzed as a poetic response to a non-human, angelic presence in the world. The mysterious truths of this 'cult of similarities' (*Ahnenkult*) can only be intuitively felt but never properly known or understood. As a source of deep wisdom, they are sharply opposed to the religious-political determinations of 'myth' and the false claims about a 'blood-relationship' (*Blutzusammenhang*) that the young Kommerell once came close to embracing: 'It is precisely the fact that the dimensions that brush up against mankind are not made clear, that no myth can overcome the not-knowing and the shudder before them, that makes up the humility and truthfulness of these elegies'.[75] It is also around this time, and along these lines, that Kommerell moves beyond both the German canon and counter-canon and professes his love for world literature. The plays of Commedia dell'Arte, for instance, recast the human body as a 'sleeping universe of gestures' that rejuvenates our sense of amazement at the world and pierces through the 'vanity of human speech, the deceit of language'.[76]

Kommerell's two essays on Cervantes, 'Humoristische Personifikationen in Don Quixote' (1938) and 'Don Quijote und Simplicissimus' (late 1930s) stem from these same viewpoints.[77] According to Kommerell, the novel is not set up as a linearly developed narrative but as a 'schema' with recurrent variations.[78] Bringing unity to the book is the theme of Don Quixote's 'adventure' that leads to a long series of unexpected situations. But, unlike the previous authors that were analyzed, Kommerell has a mostly *negative* view of Don Quixote. 'No line of the book allows for the interpretation that Don Quixote – through the supreme intensification of subjectivity – possesses insight into true being'.[79] In the reading of Kommerell, Don Quixote's madness is not redeemed by the firmness of his convictions (Lukács, Jünger), nor by the subtle, self-reflective structure that sets apart *Don Quixote* as the first truly modern novel (Adorno). Don Quixote's 'missed relations to the world (*verfehlte Weltberührungen*)'[80] are neither the token of a sustained opposition to the world, transmuting its overall meaninglessness into the instigator of existential and spiritual strength (Lukács, Jünger), nor a literary motif that 'negates' the current state of the world and lays bare its overall contingency (Bloch, Adorno). Kommerell takes issue with both the gnostic and the critical undertones that resonate in the previously discussed interpretations of *Don Quixote*. In his view, Cervantes is in no way interested in showing up the meaninglessness or injustice of the world. According to Kommerell, *Don Quixote* describes that the lifeworld *is* saturated with an existential significance, goodness, and unity; it is just that its protagonist, by his own doing, deprives himself of the possibility to meet the lifeworld in just this manner. The reason for

The Missed Conversation   111

this misapprehension lies according to Kommerell, not in Don Quixote's supposedly irrational behavior, but, to the contrary, in his excessive use of the faculty of reason. It is precisely his tendency to *overthink* everything, which impedes Don Quixote's non-mediated, intuitive, and 'soulful' interaction with the world. '(A)bove all . . . has human thought, when it turns on itself, sunk back into interpretation (*dem Deuten verfallen*)'.[81] Kommerell's interest in Don Quixote does therefore not stem from a fascination with the creative potential of *un*worldliness. Don Quixote is above all a 'personification' of a specific, though deeply flawed, 'exploration of the world and exploration of the self' (*Weltverkennung and Selbstverkennung*) and thus exemplifies a 'lived experience' (*Erlebnisform*) rather than a psychological character trait.[82] Kommerell thereby distinguishes three different phases that mark Don Quixote's (mis)adventure. In a first phase, thought and imagination, in the form of reading, take over from an intuitive grasp of life and result in a distortion of all the world's things and events. 'This is the first act of every adventure: a distorted assessment (*verfälschte Bestandsaufnahme*)'.[83] Because Don Quixote cannot help but to act on his thoughts, the second phase brings an immediate and painful revenge on the part of the world. 'The objects, resisting the interpretation imposed on them, respond according to their true nature with an action that is mentally and often physically painful for the interpreter'.[84] In the third phase of Don Quixote's dealings, his thoughts and imagination once again cloud over his sense of better judgment, explaining away the reactions of the outside world as the intervention of a wicked sorcerer.

> (T)o our surprise, the knight also absorbs the most urgent indications of the truth of his overall account by way of true epistemological leniency: one must not to be misled; It is magicians who disturb the workings of the organs of perception.[85]

The conceptual foundations of Kommerell's interpretation become most clear in his notes on the second book of *Don Quixote*. Because this second book starts from the idea that some of the people Don Quixote encounters have, in the meanwhile, read the first book, Cervantes manages to conjure a world that is no longer straightforwardly antithetical to the erring knight. To the contrary, the specific cruelty that awaits Don Quixote in the second book revolves around the attempts of figures such as the duke and the duchess to fool him into thinking that the world does actually correspond to his delusions. While Bloch is inclined to read the pranks of the ducal couple as a positive feature because they enable Don Quixote to continue perceiving the world entirely on his own terms (Bloch: 'Don Quixote . . . sees even here nothing but the embodiment of the wishful dreams in which he believes'[86]), Kommerell considers them nefarious because they

112 *Unworldliness in Twentieth Century German Thought*

obliterate any lived interaction with the world in its current state. When the world is made to comply with Don Quixote's madness, this does not create the possibility of a wholesome, *different* worldview (Bloch), but it obfuscates the very duality between the rich reality of the world and the stale peregrinations of human thought – between the spiritual spontaneity of life and the sterile abstractions of understanding. Kommerell's reference to the vacuity of the chivalric novels that cause Don Quixote's madness is, *ex negativo*, the proof of his belief in the lifeworld's existential plenitude and internal unity. 'While there was once a chivalric world, there is no "world" of chivalric books; rather, it denotes that they have run out of world'.[87] For the *Lebensphilosoph* that Kommerell has remained all along, even in the later years of his life, the destruction of life's immanent richness by pre-established thought patterns and *idées fixes* is the epitome of spiritual poverty. When Don Quixote's world is made to 'obey his idea (of that world)' this proclaims victory for the unfruitful act of reading and thinking over the soulful dynamic of life itself. Don Quixote's goings are now no more than a 'life derived from reading' (*Nachgelesenem Leben*), utterly blind to the reality of the lifeworld's own mysteries and beauties.

In Kommerell's view, hence, Don Quixote does not stand for the irrationality of genuine faith (Lukács, Jünger) or the precariousness of hope (Bloch, Adorno) but for the life-denying excesses of abstract thought and reasoning. Kommerell drives home this point in two different ways. The first one revolves around the claim that Cervantes' novel is steeped in Christian beliefs. This does not mean that Kommerell, like Bloch, turns Don Quixote into a social and political commentator who uses the Christian faith to denounce the ills of capitalism and casts a utopian light on the possibility of a just and equal society. To the contrary, Don Quixote's willingness to 'sacrifice' himself for the excesses of abstract thought and imagination make of him the quintessential 'sinner' who 'arrogates to himself a grounding and foundational position where everything is already grounded and founded by a secular and mental register'.[88] As a consequence, the novel's ending is highly important to Kommerell. It is there that Don Quixote is met by the Grace of God, enabling, at first, the transformation of his earlier distorted 'beliefs' into a most 'radical disbelief' but, subsequently and more importantly, returning him to the true belief that is the Christian faith: '(T)he second part triumphs with the profound disillusionment from the delusion, which is by no means brought about by a development or purification of the hero by his own power, but by God's intervention in his sleep'.[89]

The key to Kommerell's interpretation of Cervantes lies in a figure that, in spite of its overall presence throughout the book, plays no crucial role in the readings of Lukács, Jünger, Bloch, and Adorno: Sancho Panza. Only Lukács and Bloch hint at the importance of Don Quixote's companion, differentiating, for example, between the easily misled squire of the early

The Missed Conversation 113

books and the later governor with 'so much sound common sense'[90] and 'sober wisdom'.[91] While in Lukács' (early) reading, 'Don Quixote and Sancho Panza have no relationship with one another, at least not as human beings',[92] Kommerell stresses that they 'belong to each other'.[93] For Kommerell, that is, the presence of Sancho Panza indicates the specific lived experience that runs counter to Don Quixote's overly abstract worldview: 'both are perennial ways to get hold of the world (*ewige Weisen, die Welt zu nehmen*)'.[94] In Kommerell's reading, Sancho Panza counteracts the spiritual poverty of his master, not on account of any firm convictions or rich ideals but on account of the very absence of such strong viewpoints and values. Sancho Panza is characterized by the 'absence of an idea' (*Mangel eines Idee*): 'he withdraws from the true and spiritual' (*er hebt ab vor dem Wahren und Geistigen*).[95] Sancho Panza is a liberating presence in Cervantes' novel because, unlike his master, he lacks the imaginative power to neutralize the world's actual state. While Don Quixote can only be redeemed when the novel (and his adventure) ends, and God's Grace overturns his delusions, Sancho Panza's presence is redemptive throughout the entire book, and for this very reason that 'clinging to or abandoning a basis of ideas is not a condition of existence: his comfort in life and habits remain completely unaffected by belief and non-belief in the Lord'.[96] In other words, Sancho Panza embodies the direct, intuitive, and 'soulful' interaction with the world that is so lacking in Don Quixote's excessively mediated existence. Sancho Panza stands for the instinctive embrace of the non-rational powers of life as such, and for a lived awareness of the infinite riches of the world at large. His is a 'pure lust for life' (*reine Lebenslust*) and an 'animalistic intelligence' (*animalistische Intelligenz*), and his 'natural wit' (*Mutterwitz*) is a perpetual 'antithesis to the idea' (*Widerspruch der Idee*). In Kommerell's reading, therefore, Sancho Panza remains above all loyal to the principle of never distrusting the immediacy of his senses, seeking out pleasure, and avoiding pain wherever he goes.[97]

Like his view of Don Quixote, Kommerell's interpretation of Sancho Panza revolves around the notion of 'adventure'. Don Quixote's adventure both starts and ends with the victory of the unshakeable beliefs he gathered while reading chivalry romances, but Sancho Panza embraces the 'allure of the unpredictable' (*Reiz des Unberechenbaren*) out of an instinctive gusto for the surprises of life. The pranks of the ducal couple therefore have a very different meaning to Sancho Panza than to Don Quixote. When Sancho Panza is tricked into believing that he is the governor of the island Barataria, this is not indicative of the world's having been made fully 'obedient' to a false 'idea'. To the contrary, Sancho Panza is believed to practice an 'instinctive governing' that is inspired by the deep trust in folk wisdom and an innate feel for justice.[98] This victory of life over understanding, and of soul over thought, is corroborated by Sancho Panza's idiosyncratic

114 *Unworldliness in Twentieth Century German Thought*

use of language. His playful use of traditional sayings and proverbs ought not to be reduced to nonsensical prattle since it amounts to a 'higher language' (*hohere Sprache*) and age-old wisdom that break through the vanities of human knowledge and understanding. 'In the proverb, the mind is idle. Sancho Panza does not like thinking, he needs something to lean on: instead of the thought, it is the turning point which presents itself in him (*statt des Gedankens stellt sich bei ihm die Wendung ein*); instead of the combination (of ideas), it is memory which does the work, most vividly, but by no means nurtured by any cooperation with judgement; morally, he likewise tends to continuity, for in the proverb, the forefathers think for us and settle our dilemmas through the most simple example. It is the thought-form of experience (*die Denkform der Erfahrung*) – without the revision of the experience'.[99]

Kommerell's reading of *Don Quixote* attests to the final stage of his thinking, when he trusts art to disclose the plenitude of life. He pits the 'brilliance' of Cervantes' 'inventing, making, building' against a 'brilliance of meaning-giving' (*Genialität des Sinngebens*) and argues that the latter is lacking in the Spanish author.[100] In contrast to Lukács, Jünger, Bloch, and Adorno, Kommerell does not connect Cervantes' novel to a sustained quest for meaning in a meaningless universe (Lukács and Jünger) nor to the unsuspected retrieval of hope in a contingent world (Bloch and Adorno). For him, there is something corrupted to both the unceasing attempt to give meaning and the desperate clinging to hope, and this for the reason that the world is not all that forsaken to begin with. Neither the opposition to, nor the negation of, the world in its current state can be considered an ethical stance since both attitudes forfeit the immanent riches of the life-world itself: 'How much possibility is hidden here, chuckling behind every reality. Possibilities of interpretation that lose themselves in the innermost parts of human beings as well as in the essence of the spirit! Because it never transcends, this book is transcendent like no other (*weil es niemals transzendiert, ist dieses Buch transzendent wie kein anderes*)'.[101] Cervantes is, above all, an inventor of characters and situations that bespeak the irreducible 'versatility' (*Vielseitigkeit*) of all worldly things and events.[102] Unlike the 'unrhythmic' and fragmented novels of Jean Paul, this multiplicity does not threaten the integrity of Cervantes' work. To the contrary, *Don Quixote* is 'form-creating' (*Gestaltschopfend*) and weaves together a large variety of literary genres into a 'supreme artistic . . . understanding' (*allerhöchstem . . . Kunstverstand*).[103] By pushing Sancho Panza to the center of the stage, Kommerell reads Cervantes' comic novel as the antithesis of Jean Paul's humorous stories: the last word is now no longer for the suffocating inwardness of an alienated mind (Jean Paul's protagonists, Don Quixote) but for a spontaneous recuperation of the world's many wonders (Sancho Panza).

V

There is a second author who is drawn by the figure of Sancho Panza when he comes nearer to the end of his life: Siegfried Kracauer. In the years immediately prior to his death he sends letters to both Adorno and Bloch, claiming that 'there is . . . a good bit of Sancho Panza in (him)' (1963) and that '(Bloch's) tempestuousness takes the breath away from the Sancho Panza in (him)' (1965).[104] Unlike Kommerell, Kracauer does not write extensively about Cervantes' novel, but, as we will see, Sancho Panza does play a crucial role in the last stage of his thinking. That the later Kracauer shares the later Kommerell's discomfort with Don Quixote's grandiose idealism should come as no big surprise when we first have a closer look at his precarious position from the 1930s onward. On February 28, 1933, one day after the *Reichstag* fire, Kracauer feels forced to flee Berlin and heads for Paris. After working three years as a correspondent for the *Frankfurt Zeitung*, the newspaper, as well, deems the situation in Germany insufficiently safe for a Jewish and left-leaning journalist and makes him their correspondent for the French capital. Nonetheless, in August 1933, they remove Kracauer from this position and thereby set off a downward spiral that will include months of internment by the Vichy regime in 1939 and distressing weeks in Marseille at the start of the war.[105] In April 1941, Kracauer finally manages to cross over to New York. Jobless and without income, his fate now depends on the generosity of his contacts in the United States, including Horkheimer, Adorno, and Meyer Shapiro. At last, he lands a position as an assistant to the film curator Iris Barry at the Museum of Modern Art and, funded with money from the Rockefeller Foundation, starts working on his first study of cinema *From Caligari to Hitler: A Psychological History of the German Film*.[106] Concerned with 'the psychological pattern of a people at a particular time', Kracauer draws the parallel between the mental strains that are suffered in pre-war, crisis-ridden Germany and the films that are produced in that same era and country.[107] He thereby singles out, for instance, the a-political escapism of the so-called mountain films and the yearning for an authoritarian figure in expressionist cinema as symptoms of a proto-fascist society. Unlike both Bloch and Adorno, Kracauer is determined to position himself as an *American*-German intellectual. In 1942, when he writes an essay 'Why France Liked Our Films', it is clear which viewpoint he has adopted in little more than a year's time: 'It is no longer a European observer who is making these observations'.[108] This means that Kracauer will start reading the work of thinkers that he had had less access to in Europe, such as John Dewey and A.N. Whitehead. These American sources will gradually supplement the European framework that supported his views from the 1920s. As we will see, however, they will also inspire him to again embrace the dynamic

116   *Unworldliness in Twentieth Century German Thought*

of a 'life as such' and therewith, paradoxically, push him back into the direction of the German *Lebensphilosophie* he had once rejected in no unclear terms. His political views, as well, take on a different guise. When Kracauer endorsed the Weimar left in the 1920s, he had already avoided the more radical positions that were held by some of his friends (including Bloch and Adorno), having always been more *against anti*-revolution than downright *pro*-revolution itself. In the Cold War years, however, this rejection of clearly articulated and radical political goals leads to a marked discomfort with *all* types of ideology.[109] Alongside a renewed embrace of some of the presuppositions of *Lebensphilosophie*, it is this humanist and centrist position that enables us to draw attention to some parallels between the later Kracauer and the later Kommerell.

From the many projects that Kracauer starts working on in the United States, two books stand out for the context of our discussion: *Theory of Film. The Redemption of Physical Reality* (1960) and *History. The Last Things before the Last* (posthumously published in 1969). In contrast to *From Caligari to Hitler*, Kracauer's *Theory of Film* revolves around a self-proclaimed 'realism'. Film is now no longer seen as a crystallization of the *mental* life of a people at a particular time but as the reproduction of *material* 'things in their concreteness'.[110] On a first reading, it might seem that Kracauer's philosophical and sociological position has not changed all that much in comparison to his analyses from the 1920s. The conceptual groundwork of *Theory of Film* is provided by a like-minded theory of modernity that singles out the dangers of excessive 'abstraction', 'technology', and 'loneliness'. In this way, Kracauer seems to extend his earlier ideas about a 'culture that no longer encompasses man', once again pointing out a deeply rooted 'relativism' and the absence of a 'faith in absolutes'. Like the early essays, *Theory of Film* is steeped in a melancholic confrontation with the 'ruins of ancient beliefs' and the concomitant 'ideological shelterlessness'.[111] Moreover, in the 1960s Kracauer once again warns for the pernicious impact of the retreat into 'irreality' and the risk of 'evasion'. In line with the early diagnosis of a society that 'rationalizes not too much but rather *too little*' (cf. supra), the later texts denounce an uncritical or 'mythic' use of science and technology. Science is no longer 'synonymous with reason' and 'actually indifferent to the form of our society'.[112] Therefore, blind faith in the progress of ratio, science, and technology is now deemed more a threat than a source of societal renewal. In the final decades of his life, Kracauer retains his earlier skepticism regarding all attempt to 'kindle religious ardor in shiftless souls' and worries about 'anti-intellectualistic propositions (that) fall on fertile soil today': '(I) t appears that the will to believe is matched by the incapacity for believing. Apathy spreads like an epidemic; the 'lonely crowd' fills the vacuum with surrogates'.[113]

The Missed Conversation 117

However, the conceptual threads that link up the work of the early and the later Kracauer are more thin than they might seem, and thinner than Kracauer *makes* them seem. For, after his move to the United States, Kracauer does think an 'escape from spiritual nakedness' is possible at all times. In his later texts, that is, we are believed to be able to 'rid ourselves of . . . abstractness' by fully embracing the 'world that is ours'.[114] In his *Theory of Film*, Kracauer credits a rediscovery of 'things in their concreteness' with the power to overturn and even re-enchant the alienated situation of modern man.[115] Kracauer's renewed optimism is above all dependent on his notion of 'reality'. For the later Kracauer, concrete reality stands for an infinite potential of change: it is a 'flux' of endless becoming that installs the hope that any given state can transform into something else. Photographic and filmic images are causally and indexically related to this concrete reality and, for this reason, reveal its inherent multiplicity and changeability. As such, they play a pivotal role in the 'redemption of physical reality', that is, they reopen man to the unexhausted potential of his surroundings. In this context, Kracauer distinguishes between a formative and a realistic use of the camera. While the former refers to the photographer or filmmaker's desire to go beyond physically existing reality and depict a clearly fictitious world, an internal state of mind or a plot-based narrative, the latter reproduces the wealth of reality 'as it is'. In Kracauer's view, there ought to be no doubt whatsoever that the realistic tendency deserves priority over the formative one: 'films may claim aesthetic validity if they build from their basis properties; like photographs, that is, they must record and reveal physical reality'.[116] According to this argument, the camera is capable of retrieving an unsuspected richness in our most immediate surroundings on account of its capacity to reveal their 'unstaged', 'fortuitous', 'endless', and 'indeterminate' nature. What seems like a mere factual existence is thus revealed to be a mysterious and vital presence that cannot fail to surprise and replenish our sense of possibility: photographic media reinvigorate the feeling for a 'fringe of indistinct multiple meanings' and a 'vague meaningfulness' in the world.[117]

Kracauer's marked opposition between the 'aesthetic character of (concrete) experience' and the excessive abstraction of science and technology brings his position close to that of the later Kommerell. Like Kommerell, Kracauer bets all of his money on a supposed, specifically human ability to 'discover the material world with its psychophysical correspondences'. Like Kommerell's concept of *Betroffenheit*, Kracauer's formula 'the redemption of physical reality' is meant to describe how we can overcome and overturn the distancing effect of abstract thought and understanding. For both thinkers, rediscovering our immediate surroundings as animated by a 'vague meaningfulness' suffices to trigger a lived response on our part: 'The truly decisive reason for the elusiveness of physical reality is the habit

118   *Unworldliness in Twentieth Century German Thought*

of abstract thinking we have acquired under the reign of science and technology. . . . We literally redeem this world from its dormant state, its state of virtual nonexistence, by endeavoring to experience it through the camera'.[118] These somewhat overbearing words should not be confused with a clear-cut idealization of the world in its current state. Neither Kracauer nor Kommerell equates the material world itself with an inherent meaning or beauty. But both thinkers do argue that artworks, be it poetry (Kommerell) or photographic and filmic images (Kracauer) can lay bare an unsuspected, soulful presence *within* it. In Kracauer's *Theory of Film*, this argument receives its most extreme (and startling) expression in a reference to the horrors of World War II and the Holocaust. The crux of Kracauer's argument is that, even when confronted with such extreme realities, images can engender a sensibility for the world's dynamic of immanent renewal. Even in such cases, a direct representation of 'things in their concreteness' can renew the belief in change. According to Kracauer, that is, the fear that the gravest suffering might be devoid of meaning will be warded off, if we only avoid the traps of abstract reasoning and imagination and muster the courage to confront it directly. 'In experiencing the rows of calves' heads or the litter of tortured human bodies in the films made of the Nazi concentration camps, we redeem horror from its invisibility behind the veils of panic and imagination'.[119]

The later Kracauer's humanistic 'turn to concrete reality' is most likely at least partly the result of an interest in American pragmatism and process-thinking. Still, his argument that an artwork 'records', 'reveals', and 'exposes' an immanent dynamic of renewal is also clearly indebted to the *Lebensphilosophie* that he had denounced from the early 1920s onward. In important passages of *Theory of Film*, he takes explicit recourse to the concept of a 'life as such' as an indication of what it is precisely that the camera recaptures. In fact, it seems as if Kracauer lifts these statements straight from the pages of his one-time mentor Georg Simmel. For Simmel, life is no quasi-religious or supra-historical force but the spirited impetus behind the manifold 'constructions' (*Gebilde*) of culture, such as images, artworks, and concepts. As we have seen in the first chapter, these products are described as the 'more than life' that draws meaning from life's process of continuous self-regeneration. 'As the definition of spiritual life one can . . . declare that (life) produces something with a meaning and law unto itself'.[120] Like Kracauer, Simmel pits the constructs of a vital culture against the staleness and excessive abstraction of solidified concepts and beliefs. In Simmel's view, the path toward such a vital culture is never fully closed off since life is characterized by an unending potential to 'transcend' itself, overstepping the boundaries of any determinate form or fixed content. 'Life is . . . always more life than that accommodated in the form currently allotted to and grown from it'.[121] For this reason, an unceasing process of

The Missed Conversation 119

rejuvenation flows in and through man's most worthwhile cultural products, making sure that such artifacts replenish the belief in the world's possibilities. The constructions of a healthy culture, hence, are never truly 'alien' to life, but remain affecting by sharing in its self-transcendence. 'The absoluteness of this other, of this *more* (i.e., the constructions of culture), that life creates or into which it penetrates, is precisely the formula and condition of life as it is lived: it *is* from the outset nothing other than a reaching-out-beyond-itself'.[122] In his later books, Kracauer returns to Simmel's suggestion that cultural products derive their worth from the flux of life and its becomings. In *Theory of Film*, filmic images are a prime example of the 'more than life' that reveals the wealth of 'life as such'. They 'point beyond the physical world to the extent that the shots or combinations of shots from which they are built carry multiple meanings. Due to the continuous influx of the psychophysical correspondences thus arouse, they suggest a reality which may fittingly be called "life". . . . (O)ne may . . . say that (films) have an affinity . . . for the continuum of life or the "flow of life", which of course is identical with open-ended life'.[123]

If we want to measure the distance between these later writings and the conceptual framework Kracauer had developed before the war, it is relevant to first compare *Theory of Film* to an early essay on photography from 1927. In this early text, the photographic image is believed to render a reality that is *cut off* from the sphere of life: photos present a 'nature devoid of meaning', and the '*go-for-broke game* of history'.[124] Photographic images are here believed to destabilize the ego, explode its inner unity, and, in short, resist the lived responsiveness through which a human being is supposed to retrieve the 'vague meaningfulness' of his surroundings. From this, Kracauer builds an argument that is structurally related to Adorno and Bloch's descriptions of a constructive and critical negation: photography estranges us from the lifeworld and, by that very token, shows up its shortcomings and injustices. For the post-war Kracauer, to the contrary, fragmentation is primarily a *liberating* event that illustrates that the world is an 'attracting' and 'intoxicating' place after all: 'We are free to experience (the world) *because* we are fragmented' (emphasis added).[125]

A comparison between the published version of *Theory of Film* and the so-called Marseille Notebooks, in which Kracauer noted down his first sketches for the book, is equally telling.[126] In this *Urtext*, Kracauer still rejects the influence of the *Lebensphilosophen* of the previous generation. The earlier Kracauer's framework builds on the idea that the mechanical expression of reality through film *diminishes*, rather than expands, the reach of the self and subjective experience. According to the pre-war Kracauer the human being's self-alienation cannot just be overcome through a direct expression of a supposedly unspoiled 'life as such': 'The task [of film] is to marshal disintegration itself'.[127] In the Marseille Notebooks Kracauer

120   *Unworldliness in Twentieth Century German Thought*

applauds the penchant of early films to, as Miriam Hansen puts it, 'debunk humanistic sentiments',[128] and he describes the experience of film as one that seizes 'a human being with skin and hair'.[129] As a consequence, the Marseille Notebooks have a deep affinity with the issue of mortality, and not with any type of *Lebensphilosophie*. Instead of suggesting that the camera bestows external objects with a type of 'vague meaningfulness', Kracauer uses the notebooks to defend the viewpoint that the camera embodies an 'allegorical' outlook that 'is indifferent vis-à-vis objects'.[130] The eye of the camera is wholly *unlike* a human eye in that the camera 'is interested in the refuse, in what is just there – both in and outside the human being'. Instead of discovering 'psychophysical correspondences', Kracauer argues for a type of mortification of the world. The close-up of a 'face', for instance, 'counts for nothing in film unless it includes the *death's head* beneath'.[131]

The terms 'allegorical', 'refuse', and 'death's head' and the reference to 'marshalling disintegration itself' are directly borrowed from the work of Walter Benjamin, who was stuck in Marseille together with Kracauer. In the view of both the pre-war Kracauer and Benjamin, the recuperation of a sudden evocativeness in outside objects has nothing to do with the exploration of an immanent, non-conceptual plenitude of life. The allegorical experience of the world is at odds with the belief in a specifically human capacity to retrieve the supposed multiplicity and changeability of the external world. Rather, the mode of allegory refers to a process of fragmentation in which parts are isolated from the underlying and meaning-giving unity to which they seemingly belong. When Kracauer likens the filmic image to an allegorical element, this entails that it at once exposes the world's unredeemed and forlorn condition *and* makes visible the concomitant need for radical change. The 'revues' that took place in Berlin's 'picture palaces', for instance, 'convey precisely and openly to thousands of eyes and ears the *disorder* (*Unordnung*) of society – this is precisely what would enable them to evoke and maintain the tension that must precede the inevitable and radical change (*Umschlag*)'.[132] Neither Kracauer nor Benjamin will be interested in spelling out the clear content or goals of such a societal revolution, but it is clear that, in their view, the world in its current and concrete state lacks any and all redemptive potential. Instead of meeting inanimate objects as 'faces' that look back in an expressive manner, the allegorical operation, vice versa, exposes that even the face is in the end but the external layer of an inexpressive and inanimate object, that is, the skull. In Benjamin's well-known formula it is stated as follows: 'Everything about history that, from the very beginning, has been untimely, sorrowful, unsuccessful, is expressed in a face – or rather in a death's head'.[133] In the view of the pre-war Kracauer, hence, an *absence* of meaning on the part of history and nature alike needs to be brought to the fore in order to retrieve

The Missed Conversation 121

the belief in genuine change and innovation. This younger Kracauer is interested in films such as Jean Vigo's *L'Atalante* (1934), where 'it is as if we were suddenly confronting the decayed parts of our lived life'.[134] When physical reality is reproduced in film, its unanticipatable movements and contingencies are not the trigger for a supposed soulful experience of the world. They are the most radical antithesis of such enlivening perceptions. Rather than 'redeeming' the world by revealing its flux-like character, films and photographs expose the fact that our surroundings are, in truth, the site of an unceasing catastrophe.

Sancho Panza is only introduced in the two very last pages of Kracauer's very last (and unfinished) book, *History: The Last Things Before the Last*. Still, he plays an essential role as the thought figure that enables Kracauer to break with the framework of his pre-war writings. It is the identification with Sancho Panza that enables Kracauer to cast off his early fascination with death and the lack of meaning in history, thereby mounting the material for his late rediscovery of a humanistic version of *Lebensphilosophie*. Once more, the connection with Kracauer's one-time mentor Georg Simmel is revelatory. In late essays like 'The Problem of Historical Time' (1916), 'The Constitutive Concepts of History' (1917/1918), and 'On the Nature of Historical Understanding' (1918),[135] Simmel had sought an alternative view of history and historiography that would avoid the opposition between 'historical realism' and 'historical idealism'. While historical realism seeks to 'reproduce the events themselves' but for that reason 'sacrifices the *contents* (meaning) of the historical process', historical idealism 'holds that reality is the same as *knowledge* of the reality' but for that reason 'sacrifices (the) continuity (of the historical process itself)'.[136] In establishing a philosophy of history that stays clear of both pitfalls, Simmel had started from the assumption that 'a given aspect of reality qualifies as historical when we know how to fix it at a certain position within our temporal system'.[137] Only when we have a clear grasp of an event's position in the continuum of concrete, temporal reality can we really claim to have historical understanding. For this very reason, the human faculty of cognition cannot on its own account come to terms with the meaning of a historical event. For human cognition is aimed at specific 'ideal contents'[138] that either have or have not been actualized in history, but these contents themselves do not shed any light on the issue of their actualization or place in concrete reality: 'From the perspective of understanding . . . the question of whether these contents fall under the categories of reality or fantasy, the present or the past, is of no consequence. . . . It follows that understanding is . . . completely independent of historical time'. '*In principle, historical knowledge simply does not have the form* which would make it possible to reproduce the continuity of history'.[139] As a consequence, Simmel had dismissed all forms of historiography that interpret the flow of history from

122 Unworldliness in Twentieth Century German Thought

the sole perspective of overarching or underlying concepts. In Simmel's view, interpretations that focus on a central idea that would determine a specific historical era, or the realm of history as such, are deeply mistaken. Because no event 'as an object of real experience' has the form of such an overarching or underlying idea, these types of purely conceptual historiography are inherently 'preliminary and fragmentary'.[140] It is at this step of the argument that Simmel had once again drawn on the categories and vocabulary of *Lebensphilosophie*: if all historical events at least partially exceed the grasp of human cognition and conceptual understanding, this is because they belong to the non-rational realm of 'life as such', marked as it is by immanent multiplicity, contingency, and changeability:

> The image of life . . . lies within an epistemological plane that is different from . . . the plane of its single elements. These elements (i.e. historical events) can be comprehended within this image of life only if they are detached from their circumscribed, concrete individuality and placed in relief.[141]

A historical event, that is, cannot be separated from the 'purely immanent and objective relationships' with other events that take place before, after, or together with it. While conceptual understanding sets up only an 'external and absolute frame of reference', the true meaning of a specific historical event is inseparable from these 'reciprocal interrelationships': 'In the total complex, th[e] determinateness of temporal location is ascribed to the process as a whole'.[142] The argument that springs from Simmel's identification between the realm of history and 'life as such' thus mirrors his earlier mentioned suggestion that the 'more than life' of a vital, human culture is inseparable from the 'life' that flows through that culture: historiography can only be considered part of such a 'healthy' culture if its categories manage to capture the flux of life as such and do not reduce history to a succession of 'ideal contents' that can be *known*. Because life as such can never be an object of knowledge, Simmel had highlighted the need to supplement conceptual understanding with a *different* type of understanding, that is, with the lived (re-)experience of a given historical event from within 'the *totality* of history'. This totality of history needs to be seen as the vital unity that bridges the gap between past and present and, 'in principle' refers 'to the totality of the cosmic process in general'.[143] In other words, for Simmel, historiography always requires a 'reciprocal process of interpretation' in which the quest for knowledge goes hand in hand with a *non*-cognitive form of historical awareness: 'Historical knowledge . . . is suspended in a perpetual compromise between the following two extremes: on the one hand, the construction of comprehensive unified entities, the continuity of which reproduces the form of the event, even

The Missed Conversation 123

though it cannot be exhausted by the concrete phenomena of reality; on the other hand, the concrete phenomena of reality. From the perspective of ideal cognitive criteria, these concrete phenomena only identify a single chronological point. Precisely for this reason, the continuity of the real event cannot be ascribed to these ideal criteria'.[144]

When Sancho Panza suddenly shows up on the penultimate page of Kracauer's final book, he performs the very same conceptual move that underlies Simmel's blend of philosophy of history and *Lebensphiloso-phie*. Sancho Panza stands for a 'side by side principle' that bridges the distance between 'the timeless and the temporal' and 'the general and the particular'.[145] For Kracauer, Sancho Panza is the 'simple man' who is immune to the lure of a merely conceptual understanding and a 'pure' historical knowledge. Taking his cue from Kafka's famous fragment 'The Truth about Sancho Panza', Kracauer describes Sancho Panza as someone who 'gamble(s) with absolutes, all kinds of quixotic ideas about universal truth', using them only to 'divert . . . his demon whom he later called Don Quixote'. Sancho Panza is the quintessential 'free man' who has a 'Utopian character' that 'points to . . . the in-between – a terra incognita in the hollows between the lands we know'.[146] Like Simmel, Kracauer insists that the course of history is not governed by 'causally determined patterns' and that historiography cannot therefore be termed a 'science'.[147] Kracauer, as well, dedicates his final years to a philosophy of history that avoids the pitfalls of both the 'Scylla of philosophical speculations with their wholesale meanings' (the abstractions of historical idealism) and the 'Charybdis of the sciences with their nature laws and regularities' (the factual truths of historical realism).[148] He agrees with Simmel that the realm of history is not fully accessible to human cognition since 'science accounts . . . (only) for partial processes' and the 'peculiar material' of history 'eludes the grasp of systematic thought'.[149] Like Simmel's philosophy of history, Kracauer's view revolves around the argument that the overarching and underlying concepts that are deployed to understand the course of history are but 'provisional'. There is a clear need to 'eliminate idea oriented history'[150] and to once and for all give up the hope that the 'last things' or 'ultimate concerns' such as 'the nature of being in general, of knowledge, of the good, of beauty, and not least of history' can be retrieved from within history itself.[151] Underlying Kracauer's last book is therefore a radical rejection of all universal philosophies of history, be they theological-messianic, secular-Marxist, or scientific-positivistic. Like Simmel, he highlights the shortcomings of such grand narratives on account of the supposed 'interconnection' of all historical events.[152] These 'tiny little movements and reactions' constitute the 'residue' that make up 'life in its flux' and, as a consequence, defy conceptual understanding.[153]

124 *Unworldliness in Twentieth Century German Thought*

Kracauer's reference to Sancho Panza, and the alternative view of history that it supports, revolve around some of the same assumptions that inspired the late writings of Kommerell. Like Kommerell, Kracauer argues for a lived responsiveness to the 'world of small events'.[154] He identifies 'historical reality' with the 'camera reality' that he had earlier described in *Film Theory*: historical understanding is inseparable from the experience of a 'realm of contingencies and new beginnings' that resists all sense of determination.[155] Kracauer does not even hold back in reintroducing the jargon of Husserlian phenomenology, including the much debated notion of lifeworld. We need to 'familiariz(e) us, for the first time as it were, with "this Earth which is our habitat" (Gabriel Marcel)' and 'think through things, not above them'.[156] This radical openness of our most immediate surroundings enables us to retrieve 'life in its fullness and as we commonly experience it':

> Instead of proceeding from, or climaxing in, statements about the meaning, or, for that matter, the meaninglessness, of history as such, it is a distinctly empirical science which explores and interprets given historical reality in exactly the same manner as the photographic media render and penetrate the physical world about us. History is much closer to the practically endless, fortuitous, and indeterminate *Lebenswelt* – Husserl's term for the basic dimension of daily life – than philosophy. Consequently, the historian would not dream of assigning to his findings and conclusions the kind of generality and validity peculiar to philosophical statements. He is unconcerned for high abstractions and absolutes; at least he does not primarily care about them.[157]

With the suggestion that genuine historical understanding stems from an exploration of the hidden riches of our surroundings, Kracauer takes leave from the earlier idea that thought stems, above all, from a radical *negation* of that lifeworld – a marked change of mind that will lead to an intellectual dispute with Adorno. In August 1960, and again in July 1964, while they are working on what should become their magnum opus (Adorno's *Negative Dialectics* and Kracauer's *The Last Things Before the Last*), both men meet in Switzerland and Frankfurt.[158] Adorno will present Kracauer with the same criticism that he will level at Bloch: Kracauer has 'capitulated' to a conformist standpoint. Priding himself on his rejection of all types of ideology, Kracauer has (like Bloch) endowed the world in its current state with a redemptive potential rather than expressing the urgent need for an *Umschlag* that negates the status quo: 'In the treasure of motives of his thought, one would look in vain for protest against reification'.[159] From Kracauer's perspective, however, Adorno's negative dialectics is but empty rhetoric since in its refusal to give content to its own ideals, it has lost its roots in concrete

The Missed Conversation 125

reality. 'I told Teddie that many of his articles concocted this way made me just dizzy; that I had often the feeling that other interpretations might be as conclusive as his, or even more so; that his whole dialectics seemed inseparable from a certain arbitrariness to me; and that, in sum, my dizziness was presumably caused by the complete absence of content and direction in these series of material evaluations'.[160] For the late Kracauer, genuine understanding can indeed only stem from a 'unique encounter with (the) opaque entities' that give color to our lifeworld: the ideal historiographer is endowed with an 'active passivity' through which he opens up to the mysterious and ambivalent meanings that resonate within his surroundings.[161]

Kracauer argues that, in such an attitude of 'waiting', subjectivity is 'anything but a limiting factor'[162]: it is only by virtue of a soulful and lived reaction to the lifeworld, that the historian can 'immerse himself' into life's concrete minutiae: 'In exact analogy to the photographic approach, the "historical approach" comes true only if the historian's spontaneous intuition does not interfere with his loyalty to the evidence but, conversely, benefits his empathic absorption in it'.[163]

The later Kracauer in this way ends up taking recourse to some of the jargon of the later Kommerell's *Lebensphilosophie*. Still, it would be a mistake to simply *equate* Kracauer's own humanism with the later Kommerell's viewpoints. First of all, Kracauer does pit the concreteness of the world 'as such' against 'abstractness' but, following Simmel's lead, he does not at all cast doubt on the importance of man's quest for understanding altogether. Unlike Kommerell, who insists that the recovery of 'the feeling of life' forces man to leave behind the need to *know*, the later Kracauer argues *in favor of* the faculty of understanding, albeit one that is at all times fed by life's many minutiae. In short, Kracauer does not at all share Kommerell's optimism about an entirely *intuitive* restoration of life's immediacy and, instead, defends the constant need for *mediations*. The constructions, concepts, and categories that give shape to human thought are not to be confused with the metaphysical plenitude of life itself: they are only expressive of it. Secondly, rather than falling prey to the promise of a truly free and *un*-alienated existence, the late Kracauer will seek, as his friend Walter Benjamin once put it, a 'highly productive use of the human being's self-alienation': 'History', according to Kracauer, 'resembles photography in that it is among other things a means of alienation'.[164] Kracauer's later humanism still revolves around the condition of *Heimatlosigkeit*. In the words of von Moltke, Kracauer presents us with 'a decentered subjectivity (that) match(es) the decentered world'.[165] His ambition is not to overcome the barriers of reason in an intuitive grasp of life or 'home'; rather, he makes these barriers visible as indispensable reference-points that enable us to orient ourselves in a constantly changing and shelterless world.

126 *Unworldliness in Twentieth Century German Thought*

Notes

1 For the relationship between Kracauer and Adorno, see Martin Jay, 'Adorno and Kracauer: Notes on a Troubled Friendship', in *Salmagundi* 40 (1978): 42–66, Johannes von Moltke, 'Teddie and Friedel: Theodor W. Adorno, Siegfried Kracauer, and the Erotics of Friendship', in *Criticism* 51 (4) (2009): 683–694; Jörg Später, *Siegfried Kracauer: Eine Biographie* (Frankfurt am Main, Germany: Suhrkamp, 2016).

2 Kommerell, quoted in Martin Viallon, 'Die Konstellation Max Kommerell und Werner Krauss: *Schreiben als Sprechen über Literatur in finsteren Zeiten*', in *Max Kommerell: Leben, Werk, Aktualität*, ed. Walter Busch and Gerhart Pickerodt (Göttingen, Germany: Wallstein Verlag, 2003), 324 (314–348). For the discussion of Kommerell's connections with Nazism, see Christian Weber, *Max Kommerell: Eine intellektuelle Biographie* (Berlin and New York: Walter de Gruyter, 2011), Chapter VII; Dorothea Hölscher-Lohmeyer, 'Geist und Buchstabe der Briefe Max Kommerells: *Anmerkungen zu ihrer Gesamtedition*', in *Max Kommerell: Leben, Werk, Aktualität*, ed. Walter Busch and Gerhart Pickerodt (Göttingen, Germany: Wallstein Verlag, 2003), 15–29; Rainer Nägele, 'Vexierbild einer Kritischen Konstellation: Walter Benjamin und Max Kommerell', in *Max Kommerell: Leben, Werk, Aktualität*, ed. Walter Busch and Gerhart Pickerodt (Göttingen, Germany: Wallstein Verlag, 2003), 349–367.

3 Kommerell, quoted in Viallon, 'Die Konstellation Max Kommerell und Werner Krauss', 327.

4 Adorno, in letters from 1934 and 1968, quoted in Paul Fleming, 'Forgetting – *Faust*: Adorno and Kommerell', in *Adorno and Literature*, ed. David Cunningham and Nigel Mapp (London and New York: Continuum, 2006), 333–334 (333–344).

5 See Bernhard Böschenstein, Jürgen Egyptien, Bertram Schefold and Wolfgang Graf Vitsthum, eds., *Wissenschaftler im George-Kreis: Die Welt des Dichters und der Beruf der Wissenschaft* (Berlin and New York: Walter de Gruyter, 2005); Robert E. Norton, *Secret Germany: Stefan George and His Circle* (Ithaca, NY: Cornell University Press, 2002).

6 Harry Maync, quoted in Ulrich Port, 'Literaturgeschichte als Körperschau: Max Kommerell und die Physionomik der 1920er Jahre', in *Hofmannsthal Jahrbuch* 14 (2006): 385 (383–414).

7 Max Kommerell, 'Vorbemerkung', in *Der Dichter als Führer in der deutschen Klassik* (Berlin: Georg Bondi, 1928). For the reference to 'politics', see Elke Siegel, 'Contested Legacies of "German" Friendship: Max Kommerell's *The Poet as Leader in German Classicism*', in *Telos* 176 (2016): 81 (77–101). My discussion of Kommerell's *Der Dichter als Führer* builds on Siegel's article and is indebted to her own discussion of the central issue of friendship.

8 Kommerell, *Der Dichter als Führer*, 16.

9 Kommerell, *Der Dichter als Führer*, 12. For a discussion of Kommerell's blend between politics and aesthetics (and the inconsistencies to which this leads), see Claude Haas, 'Hölderlin contra Goethe: Gemeinschaft und Geschichte in Max Kommerells *Der Dichter als Führer in der deutschen Klassik*', in *Zeitschrift für Germanistik* 27 (1) (2017): 149–162. See also Nägele's criticism in Nägele, 'Vexierbild einer kritischen Konstellation', and Fleming's more nuanced view in Paul Fleming, 'Ein Bund von Sternen: Konstellation bei Kommerell', in *Lektürepraxis und Theoriebildung: Zur Aktualität Max Kommerells*, ed. Christoph König, Isolde Schiffermüller, Christian Benne and Gabrielle Pelloni (Göttingen, Germany: Wallstein, 2018), 105–120.

The Missed Conversation   127

10 Kommerell, *Der Dichter als Führer*, 16 (transl. Siegel and quoted in 'Contested Legacies of "German" Friendship', 86).

11 Kommerell, *Der Dichter als Führer*, 16 (transl. Siegel and quoted in 'Contested Legacies of "German" Friendship', 86) 199–200.

12 Kommerell, *Der Dichter als Führer*, 16 (transl. Siegel and quoted in 'Contested Legacies of "German" Friendship', 86) 201.

13 Kommerell, *Der Dichter als Führer*, 16 (transl. Siegel and quoted in 'Contested Legacies of "German" Friendship', 86) 203.

14 Kommerell, *Der Dichter als Führer*, 16 (transl. Siegel and quoted in 'Contested Legacies of "German" Friendship', 86) 205.

15 Kommerell, *Der Dichter als Führer*, 16 (transl. Siegel and quoted in 'Contested Legacies of "German" Friendship', 86) 206.

16 Kommerell, *Der Dichter als Führer*, 16 (transl. Siegel and quoted in 'Contested Legacies of "German" Friendship', 86) 206.

17 Kommerell, *Der Dichter als Führer*, 16 (transl. Siegel and quoted in 'Contested Legacies of "German" Friendship', 86) 240–241.

18 Siegfried Kracauer, 'Georg Simmel', in *The Mass Ornament: Weimar Essays*, transl. and ed. Thomas Y. Levin (Cambridge and London: Harvard University Press, 1995), 233–238 (225–257).

19 Siegfried Kracauer, 'Über die Freundschaft', in *Werke 5.1: Essays, Feuilletons, Rezensionen, 1906–1923*, ed. Inka Mülder-Bach and Ingrid Belke (Frankfurt am Main, Germany: Suhrkamp, 2011), 45–48 (29–59). For discussions of Kracauer's early essays on friendship, see Gerhard Richter, 'Siegfried Kracauer and the Folds of Friendship', in *The German Quarterly* 70 (3) (1997): 233–246; Harry Blatterer, 'Siegfried Kracauer's Differentiating Approach to Friendship', in *Journal of Historical Sociology* 32 (2019): 173–188.

20 Kracauer, 'Über die Freundschaft', 54–57.

21 Siegfried Kracauer, 'Those Who Wait', in *The Mass Ornament: Weimar Essays*, transl. and ed. Thomas Y. Levin (Cambridge and London: Harvard University Press, 1995), 131.

22 Kracauer, 'Georg Simmel', 251.

23 Siegfried Kracauer, 'Gedanken über Freundschaft', in *Werke 5.1: Essays, Feuilletons, Rezensionen, 1906–1923*, ed. Inka Mülder-Bach and Ingrid Belke (Frankfurt am Main, Germany: Suhrkamp, 2011), 342 (332–350).

24 Kracauer, 'Gedanken über Freundschaft', 335.

25 Kracauer, 'Gedanken über Freundschaft', 337.

26 Kracauer, 'Gedanken über Freundschaft', 337.

27 Kracauer, 'Über die Freundschaft', 43.

28 Kracauer, 'Gedanken über Freundschaft', 339.

29 For insightful discussions of Kracauer's work as a commentator of Weimar (mass)-culture, see, for example, Miriam Hansen, 'Decentric Perspectives: Kracauer's Early Writings on Film and Mass Culture', in *New German Critique* 54 (1991): 47–76, Gertrud Koch, *Siegfried Kracauer: An Introduction* (Princeton, NJ: Princeton University Press, 2000); David Frisby, *Fragments of Modernity: Theories of Modernity in the Work of Simmel, Kracauer and Benjamin* (London and New York: Routledge, 2011); Graeme Gilloch, *Siegfried Kracauer: Our Companion in Misfortune* (Cambridge, UK: Polity Press, 2015), esp. Part II.

30 This does not, however, entail that, in the 1920s, Kracauer should be regarded as a non-religious, let alone non-metaphysical thinker. As we will see, he denounces the shallowness of a religious or metaphyiscal *flânerie* (Craver) and the coldness of the modern *Ratio* alike. Moreover, many of the concepts that he develops to counter the spiritual crisis of Weimar Germany are in fact

128   *Unworldliness in Twentieth Century German Thought*

'secularized' versions of religious and metaphysical concepts (e.g. 'waiting'). For the argument that, in Kracauer's work, 'religion still had a ghostly relationship to the modern', see Harry T. Craver, *The Reluctant Skeptic: Siegfried Kracauer and the Crises of Weimar Culture* (New York and Oxford: Berghahn, 2017) (quote on p. 14); Inka Mülder, *Siegfried Kracauer-Grenzgänger zwischen Theorie und Literatur: Seine frühen Schriften 1913–1933* (Stuttgart, Germany: J.B. Metzler, 1985), e.g., p. 18.

31 Siegfried Kracauer, 'The Group as Bearer of Ideas', in *The Mass Ornament: Weimar Essays*, transl. and ed. Thomas Y. Levin (Cambridge and London: Harvard University Press, 1995), 151 (143–170).

32 Kracauer, 'The Group as Bearer of Ideas', 152.

33 Siegfried Kracauer, 'The Biography as an Art Form of the New Bourgeoisie', in *The Mass Ornament: Weimar Essays*, transl. and ed. Thomas Y. Levin (Cambridge and London: Harvard University Press, 1995), 104 (101–105).

34 Kracauer, 'The Biography as an Art Form of the New Bourgeoisie', 103.

35 Kracauer, 'The Biography as an Art Form of the New Bourgeoisie', 102.

36 Kracauer, 'The Biography as an Art Form of the New Bourgeoisie', 105.

37 Kracauer, 'The Biography as an Art Form of the New Bourgeoisie', 104.

38 Siegfried Kracauer, 'The Mass Ornament', in *The Mass Ornament: Weimar Essays*, transl. and ed. Thomas Y. Levin (Cambridge, MA and London: Harvard University Press, 1995), 86 (75–86).

39 Kracauer, 'The Mass Ornament', 81.

40 Kracauer, 'The Mass Ornament', 81.

41 Kracauer, 'The Mass Ornament', 77.

42 Kracauer, 'The Mass Ornament', 78.

43 Kracauer, 'The Mass Ornament', 76–77.

44 Kracauer, 'The Mass Ornament', 79.

45 Kracauer, 'The Mass Ornament', 86.

46 See, Weber, *Max Kommerell*, 59–64.

47 Kommerell, quoted in Weber, *Max Kommerell*, 61.

48 Kommerell, quoted in Viallon, 'Die Konstellation Max Kommerell und Werner Krauss', 324. See also Hansgeorg Schmidt-Bergman, 'Max Kommerells Weg von George zu Rilke', in *Max Kommerell: Leben, Werk, Aktualität*, ed. Walter Busch and Gerhart Pickerodt (Göttingen, Germany: Wallstein Verlag, 2003), 300–313.

49 For my discussion of Kommerell's book on Jean Paul, I build on the analyses of Paul Fleming, primarily 'The Crisis of Art: Max Kommerell and Jean Paul's Gestures', in *MLN* 115 (3) (2000): 519–543 and 'Die Moderne ohne Kunst: Max Kommerells Gattungspoetik in *Jean Paul*', in *Max Kommerell: Leben, Werk, Aktualität*, ed. Walter Busch and Gerhart Pickerodt (Göttingen, Germany: Wallstein Verlag, 2003), 54–72.

50 Max Kommerell, *Jean Paul* (Frankfurt am Main, Germany: Vittorio Klostermann, 1933), 418 (transl. Paul Fleming and quoted in 'The Crisis of Art', 522).

51 For the issue of physiognomy in Kommerell, see Port, 'Literaturgeschichte als Körperschau'.

52 Kommerell, *Jean Paul*, 48 (transl. Paul Fleming and quoted in 'The Crisis of Art', 525).

53 Kommerell, *Jean Paul*, 46 (transl. Paul Fleming and quoted in 'The Crisis of Art', 525).

54 Kommerell, *Jean Paul*, 46.

The Missed Conversation 129

55 Kommerell, *Jean Paul*, 47 (transl. Paul Fleming and quoted in 'The Crisis of Art', 534). For a discussion of these 'pure gestures', see Isolde Schiffermüller, 'Gebärde, Gestikulation und Mimus. Krisengestalten in der Poetik von Max Kommerell', in *Max Kommerell: Leben, Werk, Aktualität*, ed. Walter Busch and Gerhart Pickerodt (Göttingen, Germany: Wallstein Verlag, 2003), 98–117.

56 See, for example, Fleming, 'Die Moderne ohne Kunst'; Ulrich Port, 'Die "Sprachgebärde" und der "Umgang mit sich selbst": Literatur als Lebenskunst bei Max Kommerell', in *Max Kommerell: Leben, Werk, Aktualität*, 74–97; Eva Geulen, 'Aktualität im Übergang: Kunst und Moderne bei Max Kommerell', in *Max Kommerell: Leben, Werk, Aktualität*, 32–53.

57 Kommerell, *Jean Paul*, 41. For a discussion of Kommerell's rejection of Jean Paul's 'pure' gestures, see also Fleming, 'Die Moderne ohne Kunst', 66; Elmar Locher, 'Die Sprache und das Unaussprechliche: Kleist bei Kommerell', in *Max Kommerell: Leben, Werk, Aktualität*, 249–277; Milena Massalongo, 'Versuch zu einem kritischen Vergleich zwischen Kommerells und Benjamins Sprachgebärde', in *Max Kommerell: Leben, Werk, Aktualität*, 118–161.

58 Kommerell, *Jean Paul*, 414 (transl. Paul Fleming and quoted in 'The Crisis of Art', 538).

59 Kommerell, *Jean Paul*, 418–419 (transl. Paul Fleming and quoted in 'The Crisis of Art', 522).

60 Kommerell, *Jean Paul*, 47.

61 Max Kommerell, 'Von Wesen des Lyrischen Gedichts', in *Gedanken über Gedichte* (Frankfurt am Main, Germany: Vittorio Klostermann, 1985), 32.

62 Kommerell, 'Von Wesen des Lyrischen Gedichts', 9.

63 Kommerell, 'Von Wesen des Lyrischen Gedichts', 43, 12.

64 Kommerell, 'Von Wesen des Lyrischen Gedichts', 32. See also Max Kommerell, 'Die Dichtung in freien Rhythmen und der Gott der Dichter', in *Gedanken über Gedichte* (Frankfurt am Main, Germany: Vittorio Klostermann, 1985), 430–504.

65 Kommerell, 'Von Wesen des Lyrischen Gedichts', 47. For a discussion of the poet as a 'meaning-giver' in the work of Kommerell, see Matthias Weichelt, 'Je einsamer der Mensch, umso notwendiger die Dichtung: Kunst und Hermeneutik bei Max Kommerell', in *Lektürepraxis und Theoriebildung: Zur Aktualität Max Kommerells*, ed. Christoph König, Isolde Schiffermüller, Christian Benne and Gabrielle Pelloni (Göttingen, Germany: Wallstein, 2018), 50–67; Gabriela Pelloni, '"Veränderte Mischungen": Kommerells ästhetische Erziehung', in *Lektürepraxis und Theoriebildung: Zur Aktualität Max Kommerells*, 68–87.

66 Kommerell, 'Von Wesen des Lyrischen Gedichts', 19, 23, 46.

67 Kommerell, 'Von Wesen des Lyrischen Gedichts', 30.

68 Kommerell, 'Von Wesen des Lyrischen Gedichts', 22–23. Kommerell is most likely referring to Goethe's statement that '(t)he moment of solidescence is to be regarded as highly significant. Solidescence is the last act of becoming, leading from the liquid through the soft to the solid, representing the completion of what has become' (in 'Mountain formation as a whole and in detail' (1770s)).

69 See, for example, Kommerell, 'Von Wesen des Lyrischen Gedichts', 26, 38.

70 See, for example, Kommerell, 'Von Wesen des Lyrischen Gedichts', 36.

71 See, for example, Kommerell, 'Von Wesen des Lyrischen Gedichts', 44–46.

130 *Unworldliness in Twentieth Century German Thought*

72 See, for example, Kommerell, 'Von Wesen des Lyrischen Gedichts', 41. About the issue of the 'unsayable' in Kommerell, see Elmar Locher, 'Die Sprache und das Unaussprechliche'; Elmar Locher, 'Über das "ohne Worte sein": Kleist und Kommerell', in *Lektürepraxis und Theoriebildung: Zur Aktualität Max Kommerells*, 121–136. About the issue of *Stimmung* in Kommerell, see Michael Karlsson Pedersen, 'Der atmende Stoff: Zum Stimmungsbegriff Max Kommerells', in *Lektürepraxis und Theoriebildung: Zur Aktualität Max Kommerells*, 161–174.

73 Kommerell, 'Von Wesen des Lyrischen Gedichts', 37.

74 Kommerell, 'Von Wesen des Lyrischen Gedichts', 44 (*Zwei Eigenschaften wird man wohl nie am dichterischen Individuum, das zum lyrischen Gedicht berufen ist, vermissen: eine liebevolle Aufgeschlossenheit für das Lebendige und eine Fähigkeit zur Ergänzung, die inmitten einseitiger Tätigkeiten und Anlagen die ungeteilte Einfalt des menschlichen Daseins rettet*).

75 Max Kommerell, 'Rilkes Duineser Elegien', in *Gedanken über Gedichte* (Frankfurt am Main, Germany: Vittorio Klostermann, 1985), 499–501 (491–503). For a discussion of Kommerell's reading of Rilke, see Schmidt-Bergman, 'Max Kommerells Weg von George zu Rilke'.

76 Max Kommerell, 'Betrachtung über die Commedia dell'Arte', in *Dichterische Welterfahrung: Essays* (Frankfurt am Main, Germany: Vittorio Klostermann, 1952), 161, 169 (159–173).

77 For a brief discussion of Kommerell's reading of Cervantes, see Weber, *Max Kommerell*, 305–313.

78 Max Kommerell, 'Humoristische Personifikationen in Don Quixote', in *Dichterische Welterfahrung: Essays* (Frankfurt am Main, Germany: Vittorio Klostermann, 1952), 121; Max Kommerell, 'Don Quijote und Simplicissimus', in *Essays, Notizen, Poetische Fragmente*, ed. Inge Jens (Olten, Switzerland and Freiburg im Breisgau, Germany: Walter Verlag, 1969), 50.

79 Kommerell, 'Don Quijote und Simplicissimus', 61.

80 Kommerell, 'Don Quijote und Simplicissimus', 65.

81 Kommerell, 'Don Quijote und Simplicissimus', 61.

82 Kommerell, 'Humoristische Personifikationen in Don Quixote', 114.

83 Kommerell, 'Humoristische Personifikationen in Don Quixote', 122.

84 Kommerell, 'Humoristische Personifikationen in Don Quixote', 122.

85 Kommerell, 'Humoristische Personifikationen in Don Quixote', 122.

86 Ernst Bloch, *The Principle of Hope*, transl. Neville Plaice, Stephen Plaice and Paul Knight (Cambridge, MA: The MIT Press, 1986), *Volume 3*, 1049.

87 Kommerell, 'Humoristische Personifikationen in Don Quixote', 112.

88 Kommerell, 'Humoristische Personifikationen in Don Quixote', 126, see also Kommerell, 'Don Quijote und Simplicissimus', 46–56.

89 Kommerell, 'Humoristische Personifikationen in Don Quixote', 130, 124.

90 Bloch, *The Principle of Hope*, 1043.

91 Lukács, '*Don Quixote*: Preface', https://www.marxists.org/archive/lukacs/works/1951/don-quixote.htm.

92 Lukács, *Theory of the Novel*, 151.

93 Kommerell, 'Humoristische Personifikationen in Don Quixote', 143.

94 Kommerell, 'Humoristische Personifikationen in Don Quixote', 143.

95 Kommerell, 'Humoristische Personifikationen in Don Quixote', 118; Kommerell, 'Don Quijote und Simplicissimus', 50.

96 Kommerell, 'Humoristische Personifikationen in Don Quixote', 130.

97 Kommerell, 'Don Quijote und Simplicissimus', 50; Kommerell, 'Humoristische Personifikationen in Don Quixote', 143.

The Missed Conversation 131

 98 Kommerell, 'Don Quijote und Simplicissimus', 56.
 99 Kommerell, 'Humoristische Personifikationen in Don Quixote', 120.
100 Kommerell, 'Humoristische Personifikationen in Don Quixote', 145.
101 Kommerell, 'Humoristische Personifikationen in Don Quixote', 144.
102 Kommerell, 'Humoristische Personifikationen in Don Quixote', 144.
103 Kommerell, 'Don Quijote und Simplicissimus', 65. See also Fleming, 'Die Moderne ohne Kunst', 66–67.
104 For an excellent analysis of Kracauer's references to Quixote and Panza, see the 'Afterword: from Don Quixote to Sancho Panza', in *The Reluctant Skeptic: Siegfried Kracauer and the Crises of Weimar Culture*, ed. Harry T. Craver (New York and Oxford: Berghahn, 2017), 244–254. The quotes are on p. 248.
105 Momme Broderson, *Siegfried Kracauer* (Hamburg, Germany: Rowohlt, 2001), 94–97.
106 For an excellent analysis of Kracauer's early years in the United States, see Johannes von Moltke and Kristy Rawson, 'Introduction', in *Siegfried Kracauer's American Writings: Essays on Film and Popular Culture*, ed. Johannes von Moltke and Kristy Rawson (Berkeley, Los Angeles and London: University of California Press, 2012), 1–26; Anton Kaes, 'Siegfried Kracauer: The Film Historian in Exile', in *Escape to Life: German Intellectuals in New York: A Compendium on Exile after 1933*, ed. Eckart Goebel and Sigrid Weigel (London and New York: Walter de Gruyter, 2013), 236–269. See also Mark M. Anderson, 'Siegfried Kracauer and Meyer Schapiro: A Friendship', in *New German Critique* 54 (1991): 19–30.
107 Siegfried Kracauer, *From Caligari to Hitler: A Psychological History of the German Film* (Princeton, NJ, and Oxford: Princeton University Press, 2004), 8.
108 Siegfried Kracauer, 'Why France Liked Our Films', in *Siegfried Kracauer's American Writings: Essays on Film and Popular Culture*, ed. Johannes von Moltke and Kristy Rawson (Berkeley, Los Angeles and London: University of California Press, 2012), 40 (33–40).
109 The extent to which Kracauer's late humanism remains *political* (instead of putting forward a a-/depoliticized outlook on the world) is an open and oft-debated question. Possible answers depend on, among other things, the definition of politics itself and its relation to culture. See, e.g. the claims of Craver that, for Kracauer, "culture precedes politics", in Craver, *Reluctant Skeptic*, 4; Jay, 'Adorno and Kracauer', 43: 'But that Kracauer saw no hope for a new polis in the revolutionary rumblings to the east set him apart from many who shared his antipathy to Wilhelmian society. In the long run, Kracauer has been vindicated, at least as far as that revolution went, but his pessimism from the first shows how apolitical his hopes for redemption always tended to be. Even during the 1920's, when he moved towards an uneasy endorsement of the Weimar left, he still remained skeptical of easy political solutions to the crisis of his society'. See also von Moltke's view that, according to Kracauer, culture *is* politics in Johannes von Moltke, *The Curious Humanist: Siegfried Kracauer in America* (Oakland: The University of California Press, 1996), e.g. 35–36: 'Even a book like *Theory of Film* can hardly be considered "apolitical", as if, along with lingering Marxist identifications, it abandoned any attempt to think progressively about the politics of the aesthetic. While the book indisputably strikes a Cold War cord in some of its humanist credos, it should be read also as an attempt to rescue liberal humanism from itself by reinvesting

132   *Unworldliness in Twentieth Century German Thought*

it with notions of experience and dethroning the autonomous subject in favor of materiality and alterity'. In von Moltke's reading, *pace* Adorno's dismissive remarks about Kracauer's 'curious realism', the late Kracauer's analysis of the experiential dimension of cinema and spectatorship remains *political* because it pinpoints an anti-authoritarian type of subjectivity (see Chapter 9). None of the aforementioned authors, however, analyzes the link between the later Kracauer and *Lebensphilosophie*.

110 Siegfried Kracauer, *Theory of Film: The Redemption of Physical Reality* (London, Oxford and New York: Oxford University Press, 1965), 296. For the most comprehensive and insightful analysis of Kracauer's *Theory of Film*, see the work of Miriam Bratu Hansen, esp. her *Cinema and Experience: Siegfried Kracauer, Walter Benjamin, and Theodor W. Adorno* (Berkeley, Los Angeles and London: University of California Press, 2012).

111 Kracauer, *Theory of Film*, 'Epilogue', esp. 287–295.

112 Kracauer, *Theory of Film*, 'Epilogue', 290.

113 Kracauer, *Theory of Film*, 'Epilogue', 290–291.

114 Kracauer, *Theory of Film*, 'Epilogue', 296. On this issue, and the 'existentialist ontology' or 'magical nominalism' that it entails, see resp. Gertrud Koch, *Siegfried Kracauer* and Martin Jay, 'Afterword', in *The Reluctant Skeptic: Siegfried Kracauer and the Crises of Weimar Culture*, ed. Harry T. Craver (New York and Oxford: Berghahn, 2017), 227–235.

115 For this notion of 'enchantment', see Martin Jay, 'Magical Nominalism: Photography and the Reenchantment of the World', in *The Pictorial Turn*, ed. Neal Curtis (New York: Routledge, 2010), 69–87.

116 Kracauer, *Theory of Film*, 37.

117 Kracauer, *Theory of Film*, 20.

118 Kracauer, *Theory of Film*, 299–300.

119 Kracauer, *Theory of Film*, 306. For discussions of this passage see Hansen, *Cinema and Experience*, 257; Georges Didi-Huberman, *Images in Spite of All: Four Photographs from Auschwitz*, trans. Shane B. Lillis (Chicago: University of Chicago Press, 2008), 176–179; Gertrud Koch, '"Not Yet Accepted Anywhere": Exile, Memory and Image in Kracauer's Conception of History', in *New German Critique* 54 (1991): 95–110 (esp. 98–100).

120 Georg Simmel, 'Life as Transcendence', in *The View of Life: Four Metaphysical Essays with Journal Aphorisms*, transl. John A. Y. Andrews and Donald N. Levine (Chicago and London: The University of Chicago Press, 2010), 16.

121 Simmel, 'Life as Transcendence', 14.

122 Simmel, 'Life as Transcendence', 16.

123 Simmel, 'Life as Transcendence', 71.

124 Siegfried Kracauer, 'Photography', in *The Mass Ornament: Weimar Essays*, transl. and ed. Thomas Y. Levin, 61.

125 Kracauer, *Theory of Film*, 300, 303.

126 For a truly brilliant discussion of this topic, see Miriam Bratu Hansen, '"With Skin and Hair": Kracauer's Theory of Film, Marseille 1940', in *Critical Inquiry* 19 (3) (1993): 437–469 and her *Cinema and Experience*, 253–279. See also 'On the Face of Things: Béla Balazs and Siegfried Kracauer on Physiognomy and Film', in *The Detective of Modernity: Essays on the Work of David Frisby*, ed. Georgia Giannakopoulou and Graeme Gilloch (London and New York: Routledge, 2021), 79–90. My analysis builds further on Bratu Hansen's. The original text of the Marseille Notebooks was published in Siegfried Kracauer,

The Missed Conversation 133

'Theorie des Films: Die Errettung der aüsseren Wirklichkeit', in *Werke. Band 3*, ed. Sabine Biebl and Inka Mülder-Bach (Frankfurt am Main, Germany: Suhrkamp, 2005), 515–845. All translations in English are drawn from Bratu Hansen's text.

127 Kracauer (transl. Bratu Hansen and quoted in ' With Skin and Hair', 462).
128 Hansen, 'With Skin and Hair', 450.
129 Kracauer (transl. Bratu Hansen and quoted in 'With Skin and Hair', 458).
130 Kracauer (transl. Bratu Hansen and quoted in 'With Skin and Hair', 448).
131 Kracauer (transl. Bratu Hansen and quoted in 'With Skin and Hair', 447).
132 Siegfried Kracauer, 'Cult of Distraction' 327.
133 Walter Benjamin, *The Origin of German Tragic Drama*, trans. John Osborne (London: Verso, 2003), 166. Compare also Kracauer's concept of '*Umschlag*' with Benjamin's concept of '*Umschwung*' (p. 232). Benjamin's concept refers to a like-minded, critical moment: here as well, the unmasking of a fundamental absence of meaning in the world goes hand in hand with an expression of the need for immediate change.
134 Kracauer (transl. Bratu Hansen and quoted in '"With Skin and Hair"', 459).
135 In Georg Simmel, *Georg Simmel: Essays on Interpretation in Social Science*, transl. and ed. Guy Oakes (Manchester: Manchester University Press, 1980), resp. 127–144, 145–197, 97–126.
136 Georg Simmel, 'The Problem of Historical Time', in *Georg Simmel, Essays on Interpretation in Social Science*, transl. and ed. Guy Oakes (Manchester: Manchester University Press, 1980), 144 (my emphasis). For an interesting account of Simmel's late philosophy of history, see Gary Backhaus, 'Husserlian Affinities in Simmel's Later Philosophy of History: The 1918 Essay', in *Human Studies* 26 (2003): 223–258.
137 Simmel, 'The Problem of Historical Time', 127.
138 Simmel, 'The Problem of Historical Time', 128.
139 Simmel, 'The Problem of Historical Time', 129, 141.
140 Simmel, 'The Problem of Historical Time', 131.
141 Simmel, 'The Problem of Historical Time', 140.
142 Simmel, 'The Problem of Historical Time', 132.
143 Simmel, 'The Problem of Historical Time', 135.
144 Simmel, 'The Problem of Historical Time', 143.
145 Siegfried Kracauer, *History: The Last Things Before the Last*, completed Paul Oskar Kristeller (Princeton, NJ: Markus Wiener Publishers, 1994), 216. For insightful discussions of Kracauer's philosophy of history, see D. N. Rodowick, 'The Last Things Before the Last: Kracauer and History', in *New German Critique* 41 (1987): 109–131; Graeme Gilloch, 'Inconclusive: Penultimate Things', in *Siegfried Kracauer: Our Companion in Misfortune* (Cambridge, UK: Polity Press, 2015), 202–211.
146 Kracauer, *History: The Last Things Before the Last*, 217.
147 Kracauer, *History: The Last Things Before the Last*, 29.
148 Kracauer, *History: The Last Things Before the Last*, 45.
149 Kracauer, *History: The Last Things Before the Last*, 130, 191.
150 Kracauer, *History: The Last Things Before the Last*, 170.
151 Kracauer, *History: The Last Things Before the Last*, 193.
152 Kracauer, *History: The Last Things Before the Last*, 153.
153 Kracauer, *History: The Last Things Before the Last*, 50, 55.
154 Kracauer, *History: The Last Things Before the Last*, 121.

134 Unworldliness in Twentieth Century German Thought

155 Kracauer, *History: The Last Things Before the Last*, 37.
156 Kracauer, *History: The Last Things Before the Last*, 192.
157 Kracauer, *History: The Last Things Before the Last*, 194.
158 For the definitive analysis of the tensions and disagreements between Adorno and Kracauer, see Jay, 'Adorno and Kracauer'. See also Adorno's essay 'The Curious Realist: On Siegfried Kracauer', in *Notes on Literature: Volume 2*, ed. Rolf Tiedemann, transl. Sherry Weber Nicholsen (New York: Columbia University Press, 1992), 58–75.
159 Adorno, transl. Martin Jay and quoted in 'Adorno and Kracauer', 63.
160 Kracauer, transl. Martin Jay and quoted in 'Adorno and Kracauer', 54.
161 Kracauer, *History: The Last Things Before the Last*, 96, 83–85.
162 Kracauer, *History: The Last Things Before the Last*, 102.
163 Kracauer, *History: The Last Things Before the Last*, 56.
164 Kracauer, *History: The Last Things Before the Last*, 5.
165 von Moltke, *The Curious Humanist*, 245. See also Enzo Traverso, *Itinéraire d'un intellectuel nomade* (Paris: Éditions de la découverte, 1994), 180.

Bibliography

Adorno, Theodor W. 'The Curious Realist: On Siegfried Kracauer', in *Notes on Literature: Volume 2*, ed. Rolf Tiedemann, transl. Shierry Weber Nicholsen (New York: Columbia University Press, 1992)

Anderson, Mark M. 'Siegfried Kracauer and Meyer Schapiro: A Friendship', in *New German Critique* 54 (1991)

Backhaus, Gary. 'Husserlian Affinities in Simmel's Later Philosophy of History: The 1918 Essay', in *Human Studies* 26 (2003)

Benjamin, Walter. *The Origin of German Tragic Drama*, transl. John Osborne (London: Verso, 2003)

Blatterer, Harry. 'Siegfried Kracauer's Differentiating Approach to Friendship', in *Journal of Historical Sociology* 32 (2019)

Bloch, Ernst. *The Principle of Hope*, transl. Neville Plaice, Stephen Plaice and Paul Knight (Cambridge, MA: The MIT Press, 1986)

Böschenstein, Bernhard, Egyptien, Jürgen, Schefold, Bertram and Vitsthum, Wolf-gang Graf, eds. *Wissenschaftler im George-Kreis: Die Welt des Dichters und der Beruf der Wissenschaft* (Berlin and New York: Walter de Gruyter, 2005)

Broderson, Momme. *Siegfried Kracauer* (Hamburg: Rowohlt, 2001)

Craver, Harry T. *The Reluctant Skeptic: Siegfried Kracauer and the Crises of Weimar Culture* (New York and Oxford: Berghahn, 2017)

Didi-Huberman, Georges. *Images in Spite of All: Four Photographs from Auschwitz*, transl. Shane B. Lillis (Chicago: University of Chicago Press, 2008)

Fleming, Paul. 'The Crisis of Art: Max Kommerell and Jean Paul's Gestures', in *MLN* 115 (3) (2000)

Fleming, Paul. 'Die Moderne ohne Kunst: Max Kommerells Gattungspoetik in Jean Paul', in *Max Kommerell. Leben, Werk, Aktualität*, ed. Walter Busch and Gerhart Pickerodt (Göttingen: Wallstein Verlag, 2003)

Fleming, Paul. 'Ein Bund von Sternen. Konstellation bei Kommerell', in *Lektürepraxis und Theoriebildung: Zur Aktualität Max Kommerells*, ed. Christoph König, Isolde Schiffermüller, Christian Benne and Gabrielle Pelloni (Göttingen: Wallstein, 2018)

The Missed Conversation 135

Fleming, Paul. 'Forgetting – Faust: Adorno and Kommerell', in *Adorno and Literature*, ed. David Cunningham and Nigel Mapp (London and New York: Continuum, 2006)

Frisby, David. *Fragments of Modernity: Theories of Modernity in the Work of Simmel, Kracauer and Benjamin* (London and New York: Routledge, 2011)

Geulen, Eva. 'Aktualität im Übergang: Kunst und Moderne bei Max Kommerell', in *Max Kommerell: Leben, Werk, Aktualität*, ed. Walter Busch and Gerhart Pickerodt (Göttingen: Wallstein Verlag, 2003)

Gilloch, Graeme. *Siegfried Kracauer: Our Companion in Misfortune* (Cambridge: Polity Press, 2015)

Haas, Claude. 'Hölderlin contra Goethe: Gemeinschaft und Geschichte in Max Kommerells Der Dichter als Führer in der deutschen Klassik', in *Zeitschrift für Germanistik* 27 (1) (2017)

Hansen, Miriam Bratu. *Cinema and Experience: Siegfried Kracauer, Walter Benjamin, and Theodor W. Adorno* (Berkeley, Los Angeles and London: University of California Press, 2012)

Hansen, Miriam Bratu. 'Decentric Perspectives: Kracauer's Early Writings on Film and Mass Culture', in *New German Critique* 54 (1991)

Hansen, Miriam Bratu. '"With Skin and Hair": Kracauer's Theory of Film, Marseille 1940', in *Critical Inquiry* 19 (3) (1993)

Hölscher-Lohmeyer, Dorothea. 'Geist und Buchstabe der Briefe Max Kommerells: Anmerkungen zu ihrer Gesamtedition', in *Max Kommerell. Leben, Werk, Aktualität*, ed. Walter Busch and Gerhart Pickerodt (Göttingen: Wallstein Verlag, 2003)

Jay, Martin. 'Adorno and Kracauer: Notes on a Troubled Friendship', in *Salmagundi* 40 (1978)

Jay, Martin. 'Magical Nominalism: Photography and the Reenchantment of the World', in *The Pictorial Turn*, ed. Neal Curtis (New York: Routledge, 2010)

Kaes, Anton. 'Siegfried Kracauer: The Film Historian in Exile', in *Escape to Life. German Intellectuals in New York: A Compendium on Exile After 1933*, ed. Eckart Goebel and Sigrid Weigel (London and New York: Walter de Gruyter, 2013)

Karlsson Pedersen, Michael. 'Der atmende Stoff. Zum Stimmungsbegriff Max Kommerells', in *Lektürepraxis und Theoriebildung: Zur Aktualität Max Kommerells*, ed. Christoph König, Isolde Schiffermüller, Christian Benne and Gabrielle Pelloni (Göttingen: Wallstein, 2018)

Koch, Gertrud. '"Not Yet Accepted Anywhere": Exile, Memory and Image in Kracauer's Conception of History', in *New German Critique* 54 (1991)

Koch, Gertrud. *Siegfried Kracauer: An Introduction* (Princeton: Princeton University Press, 2000)

Kommerell, Max. 'Betrachtung über die Commedia dell'Arte', in *Dichterische Welterfahrung: Essays* (Frankfurt am Main: Vittorio Klostermann, 1952)

Kommerell, Max. *Der Dichter als Führer in der deutschen Klassik* (Berlin: Georg Bondi, 1928)

Kommerell, Max. 'Die Dichtung in freien Rhythmen und der Gott der Dichter', in *Gedanken über Gedichte* (Frankfurt am Main: Vittorio Klostermann, 1985)

Kommerell, Max. 'Don Quijote und Simplicissimus', in *Essays, Notizen, Poetische Fragmente*, ed. Inge Jens (Olten and Freiburg im Breisgau: Walter Verlag, 1969)

Kommerell, Max. 'Humoristische Personifikationen in Don Quixote', in *Dichterische Welterfahrung. Essays* (Frankfurt am Main: Vittorio Klostermann, 1952)

136 Unworldliness in Twentieth Century German Thought

Kommerell, Max. *Jean Paul* (Frankfurt am Main: Vittorio Klostermann, 1933)

Kommerell, Max. 'Rilkes Duineser Elegien', in *Gedanken über Gedichte* (Frankfurt am Main: Vittorio Klostermann, 1985)

Kommerell, Max. 'Von Wesen des Lyrischen Gedichts', in *Gedanken über Gedichte* (Frankfurt am Main: Vittorio Klostermann, 1985)

Kracauer, Siegfried. 'The Biography as an Art Form of the New Bourgeoisie', in *The Mass Ornament: Weimar Essays*, transl. and ed. Thomas Y. Levin (Cambridge, MA and London: Harvard University Press, 1995)

Kracauer, Siegfried. 'Cult of Distraction: On Berlin's Picture Places', in *The Mass Ornament: Weimar Essays*, transl. and ed. Thomas Y. Levin (Cambridge, MA and London: Harvard University Press, 1995)

Kracauer, Siegfried. *From Caligari to Hitler: A Psychological History of the German Film* (Princeton and Oxford: Princeton University Press, 2004)

Kracauer, Siegfried. 'Gedanken über Freundschaft', in *Werke 5.1: Essays, Feuilletons, Rezensionen, 1906–1923*, ed. Inka Mülder-Bach and Ingrid Belke (Frankfurt am Main: Suhrkamp, 2011)

Kracauer, Siegfried. 'Georg Simmel', in *The Mass Ornament: Weimar Essays*, transl. and ed. Thomas Y. Levin (Cambridge, MA and London: Harvard University Press, 1995)

Kracauer, Siegfried. *History: The Last Things Before the Last*, completed Paul Oskar Kristeller (Princeton: Markus Wiener Publishers, 1994)

Kracauer, Siegfried. 'The Mass Ornament', in *The Mass Ornament: Weimar Essays*, transl. and ed. Thomas Y. Levin (Cambridge, MA and London: Harvard University Press, 1995)

Kracauer, Siegfried. 'Photography', in *The Mass Ornament: Weimar Essays*, transl. and ed. Thomas Y. Levin (Cambridge, MA and London: Harvard University Press, 1995)

Kracauer, Siegfried. 'Theorie des Films. Die Errettung der aüsseren Wirklichkeit', in *Werke: Band 3*, ed. Sabine Biebl and Inka Mülder-Bach (Frankfurt am Main: Suhrkamp, 2005)

Kracauer, Siegfried. *Theory of Film: The Redemption of Physical Reality* (London, Oxford and New York: Oxford University Press, 1965)

Kracauer, Siegfried. 'Those Who Wait', in *The Mass Ornament: Weimar Essays*, transl. and ed. Thomas Y. Levin (Cambridge, MA and London: Harvard University Press, 1995)

Kracauer, Siegfried. 'Über die Freundschaft', in *Werke 5.1: Essays, Feuilletons, Rezensionen, 1906–1923*, ed. Inka Mülder-Bach and Ingrid Belke (Frankfurt am Main: Suhrkamp, 2011)

Kracauer, Siegfried. 'Why France Liked Our Films', in *Siegfried Kracauer's American Writings, Essays on Film and Popular Culture*, ed. Johannes von Moltke and Kristy Rawson (Berkeley, Los Angeles and London: University of California Press, 2012)

Locher, Elmar. 'Die Sprache und das Unaussprechliche: Kleist bei Kommerell', in *Max Kommerell: Leben, Werk, Aktualität*, ed. Walter Busch and Gerhart Pickerodt (Göttingen: Wallstein Verlag, 2003)

Locher, Elmar. 'Über das "ohne Worte sein": Kleist und Kommerell', in *Lektürepraxis und Theoriebildung: Zur Aktualität Max Kommerells*, ed. Christoph König, Isolde Schiffermüller, Christian Benne and Gabrielle Pelloni (Göttingen: Wallstein, 2018)

Massalongo, Milena. 'Versuch zu einem kritischen Vergleich zwischen Kommerells und Benjamins Sprachgebärde', in *Max Kommerell: Leben, Werk, Aktualität*, ed. Walter Busch and Gerhart Pickerodt (Göttingen: Wallstein Verlag, 2003)

The Missed Conversation 137

Mülder, Inka. *Siegfried Kracauer-Grenzgänger zwischen Theorie und Literatur: Seine frühen Schriften 1913–1933* (Stuttgart: J.B. Metzler, 1985)

Nägele, Rainer. 'Vexierbild einer Kritischen Konstellation: Walter Benjamin und Max Kommerell', in *Max Kommerell: Leben, Werk, Aktualität*, ed. Walter Busch and Gerhart Pickerodt (Göttingen: Wallstein Verlag, 2003)

Norton, Robert E. *Secret Germany: Stefan George and His Circle* (Ithaca, NY: Cornell University Press, 2002)

Pelloni, Gabrielle. '"Veränderte Mischungen": Kommerells ästhetische Erziehung', in *Lektürepraxis und Theoriebildung: Zur Aktualität Max Kommerells*, ed. Christoph König, Isolde Schiffermüller, Christian Benne and Gabrielle Pelloni (Göttingen: Wallstein, 2018)

Port, Ulrich. 'Die "Sprachgebärde" und der "Umgang mit sich selbst": Literatur als Lebenskunst bei Max Kommerell', in *Max Kommerell: Leben, Werk, Aktualität*, ed. Walter Busch and Gerhart Pickerodt (Göttingen: Wallstein Verlag, 2003)

Port, Ulrich. 'Literaturgeschichte als Körperschau: Max Kommerell und die Physionomik der 1920er Jahre', in *Hofmannsthal Jahrbuch* 14 (2006)

Richter, Gerhard. 'Siegfried Kracauer and the Folds of Friendship', in *The German Quarterly* 70 (3) (1997)

Rodowick, D. N. 'The Last Things Before the Last: Kracauer and History', in *New German Critique* 41 (1987)

Schiffermüller, Isolde. 'Gebärde, Gestikulation und Mimus: Krisengestalten in der Poetik von Max Kommerell', in *Max Kommerell: Leben, Werk, Aktualität*, ed. Walter Busch and Gerhart Pickerodt (Göttingen: Wallstein Verlag, 2003)

Schmidt-Bergman, Hansgeorg. 'Max Kommerells Weg von George zu Rilke', in *Max Kommerell: Leben, Werk, Aktualität*, ed. Walter Busch and Gerhart Pickerodt (Göttingen: Wallstein Verlag, 2003)

Siegel, Elke. 'Contested Legacies of "German" Friendship: Max Kommerell's *The Poet as Leader in German Classicism*', in *Telos* 176 (2016)

Simmel, Georg. 'Life as Transcendence', in *The View of Life: Four Metaphysical Essays with Journal Aphorisms*, transl. John A. Y. Andrews and Donald N. Levine (Chicago and London: The University of Chicago Press, 2010)

Simmel, Georg. 'The Problem of Historical Time', in *Georg Simmel, Essays on Interpretation in Social Science*, transl. and ed. Guy Oakes (Manchester: Manchester University Press, 1980)

Später, Jörg. *Siegfried Kracauer: Eine Biographie* (Frankfurt am Main: Suhrkamp, 2016)

Symons, Stéphane. 'On the Face of Things: Béla Balazs and Siegfried Kracauer on Physiognomy and Film', in *The Detective of Modernity: Essays on the Work of David Frisby*, ed. Georgia Giannakopoulou and Graeme Gilloch (London and New York: Routledge, 2021)

Traverso, Enzo. *Itinéraire d'un intellectuel nomade* (Paris: Éditions de la découverte, 1994)

Viallon, Martin. 'Die Konstellation Max Kommerell und Werner Krauss: *Schreiben als Sprechen über Literatur in finsteren Zeiten*', in *Max Kommerell: Leben, Werk, Aktualität*, ed. Walter Busch and Gerhart Pickerodt (Göttingen: Wallstein Verlag, 2003)

von Moltke, Johannes. *The Curious Humanist: Siegfried Kracauer in America* (Oakland: The University of California Press, 1996)

von Moltke, Johannes. 'Teddie and Friedel: Theodor W. Adorno, Siegfried Kracauer, and the Erotics of Friendship', in *Criticism* 51 (4) (2009)

von Moltke, Johannes and Rawson, Kristy. 'Introduction', in *Siegfried Kracauer's American Writings. Essays on Film and Popular Culture*, ed. Johannes von

138   *Unworldliness in Twentieth Century German Thought*

Moltke and Kristy Rawson (Berkeley, Los Angeles and London: University of California Press, 2012)

Weber, Christian. *Max Kommerell: Eine intellektuelle Biographie* (Berlin and New York: Walter de Gruyter, 2011)

Weichelt, Matthias. 'Je einsamer der Mensch, umso notwendiger die Dichtung: Kunst und Hermeneutik bei Max Kommerell', in *Lektürepraxis und Theoriebildung: Zur Aktualität Max Kommerells*, ed. Christoph König, Isolde Schiffermüller, Christian Benne and Gabrielle Pelloni (Göttingen: Wallstein, 2018)

Index

absolutism of reality 13
abstract idealism 43–44, 52, 72, 74–75
abstract thought 108, 112, 117
adaptability 23–24
Adorno, Theodor 25, 76–79, 80–81,
    83–85, 119, 124; on Don Quixote
    17–20; Nazism and 95–96; on
    utopianism 61–64
adventure 44, 111–113
aesthetic culture 39
aesthetic realism 47
aesthetic value 32–33
alarm clock 54
allegory 120
antirealism 24
Arendt, Hannah 11–12, 15
art 4, 66; perception and 22
art and artworks 82–83
authenticity 12, 40, 49, 79
autonomy of the artwork 32, 66
awakening 1–3, 54

Balázs, Béla 65
being-in-the-world 5, 10–12, 15
Benjamin, Walter 20, 120, 125
Binswanger, Ludwig 10–11
biographies 102–103
Bloch, Ernst 25, 80, 82, 84, 85,
    111–112, 119; on Don Quixote
    75–78; on socialism 61–64; on
    utopianism 65–73
Blumenberg, Hans 12–14, 21
body, the 11, 105, 110
bourgeoisie 75, 85–86, 103, 105

cameras 117–120
capitalism 46–47, 65, 70, 74

chivalry and chivalric romances 43, 72,
    75, 112
cognition 79, 121–123
collective ethics 46
Commedia dell'Arte 110
communism 45–48, 61, 65
community 97, 100–102, 104
conceptual personae 17
consciousness-industries 23
creativity 1–2, 97

de-selfing 10, 13, 14
de-worlding 7–8, 104
Deleuze, Gilles 15, 17
Derrida, Jacques 14
Descartes, Rene 8
despair 42, 63, 68, 71, 85
Dewey, John 115
deworlded spaces 7–8, 10–11, 13–14
dialectics of enlightenment 103
Dimitrov, Georgi 47
disillusionment 112–113
Don Quixote 17, 25, 51–54, 65,
    71–76, 83, 85–86, 110–113, 123;
    abstract idealism and 43–45; as
    erring knight 52; as novel, *Don
    Quixote* 17, 25, 43, 47, 56n43, 83,
    85–86, 96, 110, 111, 114; idealism
    and 53–54
dreams 11, 54, 69, 81–82
dream-world 73, 74, 76
Dulcinea 72, 75
dynamograms 21–22; *see also
    Pathosformeln*; Warburg, Aby

emotions 23–24, 38
Engels, Friedrich 61–62

140 *Index*

Enlightenment 51, 82–83
Erlebnis 34, 37, 49
erring knight 44, 52, 111
existence 3, 6–9, 19, 113
experience 33–34, 48, 53, 114
Expressionism 47, 67

faith 25, 54, 112, 116
fantasy 24
fascism 70–71, 115; *see also* Nazism
feelings 22–24, 98
films 115–116, 117–120
form 38–39, 50
Foucault, Michel 14
fragmentation 51, 96
Frederick II 97
free rhythms 108–109
freedom 85, 86
French thought 16; *see also* Deleuze,
  Gilles; Derrida, Jacques; Foucault,
  Michel
Freud, Sigmund 11
friendship 97–101

George, Stefan 26, 96, 104–105
gestures 105–107, 109
God 43, 113
Goethe, Johann Wolfgang von
  99, 105
Goodness 41, 44
ground in life 97

habits 1, 6, 8
Heidegger, Martin 4–6, 7–8, 10, 51
history and historical events 50, 77,
  80–81, 85, 121–124
Hitler, Adolf 84, 95
Holocaust 118
hope 63, 68–71, 76, 84
Horkheimer, Max 81, 115
humanism 125, 132n109
Husserl, Edmund 8–10, 13, 17–20,
  33, 124

Iago 33
iconography 21
idealism 18, 52–53, 63, 115
instrumental reason 81–82
interconnection 99–100
irreducible reality 79

Judaism 15
Jünger, Ernst 25, 47–49, 63–65, 72,
  76, 79, 84; on battle 51; on Don
  Quixote 52–54; on form 50

Kant, Immanuel 32–33, 65, 74
Kleist, Heinrich von 110
Kluge, Alexander 21, 22–24
Kommerell, Max 25–26, 124;
  Nazism and 95–96; on Don
  Quixote 110–113; on friendship
  97–102; on gestures 104–107; on
  poets 108–109; on Sancho Panza
  113–114
Kracauer, Siegfried 25–26, 70, 95,
  99–104, 115–123, 124–125,
  128n30, 132n109
Krüger, Horst 61

Lask, Emil 33
Lebensphilosophie 26, 33, 99, 108
Levinas, Emmanuel 15
Leznai, Anna 45
lifeworlds 9–10, 12–13, 96, 110
lightheartedness 85
liminal states 2
love 72, 98, 101
Lukács, Georg 25, 32–34, 63–68,
  73, 76, 78, 80, 84, 112–113;
  communism and 45, 49;
  misunderstanding and art 34;
  on aesthetic culture 39; on Don
  Quixote 43–45, 54; on form 50;
  on novels 56; on society 57n60;
  on standpoint 35; on tragic heroes
  40–41; on utopian art 37–38;
  realism and 57n64; theory of the
  novel 42–43
Lyotard, Jean-François 14

Marx, Karl 61–62
Marxism 45–46, 49
mass entertainment 107
mass ornaments 103–104
master-narratives 14
meaning 14, 20–21, 34–36, 38, 42–44
merging 101
metamorphosis 2–4
Middle Ages 75, 83
middle class 70–71

Index 141

milieu 15
misunderstanding 34
models 56n43
modernity 36, 41–45
more-than-life 35–36
myth 81–82, 110

nationalism 42, 48
natural history 80–81
nature 80–82, 106
Nazism 95–96, 118; *see also* fascism
negation 64, 96, 124
negative dialectics 124–125
Negt, Oskar 21, 22–24
networks 4, 8
non-simultaneity 70
novels 42–43, 66, 84, 86; models
and 56n43

objective culture 36
objects 4–5
Othello 33

Panofsky, Erwin 21
Panza, Sancho 17, 74–75, 112–114,
121, 123–124
Pathosformeln 21–22; *see also*
dynamograms; Warburg, Aby
Paul, Jean 26, 105–109
peasantry 70–71
philosophy 78–80
photography 117, 119
poets and poetry 108–109
political action 57n64
positivism 9
practical use 5
Proust, Marcel 1–4, 6–7
psychology 33—34
pure forms 108–109
pure gestures 106, 109

Quixote, Don *see* Don Quixote

realism 46–47, 57n64, 116
reality 117–118
reality-concepts 13
reason 78, 81–83, 85–86, 103
reconciliation 78, 84, 86
redemption 85, 103, 121

reform 86n60, 89n61
religion 128n30
Rilke, Rainer Maria 110
romanticism 78–79

Schiller, Friedrich 97–99
science 116
self-perception 2–4, 7
self-reflective reason 82
selves 3–4, 102
semblance 83
Shakespeare, William 33
Simmel, Georg 35–37, 42, 64, 99, 118,
121–123, 125
socialism 61–62
soldiers 48–49
soul 105–106, 108
Stalinism 76
standpoint 35, 46
subjective culture 36
surrounding world 7, 9, 16, 64
symbolic intentions 68, 74

Tiller Girls 103, 107
total mobilization 50
totalitarianism 61
totality 37, 46, 50, 57n60, 78
totality of history 122–123
tragic heroes 39–41, 47
truth 18, 20 78–81, 110, 123

United States 115, 117
untruths 18
utopianism and utopian art 37–38, 51,
61–66, 72, 77, 80

Van Gogh, Vincent 69
Vigo, Jean 121

Warburg, Aby 21–22, 24–25
Weber, Marianne 41, 65
Weber, Max 32, 42
Weimar left 116, 132n109
Whitehead, A.N. 115
worldliness 4–6
working class 104
World War I 32, 41–42, 48–49, 51,
70, 76
world-alienation 11–12

Printed in the United States
by Baker & Taylor Publisher Services